LIVING THE 100-YEAR LIFE

Lynda Gratton

LIVING THE 100-YEAR LIFE

How to build a career that lasts and a life you love

BLOOMSBURY CONTINUUM
LONDON • OXFORD • NEW YORK • NEW DELHI • SYDNEY

BLOOMSBURY CONTINUUM
Bloomsbury Publishing Plc
50 Bedford Square, London, WC1B 3DP, UK
Bloomsbury Publishing Ireland Limited,
29 Earlsfort Terrace, Dublin 2, D02 AY28, Ireland

BLOOMSBURY, BLOOMSBURY CONTINUUM and the
Diana logo are trademarks of Bloomsbury Publishing Plc

First published in Great Britain 2026

For legal purposes the Acknowledgements on p. 270
constitute an extension of this copyright page

A catalogue record for this book is available from the British Library

Library of Congress Cataloging-in-Publication data has been applied for

ISBN: HB: 978-1-3994-3295-5; TPB: 978-1-3994-3296-2 eBook: 978-1-3994-3298-6;
ePDF: 978-1-3994-3299-3

2 4 6 8 10 9 7 5 3 1

Typeset by Lumina Datamatics Ltd
Text design by George Saad
Printed and bound in Great Britain by Clays Ltd, Elcograf S.p.A.

MIX
Paper | Supporting responsible forestry
FSC® C018072

To find out more about our authors and books
visit www.bloomsbury.com and sign up for our newsletters
For product safety related questions contact productsafety@bloomsbury.com

To My Beloved
Husband Nigel

CONTENTS

PREFACE

Living the 100-Year Life – Starting Now

Ten years ago, Andrew Scott and I wrote *The 100-Year Life:*[1] *Living and Working in an age of Longevity.* We were among the first to suggest something rather radical: that many of us could live to 100 and that this wasn't a problem to be solved but a possibility to be embraced. The book found an audience far larger and more diverse than we could ever have imagined – over a million readers across the globe. It sparked conversations in companies, classrooms and around kitchen tables. Readers told us, 'I can't think about work the same way anymore.' But they also asked: 'So what should I actually do?'

Living The 100-Year Life begins where the first book left off – but it's not a book specifically for later life - it is a book for right now, wherever you are in your journey. The promise and challenge of a long life start early, shaping every stage: how you build skills, how you sustain energy, how you navigate relationships, how you recover from setbacks, and how you make choices that accumulate into a life well lived.

If *The 100-Year Life* offered the map, this book is the guidebook. It's a practical, human exploration of how to live not just longer, but wiser – how to make good decisions in a world where careers are non-linear, roles and identities shift, and technology continues to transform the way we work. In the years since we published that first book, change has only accelerated. Generative AI has reshaped the nature of work. People are living longer with fewer predictable paths to follow. Life itself – our relationships, our roles, our rhythms – has become more fluid and less scripted.

A long life is a gift, but it also asks more of us. It asks us to evolve, to adapt, and to make choices that accumulate over time. That is what this book is about.

Here, you'll find questions to reflect on, stories to connect with, and actions you can take – now and for your future self. Whether you're 25 or 75, starting out, transitioning or reimagining what comes next, this is your invitation to work not just hard, but wisely.

Welcome to living your 100-Year Life.

INTRODUCTION

The New Reality of a Long Life

How a longer life reshapes how we work, grow and define meaning

A Story of Walking with Dad – France, August 2022

August in southwest France, life moves at a slow tempo. I walk early this morning before the heat overwhelms. Tracing ancient lanes worn smooth by cattle and sheep, I ascend the valley path with measured steps. First, a steep climb up the valley face, then near the summit of this little hill, plunging into the scrub oak forest. Walking this path in spring, I was surrounded by green shoots and lush grasses, but now the earth lies parched and dry.

Jumping from rock to rock, the steep path winds down to the convent, the bells calling the nuns to prayer. I watch as two young nuns clad in white robes carefully hang out their morning washing. Then a sharp right turn as the path hugs the valley of the little stream. I pause at the tiny strip of dappled ground by the stream – always a glorious, peaceful sight. As I push through the thicket into the nearby field, I enter what I always think of as 'the universe of flies', who love the damp of the valley as much as the birds.

Today, my thoughts are tinged with sadness. It's a subtle presence, hovering at the edge of my mind. Earlier, as I climbed the forest path to the plateau, unexplained tears rolled down my cheeks – a sense of foreboding and disquiet. I realise these solitary tears are more than the accumulation of a hectic year. They are true sorrow and I try to locate its source: the sadness closest to my heart is about my father. It seems odd: my dad passed away many years ago and I thought my period of mourning had ended yet deep down, I know he became ill more than a decade younger than I am now. As I walk these ancient paths, I feel Dad walking beside me. We who walked so often together along steep paths find ourselves in quiet conversation. I experience this silent parallel life, of what might have been for him and is for me, occasionally collides with my present. It is this collision I feel as I walk my morning forest track – a deep sense of Dad beside me. I feel almost ashamed of these precious extra years I expect to have and which he did not – I know I must make the most of them.

This is my first story. As tears surprised me on the ascent, I realised I was standing at the edge of a transition. Mourning not only my father, but a phase of my own life: one chapter closing, another waiting to begin. I was approaching 70. When Andrew and I wrote *The 100-Year Life*, we suggested that many of us would live into our nineties and beyond. At the time, that felt conceptual. Now approaching 70, I could feel it in my bones. These could be almost 40 extra years my father didn't get. And they demanded something more of me – more reflection, more care, more intention. I knew that if I wanted my next decades to be vital and meaningful, I had to reshape how I worked, how I contributed and how I lived – because in a 100-Year Life, those extra decades are not a footnote, but a full chapter.

This book is the practical continuation of *The 100-Year Life*. If that first book helped you understand that your life might be longer than expected, this one helps you figure out how to live it. Whether you are in your thirties, forties, fifties, sixties – or like me in your seventies – or even in your eighties or nineties and beyond – it shows how to live a long, purposeful life – day by day, year by year – with reflection and purpose.

OUR QUESTIONS, OUR STORIES

For me, this story in August 2022 marked a period of transition and deep reflection. I turned to my habitual way of navigating transitions – walking, thinking, writing. In the solitude of my reflective walks, memories and stories from the decades of my working life began to surface. These stories emerged not as a biographical past, ordered and complete, but from my unconscious in a seemingly random manner. One day, a story of waitressing in my teens; the next, teaching an MBA class; then assembling my consultancy team. Over the year I continued to collect these stories, and as I did so I began to see themes emerge.

For decades I've studied others' working lives, listened to executives and MBA students, and counselled leaders. Heard their stories and talked through their questions. They, too, search for wise work as they face significant life challenges and choices. Some question how to boost their productivity: What career to choose? How to make the most of their skills and find work they love. How to convert energy and skills into a monthly paycheque. What does it take to stay productive through what might be a 50-year working life? Some confront work challenges: the frustration of a missed promotion, the agony of being in the wrong job, and the annoyance of a repetitive loop when all you crave is adventure and change.

Others meanwhile ask how best to nurture themselves and others: Is it time to step back a little from work? How to balance getting on in a career and spending time with family, friends and loved ones. Some are facing life challenges: dealing with the fallout from a relationship breaking up when they are head down at work, balancing work with supporting a child or perhaps an elderly parent needing extra care. They share existential challenges: outrunning technology, preparing for a world with constant transitions.

As I thought about these decades of conversations, mentoring and reflection, a pattern emerged. The decisions shaping my career – and the questions I hear from clients, students and friends – all point to three Guiding Questions. Perhaps you're asking them too.

Who am I? This question asks: *What are the stories I tell about myself and the values and beliefs that shape who I am?* This is important because understanding yourself helps you face hard choices in a way that aligns to your strengths and aspirations; to navigate the hard choices that define your working life.

How am I working now? *How does it feel to be working now: what are the skills I am developing, the relationships I am building, the tasks I am completing?* Understanding the dynamic interplay between your identity and work helps you better understand your priorities.

What actions should I take now and what promises am I making to my future self? *What are my plans – my immediate actions and longer-term promises?* These insights help you expand your sense of self through new opportunities.

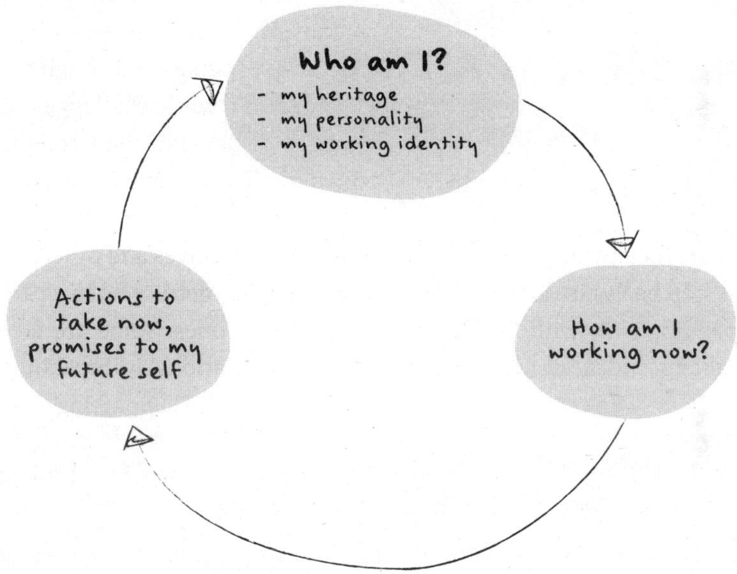

The Three Guiding Questions

These three Guiding Questions are not linear action steps, but rather a continuous process that adapts to changing circumstances and aspirations. At first glance they might seem deceptively simple questions but if you sit with them – really sit with them – they open up profound insight and possibility. They help you face transitions with intention, handle disruptions with resilience and navigate the long arc of your working life with wisdom.

Together, we will explore these three Guiding Questions through stories – the stories we tell about our past, the stories we tell about who we are now and the stories we tell about who we want to be. Storytelling is at the heart of this book. Stories are how we make sense of our lives; they help us make the connection between what happened and what it meant. A story can reveal patterns you hadn't seen, values you've inherited, or shifts that felt small at the time but changed everything. Unlike data or theory, stories stay with us. Stories move us, provoke us and help us imagine who we might become. I will tell you stories of my working life and ask you to reflect on your own stories.

When you tell your own story – honestly, messily, thoughtfully – you're not just recalling the past. You're shaping the meaning of your present and creating new possibilities for your future.

YOU ARE NOT ALONE

We each carry our own story, yet sometimes our questions and experiences echo in the lives of others. In this book, I'll share some of my own stories and the questions I'm grappling with. Some may feel familiar, others may not, but my aim is to help you reflect on your own life. To do that, I've created four fictional characters – Lucia, Nico, Ben and Mira. For each one I explore the same three guiding questions: *Who am I? How am I working now?* and *What actions will I take now and what promises will I make to my future self?* Their stories broaden the perspective of this book – from one life to many. Like all of us, they face transitions, hard choices, disruptions and uncertainties. My hope is that somewhere within their stories, you'll recognise something of yourself.

The Stories of Lucia and Nico

So many of my memories of being in my twenties are about hanging out with friends. As we grew and developed, we compared, discussed and argued. We became living experiments for weaving a life – watching up close as our friends' made choices and seeing how those choices played out. Perhaps you've had the same experience. That's why the first character isn't an individual – it's a pair of friends. Born in 1993, now in their early thirties, Lucia and Nico have spent their adult lives watching, debating and sometimes judging each other.

They grew up in the same small town where everyone knew everyone, just five minutes apart. Nico's parents ran a small business in the town – a different rhythm to the business he was to build – but the seed of independence was always there. Lucia and Nico shared late-night playlists and long bike rides to the corner café. After school, their paths diverged. Lucia moved to Europe to study social impact, eventually joining a consultancy focused on education and inclusion. Nico took a different route: after college he joined one of the tech giants first in sales, then twice swapping companies to land in product marketing. He moved around for his work – Lucia remembers late-night calls from Dublin, Hyderabad, London, San Francisco. To her, it looked as though Nico had a stellar working path ahead of him. Yet even though the jobs looked great, she remembers a phrase she heard constantly from Nico at that time: 'I feel like a tiny element of this colossal machine.' He was itching to start something on his own. His first venture did not work out but now he'd just begun his second startup, one he's built slowly and deliberately from the ground up.

Lucia and Nico stay in touch, trading voice notes at strange hours, picking up the thread of conversation without needing context. Both are now reckoning with what they imagined adult life would feel like by now, and what it really is.

Lucia's work appears purposeful. She speaks Spanish and English, spent time volunteering in Ethiopia and feels globally mobile. But inside, she feels she's drifting. Her jobs feel more reactive than visionary. The idealism she once held so fiercely has dulled. She's wondering what's next – whether to start a family, how long to keep saying yes to roles that don't quite fit. And Nico has his own questions: How ambitious should I be? What does 'success' look like if I'm not chasing scale? Some nights he lies awake, not stressed but alert; imagining the next iteration of his life.

Lucia envies Nico's autonomy and direction. Nico envies her conviction and her broader view. Both are discovering that the script they were handed – study hard, get a good job, build something meaningful – has turned out to be more complicated than they expected. Like many in their early thirties, they're beginning to grasp just how long life might be and how complex too. Their parents' careers feel distant and fixed, while their own paths feel flexible but unstable.

I am familiar with the stories of Lucia and Nico – they are the same age as many of the MBA students I teach and counsel, and I hear their stories in the narratives of my own children, now also in their thirties.

Like Lucia and Nico, are you asking: Am I building something that matters? What kind of life can I afford to live? And what does success mean now – and to whom?

Ben's Story

Ben is 42 and a senior executive at a global retail bank, leading large-scale digital transformation projects. He lives with his partner, Yuki, and their two young children in a commuter town outside a major city. His days are tightly structured – team meetings, leadership updates, family dinners, bedtime routines.

At work, Ben is known as calm, competent and reliable. Back home, he's the one who resets the Wi-Fi, keeps track of school forms and tidies the kitchen late at night. But lately, that rhythm has started to fray. He's sleeping less, questioning more. The mental load is constant and the space to think, let alone plan, feels increasingly scarce. On the train home, he sometimes stares out the window, wondering how he got here and whether this version of life is the one he wants to keep living but he's also grateful he has a good job at a time when so many of his university friends have been laid off and are struggling to get back into a well-paid, stable job.

I know many Bens – I teach them at London Business School, I coach them in teams and for some, support their journey to leadership. I've heard Ben's story many times and his experience is familiar to many in their forties. Perhaps like him, you're caught between youthful ambition and the weight of responsibility. As part of the so-called 'sandwich generation', Ben's navigating the needs of young children, a tough career and in his case, ageing parents.

Like Ben, have you ever found yourself caught between responsibility and exhaustion – knowing something needs to shift, but unsure where to begin?

Mira's Story

Mira is 53 and lives in a secluded flat on the edge of the city. Until recently, she shared a home with her husband of 25 years, raising two children, now in their twenties. One daughter lives nearby, the other has moved to Melbourne. Mira had a full-time job until her children were born, and since then has worked part-time as an accounts manager, handling logistics and scheduling.

The divorce was amicable, but financially destabilising. She's left with just enough to get by, but not enough for extras. A holiday. A flight to visit her daughter. Mira has made the calculations – she needs to keep working for at least another decade and frankly, she wants to do so, but her applications for full-time jobs often vanish into silence.

Perhaps Mira's story resonates with you, perhaps not. Or at least not at the moment.

As we go through our working lives, so our experiences begin to diverge from our peers. It's the widening diversity of experience that Lucia and Nico have already noticed as they track each other's career. By the age of 50, there will be some people who appear to have sterling working lives that will take them through into their seventies. But for many, like Mira, this is a decade that, for a variety of reasons, they are trying to re-enter or reimagine their working life. Mira is wondering if she's invested enough in her skills and connections and is perplexed by how tough it is to get a job. If she's going to commit to developing herself, where should she begin?

Like Mira, have you ever faced a future that looked different from what you imagined – and wondered what it would take to make it yours?

Then there's me – Lynda – just turned 70 and planning on working productively into my eighties. Perhaps you are planning to do the same. For as Lucia and Nico realise as they talk about living the 100-Year Life – even at 80 – there could still be 20 more years.

Whether you're in your thirties like Lucia and Nico, your forties like Ben, your fifties like Mira or your seventies like me, this book is your companion for the second, third and fourth acts of a 100-Year Life. And while these times of transition, hard choices, disruption and uncertainty may be daunting, they also hold immense potential. When approached with intention and reflection, they can become periods of deep renewal.

This promise of rejuvenation is the thread that runs through this book.

EXPERT VOICES

As I think more deeply about the memories of my own working life and how best to support you, I realise there are conversations I need to have. You will find these conversations with experts throughout this book – some are colleagues I've worked with, others are people I have reached out to and some are friends I know well. At www.livingthe100yearlife.com you'll be able to hear some of these conversations first-hand. They're not interviews, they're shared reflections.

MAKE THE MOST OF *LIVING THE 100-YEAR LIFE*

Living the 100-Year Life requires dynamic resilience so this book is not about hacks or quick fixes, but reflection, agency and craft. It's a call to pause and think deeply about the choices that shape our working lives – what you build, what you value and who you become.

The book is designed to be flexible – just like your working life. You don't have to read it all at once or in a set order. In fact, you may find more value by reading it like a map, not a novel: start where you are, skip to what calls you, then return to what matters most. At any point go to www.livingthe100yearlife.com our dedicated website. There you will find a host of resources to inspire and support.

Perhaps start with *The Living the 100-Year Life Assessment: Thread Strength Test*, a free, online tool to assess the strength of your eight threads. You'll receive a personalised assessment showing which threads are strong, which ones may be fraying and areas to focus on. Then go to *The Living the 100-Year Life Workbook: Life Design Guide* a free downloadable workbook to help you revisit our three Guiding Questions: *Who am I? How am I working now? What actions will I take – and what promises will I make to my future self?* Use it in your own time or return to it at every turning point.

This could be a time when you are inspired to really focus on strengthening your personal resilience. *The Living the 100-Year Life Journal: Reflect, Reimagine, Renew* is inspired by my own desk – with drawings, ideas, reflections. I've created in the journal a space for you to pause and reflect and a journey for you to take over the coming months. In it you will find exercises, prompts and room to reflect on each of your eight threads and the actions you want to take to strengthen and renew. Beautiful and practical, it's designed to sit beside you as you weave forward – to inspire you to renew.

Here's how the book unfolds. We begin with the first guiding question: Who am I?

Part One: Who Am I? *Know Yourself Across a Long Life*

This guiding question is important because before you can shape a working life that's meaningful and sustainable, you need to understand the person shaping it: you. That might sound obvious but in reality, many of us make major life and career decisions based on urgency, pressure or comparison without ever stopping to ask: *What really matters to me? What drives me? What's shaped me?*

I think of these questions as a triangle with three powerful dimensions: Your Heritage – the family, culture and history that brought you here. Your Personality – your natural preferences, habits and patterns. Your Working Identity – how work has shaped you and how it could evolve. We explore all three dimensions and hear from experts; I will share some of my stories, and we will return to Lucia, Nico, Ben and Mira with their stories and then ask you to reflect on yours.

These three dimensions don't define everything about you but together, they offer a strong foundation for understanding: Why you work the way you do. Why some things light you up and others leave you drained. And why certain changes feel so difficult – or so urgent.

This question of 'Who am I?' is foundational. You might be tempted to skip this part of the book and head straight for action in the second Guiding Question but without knowing who you are, you risk building the wrong capabilities – or solving the wrong problems.

This brings us to the second guiding question...

Part Two: How Am I Working Now? *Weaving a Working Life Across Decades*

Look closely and you'll begin to see weaves and weaving everywhere. Artists entwine materials to give shape to feeling. Architects design vast ceilings that interlace light and form. Craftspeople turn thread into texture and textiles into stories. Nature, too, is a weaver – birds braid twigs into nests, vines spiral around trees, bark folds like cloth upon itself. Sometimes, in a forest or a city street, you'll catch a glimpse of something woven.

I've been noticing weaves for decades and I've captured them in photographs in places across the world, gathering them as moments. If like me you are intrigued by weaves, visit www.livingthe100yearlife.com Here, you'll see my pictures of the many forms weaves take.

Weaving takes time. It brings strength and coherence yet remains supple – always attuned to the hand that shapes it.

This mindful noticing has shaped how I think about working lives across time. Over the years, as I've listened to people describe their hopes, detours, habits and ambitions, I've come to see their working lives not as linear paths, but as something more fluid, textured – and woven.

That is why when I imagine a working life, I think of it as a weave. A fabric we cannot fully see but that we can always feel. Each day, month and year adds to the texture. Some threads in the weave are strong, others are fraying. Some shine brightly, others anchor. And through it all, we are the weavers – choosing, knotting, stitching the patterns of our lives.

This is my invitation to you: to begin seeing your own life as a woven fabric. And to recognise yourself as the weaver. Below, I've illustrated what I imagine when I think about a working life. Think of these vertical threads on the loom as bringing form to the structure.

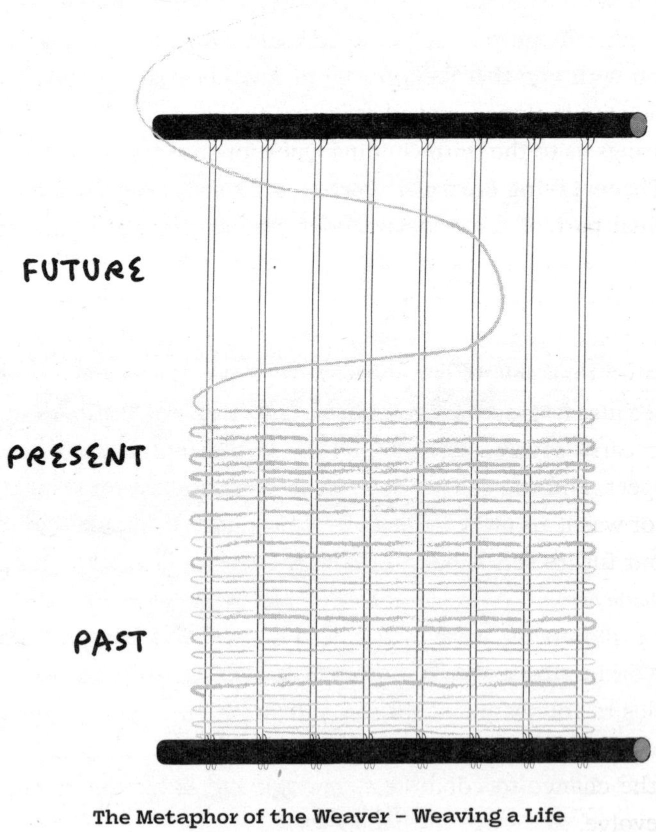

The Metaphor of the Weaver – Weaving a Life

As I will explain in Part Two of this book, four threads support productivity. *Mastery* – the ongoing pursuit of skill, depth and professional growth. *Knowing* – the development of insights about yourself, others and the wider world. *Cooperating* – the ability to work with and through others to create something greater. *Amplifying* – the use of technology to extend your reach, creativity and impact.

Four threads sustain nurture. *Friendship* – the sustaining power of connection, trust and mutual support. *Intimacy* – the deep relationships that root you in love, care and belonging. *Calm* – the intentional creation of space for rest, reflection and renewal. *Adventure* – the spark of curiosity and courage that keeps life energised and open. Over a working life you will strengthen these threads, neglect them, repair or reweave them. No one else has your exact pattern, your fabric is uniquely yours.

Each chapter in this book explores one of the threads. I will show you the shape of the thread, share ideas of how it develops and provide examples of what you can do, both in the short and longer term, to strengthen each thread. You don't need to start with all of the threads, you might begin with one that feels frayed or another that sparks curiosity. Each thread stands alone – and all are yours to shape.

This brings us to the third Guiding Question...

Part Three: Living Forward *Short-Term Choices, Long-Term Promises*

This final part of the book is about stepping into the future with clarity and courage. You've seen how a long life is woven thread by thread, and now comes the question: how do you act wisely in the present while shaping the person you want to become – your future self?

Imagining that self is not always easy. Sometimes the picture is vivid, sometimes fragmentary, sometimes blurred. Psychologists remind us that we carry several versions within us: the self we hope for, the self we expect, and the self we fear. Each pulls us forward, grounds us in reality, or warns us away from paths we'd rather not take. Even if the image of our future self is hazy, reflecting on it helps us act with more intention today.

As we explore this, we'll look at the patterns people have created for their working lives – three-stage, ladder, portfolio. These patterns are not rules to follow, but ways of seeing: structures that shape time, energy and identity. In a long life, no single pattern suffices. Instead, you have the chance to combine them, shifting as circumstances and priorities evolve.

I will show how the contract between individual and institution is also changing. The old parent–child model of security and dependence has given way to a more adult–adult relationship of responsibility and choice. That freedom can feel daunting, but it offers the opportunity to take agency: to strengthen the threads that matter most, to prepare for what lies ahead, and to build resilience for when life shifts unexpectedly.

And so Part Three closes with a challenge and an invitation: to notice where you are now, to choose a thread, and to make a promise to your future self. The path will not always be visible, but step by step, choice by choice, you can design a life that is truly your own.

MAKE THE MOST OF *LIVING THE 100-YEAR LIFE* AT ANY AGE

This is not a book to be read from start to finish like a novel, nor is it a rigid manual. It's a companion for the long and winding journey of work across a longer life. Wherever you are in weaving the fabric of your life, this book meets you there.

Weave Your 100-Year Life in Your Twenties and Thirties

You may be exploring questions like, 'What do I want from work?' or wondering how to stay open in a world of rapid change. You'll recognise Nico, who's just started building a business and feeling the strain and Lucia, balancing passion and purpose as she tries to stay true to her values.

The threads that might speak to you now are *Adventure*, *Mastery*, *Amplifying* and *Cooperation*. Turn to these chapters if you're seeking growth, building your network or daring to imagine a working life on your own terms.

Or, if you want to learn more about where you are right now, go to The Living the 100-Year Life Assessment: Thread Strength Test to assess the strength of your eight threads. The personalised assessment will show which threads are strong, which ones may be fraying and areas to focus on. Then go straight to the thread that feels weakest and see what actions or promises might shift it. The Living the 100-Year Life Workbook: Life Design Guide will help you revisit our three Guiding Questions: Who am I? How am I working now? What actions will I take – and what promises will I make to my future self? This will give you space to reflect and plan.

Weave Your 100-Year Life in Your Forties and Fifties

This may be a time of complexity: career peaks, care responsibilities, the sense that you've been running on autopilot. Ben may feel familiar, a conscientious professional questioning legacy and meaning. Yuki, his partner, navigating work while parenting and carrying the emotional weight of being an immigrant far from her own family.

Here, *Calm*, *Intimacy* and *Knowing* often come into focus. These chapters offer pathways to reconnect with your inner life, your most important relationships and your sense of self.

Use the 'Promises to My Future Self' section you will find after each thread as journaling prompts. They're designed to help you pause and recalibrate.

If this feels like the right time to make a personal commitment to growth - The Living the 100-Year Life Journal: Reflect, Reimagine, Renew is there to support you. It's full of exercises, prompts and room to reflect on each of your eight threads. Over the coming months the journal will provide a space for you to write your reflections, imagine what is possible and honour your commitments. It's a place to track your thinking, revisit your commitments and record the stories you don't want to forget.

Weave Your 100-Year Life in Your Fifties, Sixties, Seventies and Beyond

You may be stepping away from formal work, or finding your work reshaped by freedom, purpose or constraint. Meet Mira, divorced and entering a new phase with grown children; and Ben, again, now in a different life chapter – reimagining how he contributes and how he stays alive to change. Then there's me, Lynda, now in my seventies and determinedly living the 100-Year Life.

The threads of *Knowing*, *Friendship* and *Intimacy* often come into sharper relief. These are chapters about sharing wisdom, rekindling relationships and staying connected to what gives you joy. This might be a time when the thread of *Adventure* can really come to the fore.

Think of your life as a tapestry. Ask yourself, which threads have grown strong? Which ones have frayed? Use the stories to reflect – and to reweave.

LET'S BEGIN OUR CONVERSATION

As we draw this introduction to a close, I want to speak directly to you. This book is crafted as a companion – to walk alongside you as you navigate the twists, transitions and opportunities of your working life. I imagine it as a conversation between us: thoughtful, honest and provocative. At the heart of our dialogue are the three guiding questions: *Who am I? How am I working now? What actions should I take now and what promises am I making to my future self?*

These three Guiding Questions aren't meant to be answered once and for all. They're questions to return to as your life changes and deepens. Together, we'll explore the fabric of your working life: the threads you've already woven, the ones you're strengthening now and the possibilities still to come. In the spirit of the weaver, I invite you to see your working life not as something fixed but *actively shaped by your hands.* You are the weaver: the choices you make, the threads you pull tight or let go, create the pattern of your life.

Some of what you read here may comfort you, some may challenge you. My hope is that you come away not with a list of things to copy, but a deeper sense of how to make your working life *yours,* reflective of your values, strengths and possibilities. We're living through extraordinary times: climate change, AI, economic shifts, new models of family and work. These forces are reshaping how we live and what work means. You will need courage and self-awareness to respond.

I've spent decades studying work and talking with people navigating complex lives: executives, students, caregivers, freelancers, parents, founders. I've heard their questions, their doubts, their breakthroughs; I've also lived them myself. My own journey is threaded throughout this book. Not as a blueprint, but as a gesture of honesty. What I can offer here is not perfection, but presence. And a reminder: you don't have to figure this out alone.

Consider reading this book with someone else – a colleague, a partner, a friend. Or even with a reading group. Share your stories. Talk about the questions that come up. Reflect out loud. Wisdom doesn't grow in isolation; it deepens in conversation.

I hope you want to go deeper, and to support you in doing this I've created a free workbook and resources that you can find at www.livingthe100yearlife.com. To gain a foresight of what's to come, turn to the final section of this book, Step into the Weave: *Join the Living the 100-Year Life Community* to learn more about how I will support you. If you want to make a real investment in your development, then purchase *The Living the 100-Year Life Journal: Reflect, Reimagine, Renew* – which over the coming months will take you on a journey to build resilience into your life.

We're about to begin a journey through your past, present and possible future. My hope is that this journey brings clarity, courage – and I hope, a sense of calm.

PART ONE:

Know Yourself Across a Long Life

WHO AM I?

Let's start with you – not the CV or social media version, but the deeper story of who you are.

Living a long life means you'll experience more identity shifts, more personal reinvention and more time to deepen who you are. Part One helps you explore not just who you've been but who you could become across the decades ahead. Before you can shape a working life that's meaningful and sustainable, you need to understand the person shaping it: *you*. That might sound obvious but in reality, many of us make major life and career decisions based on urgency, pressure or comparison without ever stopping to ask:

What really matters to me? What drives me? What's shaped me?

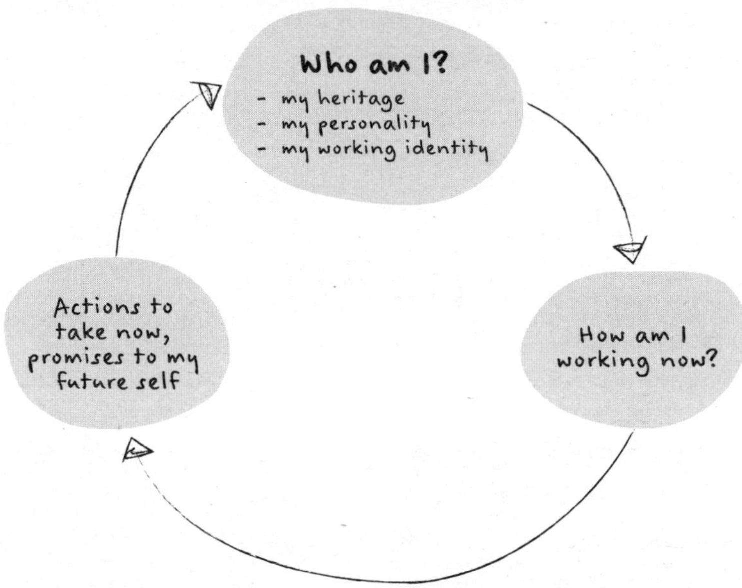

To answer the question 'Who am I?', we'll explore three powerful dimensions of your identity:

→ **Your Heritage:** roots you in your legacy, family and fate.
→ **Your Personality:** explores your natural preferences, habits and patterns
→ **Your Working Identity**: shows how work and your identity evolves through context and action.

These three dimensions don't define everything about you but together, they offer a strong foundation for understanding: Why you work the way you do; Why some things light you up, while others leave you drained. And why certain changes feel so difficult – or so urgent.

If you're in transition, stuck in repetition or sensing that something isn't quite working, start here. The better you know yourself, the wiser your working life can become.

CHAPTER 1

MY HERITAGE: The Family, Culture and History That Brought Me Here

We all come from somewhere. Behind every working life are the lives that shaped it – parents, grandparents, sometimes great-grandparents. Their choices, struggles, values and even their silence live on in us. You may not talk about them often, but they show up in your ambition. In your caution. In how you spend your time. In what you believe you're allowed to want. These multi-generational patterns play out all the time – and you would be wise to understand how they are playing out now.

Understanding your heritage isn't about nostalgia, it's about clarity.

Ask yourself: What patterns am I carrying? What values were handed down – almost invisible or loudly? What parts of my past do I want to honour – and what do I prefer to leave behind?

This part of the book is your chance to look back – not for the sake of the past, but to build a more intentional future. In a 100-Year Life, your past isn't just history, it's a foundation. The stories, habits and values you carry forward will shape not just the next few years, but the decades still to come.

Here's a simple starting point: Imagine being asked, *'Tell me something about you.'* Maybe in a job interview, or on a date, or perhaps there's a friend who really wants to understand you. What would you say? You might talk about your work, but if you had to go deeper, what would you say about the family or community you came from? What stories would you tell? Who would you include? Who's standing behind you, metaphorically placing their hands on your shoulders? Let's take this idea a little further with the thought exercise below:

Imagine standing before me. Close your eyes and picture this:

First, feel your mother's hand on your right shoulder and your father's hand on your left.

Now, behind them, their parents place their hands on their shoulders.

Then, their parents' hands rest on their shoulders.

Your Story: About Your Heritage

As you think about the people who came before you, what stories would you tell of them? Perhaps a time someone took a risk or made a sacrifice. Or moments that reveal a (spoken or unspoken) rule they lived by. A job they loved – or hated. Perhaps a family motto, habit or myth that shaped you. Or a loss or moment of survival. *What do these stories reveal about what became important to you?*

When I looked at my own stories, I discovered many about my parents and grandparents. Your own stories of your heritage are sure to have these characters.

I've selected three little stories about the three women standing at my shoulder: my mother – Barbara, her mother – Anne – and Anne's mother – Lily. I've chosen these stories because they illustrate events that shaped them and that, through their heritage, shaped me too.

My first story is about my mother Barbara, who was born in Liverpool in 1934, where her parents, Anne and Arthur, ran The Duke of York pub. In 1939, with the Second World War looming, Barbara's father volunteered for active service in the Air Force and was gone for four years. Nine days after war was declared, her mother gave birth to a boy.

A Story of Loss – Liverpool, 1941

On 6 May 1941, the three-day Blitz of the port city of Liverpool began. For these three nights, the German Luftwaffe bombed the city. With sirens blaring, the terrified citizens took shelter wherever they could. On one balmy night with a clear sky, the pub took a direct hit. It was completely destroyed. Sheltering under the staircase as they had done every night, seven-year-old Barbara heard the deafening noise of crashing masonry. Crawling out of her makeshift shelter, she saw the bright stars shining through the jagged edges of what was her home. Then in the pitch dark of the blackout, her mother and grandmother, Anne clutching her baby son, they struggled to a tram stop, taking a tram to a relative's house.

As I think about my mother, I cannot imagine what it is as a child to lose everything in a fire storm. Mum rarely mentioned this story, but I'm sure it significantly shaped her deep, deep desire to bring stability to her own family.

How did you feel when you read this story? Does it resonate with any of your stories of your own heritage – of lives shattered by war or forced immigration? What impact did your stories have on you?

For myself I think it created a family motto – at the heart of how we lived as a family. The motto was 'Don't make a fuss.' That translated into: don't show you're frightened or exhausted; don't complain about feeling ill, just get on with it.

What was your family motto? And how did it show up in your working life?

My second story is about the relationship between Mum and her mother, Anne.

A Story of Invisible Children – Liverpool, 1945

Mum is now 11 years old. She's a bright girl and has won a scholarship to Holly Lodge, a fee-paying school in Liverpool that prepares girls for their university entrance exams. Every school day she rushes home to look after her younger brother and to prepare the evening meal for the family. Her mother, Anne, is now a midwife, supporting pregnant women in some of Liverpool's worst slums. Anne arrives home late, often exhausted by her day. Importantly, as a nurse, Anne is discouraged from working if she has children, so she keeps her little family a secret – even from her colleagues at work. Mum feels resentful at having to look after her brother and the family at a time in her life when her friends at Holly Lodge go home to a mother cooking a dinner. She's the only girl at school with a working mother and it's something she hides.

What strikes me about this story is that it marks the beginnings of what became over time a family rule. If you are a working woman, your work must be invisible and not acknowledged, and importantly, you cannot be too proud about work and don't expect too much from it. The women in my family always worked – Anne as a midwife; her mother Lily, widowed with seven daughters after her husband was killed in the First World War, cleaned houses. Then every evening, Lily with her daughters (including Anne), went to the wash house in the yard to wash and iron other people's laundry.

Are any of your heritage stories about how your ancestors worked – did any of this come down through the generation to how you feel about work or your expectations of work?

Here is my third little story that in a sense closes this theme.

A Story of a Secret Marriage – Zermatt, 1954

In her youth, Mum spent all her weekends at the youth club of a local church, where she was falling in love with David. She's passed her entrance exam to university and goes up for the start of the term. She's the first person in our family ever to go to university. Later that year, she becomes pregnant.

Motherhood is not allowed for university students and Barbara must leave. Now five months pregnant, she elopes with David to a little church in Zermatt, where they marry with their youth club friends around them. Their daughter Lynda is born four months later. Anne does not approve.

I'm reflecting on what has been passed down by this story. In part, it's a love story to friendship – my mother stayed friends with the group from the youth club all her life. But there is a deeper story here about marriage and family: Marriage is sacred and sacrifices have to be made. Indeed, my mother had sacrificed her university position to give birth to me.

These stories weren't easy to uncover – I had to piece them together slowly. But now I see how they helped shape me, not just my choices but my instincts.

I began this part of the chapter by inviting you to tell your first story, a story about your heritage. I've told you three little stories about the three women standing to the right of my shoulder.

As I pieced together these fragments, I began to see how my heritage shaped more than just my childhood, it shaped my working life, my values, even how I imagined the future. In a 100-Year Life, these early imprints don't fade with time. They echo forward, influencing what we believe is possible at every stage.

MAKE SENSE OF YOUR HERITAGE

How do you understand your heritage and put it into the context of who you are now and who you could become? To understand your ancestors' context is to shed light on your own, to imagine the era that shaped them, the social norms they lived by and the role that fate played.

Eras: The Times That Shape Us

I can see from my own history that the course of a working life is never shaped by personal choices alone. It's always entwined with the wider forces of history – of era-defining events: The wars, recessions, pandemics and technological shifts that alter the landscape of life and work, sometimes gradually, sometimes overnight.

My grandmother and great-grandmother lived through brutal, war-torn times and I feel an overwhelming sense of appreciation of the hardships they faced. They are not alone – their stories were replicated around the world and in some regions of the world are being played out right now. Era events continue to shape every working life and in a 100-Year Life there will be many era events.

What about you? How have era events shaped your own story?

Maybe you started your career in a financial crash, graduated during a pandemic or built your first team entirely online. Some events are slow-burning, like the climate crisis while others, such as COVID-19, strike without warning, and some, like AI, appear at an extraordinary speed. Either way, these moments leave a mark.

Earlier, I introduced Lucia and Nico. Born in 1993, Lucia is the daughter of two people born in South America, who emigrated in the late 1980s. Just as her parents' lives were shaped by era-defining events, so too Lucia's life has been shaped by two major shifts – one anticipated, the other sudden and disorienting.

The anticipated shift is technology. If, like Lucia and Nico, you are in your twenties or early thirties, then technology has been an era-defining shift from the start. As a teenager, you lived through the social media boom, used digital platforms for connection, expression and learning. Your smartphone wasn't just a tool, it was a gateway. This shaped how you communicate and how you imagine your career: mobile, flexible, connected. And technology continues to define us – whatever our age.

Then came the unanticipated era event – the global pandemic that began in January 2020 and lasted until May 2023. Everything changed for all of us. The borders closed. Much of our work went virtual. For Nico, his work happened from his childhood bedroom. He adapted quickly but noticed the cost. His social world shrank. The adventure he and Lucia had planned evaporated.

During those early lockdown months, Lucia and Nico talked more – both working remotely, both adjusting to a reality that felt suspended and intensified. They described what they each missed: Lucia missed movement and meaning. Nico missed the rhythm of clear goals and forward motion – something to anchor the day.

You've already experienced significant era events – astonishing technological developments and the pandemic. And there are sure to be more to come – especially from climate change and AI. What will future jobs look like, how do you prepare for careers that don't yet exist? How many times will you reinvent yourself?

As you reflect on your working life, ask yourself:

- → What global or national events shaped my experience of work – pandemics, recessions, technological shifts?
- → How did they influence my choices, values or direction?
- → What changes are unfolding now – and how might they shape the future I'm building?

Whether you're just beginning or already decades into your career, it's worth pausing to consider these questions. A wise working life is not one free from disruption, it is one that builds in resilience – knowing the next era-defining event is not an 'if' but a 'when'. Throughout this book we will explore ways to strengthen this resilience, knowing the future will almost certainly surprise you.

Social Norms: The Rules We Live By

Let me tell you a story about a blue cake tin.

A Story of a Blue Cake Tin – School Day, 1962

Mum sews many of her own clothes and those of us children too. On the mantelpiece, there's a photo of her arriving at Dad's company ball, arm in arm, proud. She looks glorious in a gown she made herself: tight at the waist, flaring into a wide skirt. It's the 'New Look' from Christian Dior, brought to a factory dance in the north of England.

Mum also cooks everything from scratch, much to the irritation of her children. We dream of the new wave of convenience foods: tins of beans and Spam, packets of dried mashed potato, sachets of fluffy desserts whipped up in minutes with cold milk ... Our friends speak of them in rapture. But not in our house. Mum, unbending in the face of food fads, makes everything by hand. Yet we are delighted that when we rush home from school, the pale blue multi-tiered cake tin is always waiting – cake on the top tier, homemade biscuits below.

Mum's views were strong. *Shop-bought* was a dirty phrase. To her, it meant poor nutrition – and worse, that someone had failed in their duty of care. She chose nurturing, fiercely and proudly.

The blue cake tin lives vividly in my memory. It came to represent something more than the baking inside: it stood for certainty. For a clear belief about how life should be lived. About what it meant to be a good mother, a good neighbour, a good woman.

Perhaps you have an object like that – a dinner set, a school blazer, a diary – that represents what a 'good' life should look like.

The story of Mum's cake tin and her baking was in part a reflection of her personal choice. It was also a rejection of her own mother as a role model. Her mother Anne worked throughout her childhood. There was no cake tin waiting after school. I sensed Mum wanted something different for us. Anne became a role model she wished to avoid, not emulate. Yet the cake tin also carried something bigger: it signified social norms. In 1950s Britain, most mothers didn't have careers. A few had part-time jobs, but full-time work, especially with children, was rare. The dominant norm was homemaker. Just look at the ads from the time: women in aprons, cinched waists, smiling sweetly as they served a husband returning from work. Children quiet, the dinner warm.

These social norms shaped Mum's world and they also shaped mine; they are shaping yours too. They're the unwritten rules you absorb early: about what work is and when and where work takes place, about how to parent, when to rest and what ambition should look like. They influence who you admire, who you model yourself after. Some role models we emulate, others we resist – and many we absorb more deeply than we realise. Norms show up in what's praised, what's unspoken, what's assumed. They can offer structure or limit possibility.

You've already met Ben. His story makes this real. He grew up admiring a father who provided well and built a stable life but was rarely home. This was the social norm for fathers at the time. And as a role model for Ben, fatherhood came to mean financial support. But now, as a father himself, Ben wants something different: to be emotionally present, not just economically dependable. Still, the pressure to succeed, to meet those inherited expectations, remains.

Look around your own life. What are the social norms at play? Norms about when to retire, about whether long hours are a badge of honour, whether caregiving earns praise or penalty.

Some people reject norms entirely. Others embrace them, finding comfort or identity in their structure. But most of us live somewhere in between – negotiating, adapting, questioning.

I find myself both echoing and rejecting my mother's blue cake tin and the social norms and role models this represented.

In the 20-odd years between Mum and me, the world and social norms shifted. More girls went to university and more women entered business. Just as Mum had looked at her own mother, Anne, and thought, *I want something different*, I did the same. I saw her devoted to our family, proud of her nurturing, but often frustrated and worn down by the repetition of motherhood. By baking daily, for that cake tin.

But I chose differently. I rejected full-time caregiving and part-time work. Instead, I pursued a career with intensity. And yet, and yet, part of Mum stayed with me. I became a decent cook. I shunned processed foods. I tried to do it all. And like her, I sometimes found myself distracted, resentful, exhausted.

I still remember envying a colleague who once said, unapologetically about preparing family meals 'I don't cook.' I could never say that. Not without guilt. Not with Mum as my role model. Many of us live in that space: between admiration and reinvention. Between carrying forward what served us and rewriting what didn't. We don't get to choose our social norms or our role models, but we do get to choose how we respond to them and in that choice, we shape our own legacy.

As you reflect on your own life, ask yourself:

→ What were the unspoken rules about work, ambition and success in my family or culture?
→ Which of those patterns have I inherited – and which have I chosen to release?
→ As the world shifts, which old expectations are worth revisiting?
→ What kind of role model do I want to be – for others, and for my future self?

Fate: The Hand We're Given

Beyond social norms and era-defining events, there is another force shaping our lives: fate. Fate is the job you never applied for but landed anyway. The diagnosis you didn't expect. The person you met who changed your course. Sometimes fate lifts us, other times it alters the path entirely.

In the stories you told of your heritage, could you see how fate shaped choices and decisions? One of my own stories is of my father, David – it's a story of fate.

A Story of Dad and Fate, Lorton, 1995

Over the last few months my father David has found his breathing has become more difficult. His doctors are perplexed. Dad is incredibly fit – he strides up mountains, sails in the local lake every weekend, has never smoked and lives a very healthy life. So why the breathing difficulty? Eventually, after many tests, the doctors examining his lung tissues in high-res X-rays discover threading through his lungs tiny filaments of asbestosis. His diagnosis is mesothelioma, a truly terrible lung disease. Over the following years an ever-growing tumour in Dad's lungs overwhelms his breathing capacity. He can only use an oxygen mask to breathe. Now, no longer able to breathe, he passes away, my mother by his side.

The doctors had given Dad five months to live. This was his fate, and he bore it with extraordinary determination and goodwill. When Dad worked with asbestos in his early twenties, he had no idea that in choosing his first job as an engineer, he was also signing his death certificate.

Earlier, I introduced you to Mira. Her life has been touched by fate. In her twenties, Mira imagined a future of love, security and shared retirement. By her late forties, that vision was unravelling. Her unexpected divorce altered not just her emotional life, but her financial one too. Work, once optional, became essential. The future she planned was gone. A new one – uncertain, unsought – had taken its place.

Have you seen fate in your own heritage stories? Perhaps you've already experienced fate yourself. What has this meant to you – what have you taken away from this as you think about your own working life?

EXPERT VOICES: Robert Rowland Smith, Philosopher

Across this book I have sought the counsel of experts. Here, I turn to Robert Rowland Smith, a philosopher who brings philosophy into our understanding of everyday life.[1] Robert studied at All Souls, Oxford and over the last few decades has helped many people to see how philosophy can illuminate their choices. I was struck by Robert's reflections on fate in his autobiography, *Autobiophilosophy: An Intimate Story of What*

It Means to Be Human. As we spoke together, Robert explored what the guiding question: *Who am I?* means to him:

> When we look at our parents' stories, about their lives before us, they take on the quality of a fable. Their stories are not quite history, although there is plenty of historical data, they produce in us a state of wonder. For all our natural, biological proximity to them, they are foreigners in time. We all live in the flow of time that none of us can interrupt. Their stories hail from a time that is not ours. Perhaps this semi-disconnect from the past of our parents is why our own lives can at times feel so random – we are 'thrown' into the world.
>
> This is fundamentally a question of what it is to be a human being. There is a vague notion, but when we look deeply at ourselves and bring a real person into the picture, we gain some initial purchase on what a human being might actually do. None of us has an ideal, perfect or general self. We have the self we have, with its irreducible specificity, its one-of-a-kind combination of history, biology and character.
>
> When I look at my own father, his preference would surely have been for a life of presence, identity, connection and value. For the embroidery of the self to weave its threads until it had assumed the form and colour that most people are able to enjoy. But that was not his life. In his 40s my father contracted multiple sclerosis and that shaped the rest of his life. I am reminded of the Greek philosopher Heraclitus who wrote 'man's character is his fate'. Who we are, as much as the action of any external influence, determines what will happen to us.
>
> Being human means dealing with our fate. We cannot change our fate. How we contend with our fate is what matters. Whether our fate is lucky or unlucky, we are dealt a hand. We might be born into poverty or affluence, good or bad health, peace or war – but the playing of that hand is up to us.
> And so it is that the tension between being determined by our circumstances and determining ourselves which is the essential part of being human.

Pause to consider how Robert's words land with your experience. As you looked at the lives of your ancestors could you see the hand of fate. And the notion that our character is our fate.

As you think about the unexpected turns in your life, consider:

→ What moments of fate have altered your course?
→ What has been asked of you that you didn't choose?
→ How have you responded – and how has that response shaped who you are becoming?

Fate humbles us, but it also reveals us.

You've understood the forces that shaped your life – family roles, cultural expectations, historical events and moments of fate. These influences may not fully define you, but they leave a lasting imprint on how you see the world and what you believe is possible. As you reflect on what you've inherited – values, behaviours, beliefs – you gain more choice over what to carry forward.

In the next chapter, we shift the focus from where you come from to who you are: your personality and how it shapes the way you live and work. But before we do that, let's pause to consider actions you can take now and promises to your future self.

MY HERITAGE: Putting it into Practice

Three Actions to Take Now

1. **Tell one story aloud.**
   Choose one family story – of sacrifice, resilience or everyday life – and share it with a friend, child or colleague. Notice how it feels to give voice to the past.
2. **Identify a family motto.**
   Reflect on the unspoken rules or sayings that shaped you: *Don't make a fuss, Education first, Work hard, stay quiet.* Write one down and ask yourself: does it still serve me?
3. **Name an era event.**
   Pick one historical or global event that influenced your working life – a recession, a war, a pandemic, a technological change – and jot down how it altered your path or values.

Three Promises to My Future Self

1. **I will honour what strengthens me.**
   I will carry forward the values and practices from my heritage that give me resilience, clarity and purpose.
2. **I will release what no longer fits.**
   I will notice inherited rules or norms that limit me – and consciously choose not to pass them on.
3. **I will weave my own story.**
   I will recognise the hand of fate and the influence of history, but I will also claim my agency – shaping a life that future generations may one day look back on with gratitude.

Heritage is never just the past. In a 100-Year Life, the stories, values and mottos you inherit are not fixed scripts but living threads. Over time, you can choose which to carry forward, which to release, and which to rewrite. In doing so, you weave your ancestors' struggles and strengths into a foundation that supports reinvention, resilience and meaning across the decades ahead.

CHAPTER 2

MY PERSONALITY: My Natural Preferences, Habits and Patterns

If your heritage shows you where you've come from, your personality offers insights into how you move through the world today. Your heritage, the era events you experience, the social norms you observe and the role models you are attracted to or repelled by together make you who you are. Yet there is one other aspect you need to consider, the aspect of yourself that is more nature than nurture: Your personality traits.

In a 100-Year Life, your personality traits don't just shape how you work today, they influence how you adapt over time. Some traits, like curiosity or steadiness, can become powerful allies across a long, evolving working life. Others may need more conscious attention if they create patterns that no longer serve you as your context changes. In this chapter we will explore a model of personality, dive into how your personality leads you to make choices at work and discover that a tight fit between your personality and your work is not always advantageous.

Your Story: Your Personality

How would you describe the essence of your personality and character – the qualities that define you and guide your actions? Moments that reveal your personality capture the essence of who you are and how you move through the world. *As you recall this story, ask yourself what it says about who you are becoming.*

I've chosen a story from my adolescence: I am around 13 years old. It's not a memory that I often think about, but when I wrote my stories in the summer of 2022, it was one of the first to surface out of my unconscious.

A Story of an Artichoke – Italy, August 1968

It is the longed-for summer holiday and my family embarks on the journey from the north of England through France to our destination – northern Italy and the glorious, fragrant shores of Lake Como. Thoughts of lemons and ice cream fill my mind as we drive through France, bundled into our old estate car. But first, let me provide a little more context. By 'drive', I mean Dad navigates the 1,000 miles from Cockermouth, Cumbria, across the channel, through the expanse of France and finally into Italy. By 'bundle', I mean we four children – aged from 13 down to three – sit on wooden boxes in the rear of the car. Designed and made by Dad to accommodate the camping equipment, these boxes, arrayed with sleeping bags, are our seats for the journey.

Money is tight. Dad has a reasonably paid job as a factory manager but every penny is counted and with Britain in a currency crisis, only a very limited amount of sterling can be brought, so my budget-conscious mum has packed any crevices with provisions.

At last, we reach the campsite on Lake Como, our final destination. Nestled beneath a grove of trees is a simple cafeteria. Although I know eating from the canteen is not on the agenda for our cash-strapped family, I stealthily take a look. Pride of place is a plate of cooked artichokes. I'd read about this vegetable in my mother's recently bought copy of Claudia Roden's *A Book of Middle East Cooking' Cookery*.[1] But this was my first sighting of a real artichoke, being more familiar with the seasonal vegetables of northern England – winter carrots and potatoes, and in summer, peas and endless courgettes.

I gaze at an artichoke. A particularly fine specimen, its large glistening green leaves are laid out in precise formation, the perfectly overlapping leaves form a glorious globe. At that moment, I want nothing more than to taste the artichoke.

Not unreasonably, we are on a tight budget and there is no assurance I will enjoy the artichoke – my mother says no, she cannot buy it. Frustration and sadness overwhelm me. Part of my teenage brain whispers (as teenage brains are wont to do), this is my only chance ever to eat this extraordinary vegetable. It's a once-in-a-lifetime opportunity, taken from me by my tough-minded mother.

At that moment, faced with the frustration of the artichoke, I make three vows to myself, or more accurately to my future self: I will earn enough to choose what I eat, I will enjoy eating artichokes whenever I want to and I will never, ever go camping with my family again.

What did your story tell you about your personality? Can you see how these traits play forward to what you have become?

For me, the artichoke story captures the teenage mix of anguish and opportunities to be grasped. Of course, like many teenagers, I had periods of being insufferable and I can only imagine what my mother was feeling about her wilful daughter although she should have known that I might have had in mind Dad's mantra, 'never conform'. Yet I feel there is something else here, something peeking out that was then and was to become 'me'. It reveals a glimpse of 'me' – adventurous, curious, determined, annoying and independent.

As you think about the story that captures 'you', what five words define you? As we explore the threads of your working life, these descriptors will shape your choices and motivations.

THE FIVE TRAITS THAT SHAPE US

Let's take a closer look at the traits that shape you. To do so, I will show a model of these traits, share a conversation with an expert on personality and consider what this means for how you work.

These personality traits are what psychologists call 'the Big Five' – *Openness to experience, Conscientiousness, Extraversion, Agreeableness* and *Neuroticism* (emotional instability). The five traits are universal – found across cultures and demographics, and more recent research has shown some have a clear biological underpinning. For example, studies show that high levels of cortisol are associated with neurotic traits, highlighting the interplay between biology and behaviour.

Think about each trait as a dimension of personality, ranging from high to low. High *openness to experience* reflects a willingness to embrace new experiences, ideas and change – low scores reflect consistency and cautiousness. High *conscientiousness* suggests efficiency and a tendency towards organisation, whereas low *conscientiousness* is a tendency towards extravagance and carelessness. *Extraverts* tend to be outgoing and energetic, introverts more likely to be solitary and reserved. High *agreeableness* involves a propensity for empathy, cooperation and compassion, while low scores suggest critical and rational tendencies. If you score high in *neuroticism*, you are more likely to be sensitive and nervous, while low scores reflect resilience and confidence.

As your roles, needs and environments shift, you'll find different parts of your personality come forward. A trait that felt limiting at one stage might become a strength at another. In a 100-Year Life, personality isn't just a profile, it's a resource for reinvention.

Over the years I have completed the Big Five Personality diagnostic. In general, I score high on openness to experience, tend towards agreeableness, am more introverted (I like solitude and walks are part of this search for calm), am conscientious, and am relatively low in neuroticism. Reflecting on the artichoke story, openness to experience stands out as a key trait.

Do you have a key trait that drives how you approach work and what you enjoy?

Now, let's look more deeply at how these personality traits can influence your behaviours and interactions.

EXPERT VOICES: Randall Peterson, Psychologist

Across this book I have sought the counsel of experts. Here, I turn to Randall Peterson, a psychologist and long-time colleague of mine at London Business School.[2] For over 20 years, Randall has researched the interface between personality and work, helping MBA students and executives use personality assessments to build greater self-knowledge. His perspective is especially valuable here as we explore whether examining our personality traits can give us useful insight into who we are and how we work. Here is how he sees it:

Understanding your personality preferences is crucial to crafting a good working life. Knowing yourself enhances self-understanding, helping you navigate interactions and decisions. For example, if you know you are introverted, you can acknowledge your preference will be to step back in team settings. Yet there may be circumstances when stepping forward would be beneficial. Realising this helps you make an effort beyond your preferences. Similarly, an extrovert will realise there will be times when they are better served by stepping back and listening rather than being the first person to speak.

Personality traits are generally stable, but they evolve with life experiences and responsibilities. Take the trait conscientiousness, where the first shift happens during young adulthood at a time when people get a job, perhaps start thinking about having a family, move out from their parents' home. Situations of responsibility like this begin to change us and as we accumulate more responsibilities, so we become more conscientious. Our context influences our personality traits.

Our personality draws us to work that fits our preferences – you bring your personality to work. For example, if you are high on neuroticism, you're more likely to worry at work and feel stressed so it makes sense to find work that does not have a great deal of stress in it. Extraverts thrive in social settings, enjoy being with others and feel positive emotions when around others. Those high on openness crave work that brings novelty. Those who are high on agreeableness want to please others at work, will avoid confrontation and fear changing the status quo. High on conscientiousness? As Randall notes, 'for managers this is the dream worker – self-motivated and prepared to go that extra mile'. Extreme traits can work against you. Take *conscientiousness*, where studies show those who are very conscientious at work are prone to burn out as they become overly determined to meet their goals. They are likely to thrive when the working environment is organised and stable but suffer when the working environment becomes turbulent or ambiguous.

What are your reflections on this – can you see situations where your personality has shaped the way you work? Are you drawn to particular work? What type of work was that, how did you feel about it?

Your personality is not destiny, but it is a compass. As you explore your threads and future choices, notice not just what comes naturally, but what might emerge if you are stretched beyond your habitual ways of being.

PERSONALITY THROUGH MIRA, BEN, LUCIA AND NICO

Let's take a closer look at this range of personalities – you may find something that resonates with you in the descriptions below.

Mira in Focus

Now in her mid-fifties and recently divorced, Mira's looking for a new challenge and wondering what will suit her best. What does Mira have to take into account as she thinks about her next move?

She has always been introverted, meticulous and loyal to her work. She's high on conscientiousness: organised, detail-focused and diligent. When given a task, she completes it with quiet precision. Her colleagues often rely on her to bring calm structure to moments of disarray.

Mira's also high in neuroticism, tends to internalise stress, to ruminate when things go wrong, to feel responsible even when it's not her burden. She has trouble switching off. Even now, she sometimes lies awake mentally editing documents or replaying conversations from long ago.

Her introversion runs deep. Mira doesn't seek out large groups or fast-paced meetings. She prefers depth over breadth – small gatherings, one-on-one conversations, solo problem-solving. She's reflective, not reactive. And while she has strong emotional intelligence, she rarely shows her inner world unless invited.

So, as Mira reflects on what is next, she would be wise to consider a role that gives her an opportunity to develop her mastery, but that does not put her under too much pressure.

Ben in Focus

A senior executive at a crossroads, Ben is trying to do well in his career and be a good father. What can his personality traits tell us about what he should take into account?

Ben sits close to the middle of the introversion–extraversion scale. He enjoys a good conversation over coffee, can hold a room when needed and often finds his energy lifted by time with the right people. But he also needs space – mornings alone to think, walks to reset, quiet time to recharge after busy days. It's not that he avoids others, he just knows how to pace himself. Ben scores high on conscientiousness. Disciplined, dependable and organised, he is the person who preps the agenda, checks in on the detail and shows up when it counts. His conscientiousness also extends to his relationships – he wants the team to succeed, the meeting to land, the tone to be right.

Emotionally, Ben is steady but inwardly self-critical. He's medium on neuroticism, which means he worries – mostly about whether he's living up to his own standards.

As Ben reflects on the future, he realises that working with a team is central to his identity, and that his conscientiousness will serve him well in complex, dynamic circumstances.

Lucia in Focus

Lucia, now in her early thirties feels she is drifting. As she imagines what she could become, understanding her personality will help her think through this with clarity.

She scores high on openness to experience. It was her curiosity and her love of ideas that stretch the imagination that took her to a year's volunteering at a children's school in rural Ethiopia. She's the kind of person who has a dozen browser tabs open at once – on education reform, regenerative agriculture and poetry. She learns quickly, dreams widely and cares deeply.

But her conscientiousness is at the low end of the scale. She starts things and sometimes doesn't finish them. She prefers fluidity and creative freedom. This is both a strength and a challenge: she generates rich ideas but occasionally lacks the scaffolding to bring them to life.

Lucia is an introvert by nature, but not shy. She values solitude and deep conversation over surface-level chatter. Thoughtful in groups, she is perceptive in conflict and tends to observe before she speaks. She prefers to be invited in than to assert herself. Emotionally, she's grounded. She has a relatively low level of neuroticism and she's calm in the face of uncertainty, rarely overwhelmed by anxiety.

Her personality – open, reflective, values-driven – gives Lucia depth. But, low on conscientiousness, she's prone to periods of drift. Her work has meaning, but not momentum. She is beginning to realise that if she wants to achieve what she hopes for she will need to set herself clear goals and even ensure that a more conscientious friend (like Nico) holds her accountable.

Nico in Focus

Nico, growing up with Lucia has seen their similarities and differences. He scores high on conscientiousness. Deliberate, organised and goal-oriented, he saved a portion of his salary for a future startup and steadily acquiring skills to support his ambitions. Sometimes Lucia's drift worries him and he can see their differences become clearer over time. Yet whilst Lucia is high in openness to experience, Nico is moderate: yes, he's curious about systems and ideas, especially in knowledge work and technology, but prefers grounded experimentation over wild leaps.

He is more introverted than extrovert, more reflective than gregarious. Nico notices how he tends to thrive in small circles and prefers deep, purposeful collaboration to broad networking. Nico is low on neuroticism. He feels alert rather than anxious, and setbacks (like his failed first venture) trigger reflection rather than panic.

Nico is beginning to get a real sense of who he is – how his personality has shaped the choices he has made and how they could constrain him over time.

Do any of these descriptions resonate with you – can you imagine writing a descriptive paragraph about how you work in the way I have written them out for these four characters? What would you accentuate and what would you take away from this description?

In a long life, your personality becomes part of the threads you weave over time. What traits have helped you navigate challenge or transition? Which ones have kept you grounded or held you back? And how might your future self draw on different parts of your personality to evolve?

YOUR CHARACTER AT WORK

Let's now connect personality with the choices you've made – or might make – in your working life.

Have there been occasions when you can see how your personality traits drew you towards a certain type of work? I've thought about this question from my own perspective and here's what I discovered as I look across the first decades of my working life.

My first 'real' job was in 1982 in the Human Resources function of British Airways. It was a managerial role that, after three years, I didn't truly enjoy. I switched to a consulting role at PA Consultants, partly to earn more money (remember the artichoke?) and partly to become more of an advisor and less of a manager. Then, in my mid-thirties, autonomy and curiosity became my drivers. Now I sought a relatively non-hierarchical and autonomous environment and academia fitted that need, so I joined London Business School. The move involved significant trade-offs, including a salary reduction of 80 per cent. I lost my corporate car and the chance to swim in the large pond of management consultancy yet ultimately, my personality preferences gave me the courage to act on this feeling.

Finding a job that suits your personality has benefits, but in conversation with Randall, he offers a warning: as you discover work that fits you, your personality traits become entrenched. Preferences are reinforced through habits and behaviours in everyday work that bring satisfaction. However, consider whether seeking work that 'fits' narrows your options. Should you instead be making choices that challenge your preferences?

Longer life opens new choices and makes reinvention not just possible, but necessary. But reinvention doesn't begin with a clean slate, it begins with who you are now. That's what this chapter has explored: your personality. Those stable yet evolving traits that shape how you move through the world. We've seen how traits such as conscientiousness, openness or introversion can influence the work you gravitate towards, the environments where you thrive and the patterns you create over time. We've also witnessed how these traits shift with age, experience and responsibility, and how moments of transition can bring out new aspects of who you are.

MY PERSONALITY: Putting it into Practice

Three Actions to Take Now

1. **Write your five words.**
   Choose five adjectives that best describe your personality today. Keep them somewhere visible – on your desk, in your journal – and reflect on how they show up in your daily work.

2. **Spot your trait in action.**
   Over the next week, notice one moment when your personality shaped your behaviour – perhaps your introversion guided you to listen deeply, or your conscientiousness helped you stay organised. Capture it in a sentence.
3. **Stretch beyond your default.**
   Pick one trait you lean on heavily and do the opposite, just once. If you're extroverted, practice listening without speaking first. If you're conscientious, let a small detail go. See what you learn.

Three Promises to My Future Self

1. **I will know myself clearly.**
   I will continue to deepen my understanding of my natural traits and preferences, using that self-knowledge as a guide for choices ahead.
2. **I will evolve with experience.**
   I will recognise that personality shifts with time and responsibility – and I will welcome the growth that comes with new stages of life.
3. **I will not let traits become limits.**
   I will notice when I cling too tightly to what feels natural and instead give myself permission to stretch, experiment and reinvent.

Personality is never fixed. In a 100-Year Life, your natural traits are a foundation – shaping how you respond, connect and create. But across the decades, new experiences will stretch you, responsibilities will reshape you, and different parts of your character will come forward. By knowing yourself clearly and allowing room to evolve, you turn personality into a lifelong resource – helping you adapt, grow and flourish in ways you cannot yet imagine.

In a longer life, this self-knowledge becomes a crucial resource. It helps you recognise the roles that fit, those that stretch you and the ones that hold you back. But personality is not a blueprint, it's a compass. It can point to what feels authentic, but it can't always tell you what's next.

That's the question we turn to now. In the next chapter, we'll explore your identity – how you reshape your sense of self over time, not through planning alone but through action, experimentation and reflection. Your personality gives you a starting point, your identity is what comes next.

CHAPTER 3

MY WORKING IDENTITY: How Work Has Shaped Me – and How It Could Evolve

It is this 'one-of-a-kind combination' which makes up who we are. Together we have glimpsed how the stories of your past shape who you are, and we've dived into personality traits to get a sense of how you approach your work. Finally, let's take a closer look at how work has shaped you – and how you have shaped the work you do.

While we often think of work as something we choose, work in turn also chooses us – it moulds our language, shapes our habits and shifts our sense of self. In this chapter, we'll explore how work not only reflects our identity but transforms it. Whether through major transitions, subtle adaptations, or small side projects, your working life has likely played a profound role in who you've become – and who you might yet be.

In a 100-Year Life, our working identity doesn't stay still. It stretches across decades, adapts to new roles and deepens through reinvention. You may find yourself growing into – and out of – multiple professional identities, each one shaped by where you are in life, what you care about and how you respond to the world around you. Work constantly shapes who we are, yet there are two occasions when this shaping is particularly strong: When you make a switch between one job and another – creating an opportunity for you to explore your multiple selves. And when you take a 'side project' – times when you test out a new identity.

Let's take a closer look at both...

SWITCHING: Make Room for Multiple Selves

Some changes in our working lives are gradual. We drift into new habits, pick up new skills and adapt subtly over time. But other changes in our working life feel sharper – marked by a clear 'before' and 'after'. One of the most powerful moments of identity transformation comes when we switch – from one job to another, from one function or company to another, or across countries and cultures. These moments are rarely just about new job titles or fresh email signatures, often they demand a deeper shift. A change in how we see ourselves. A change in how others see us. A change in the language we use, the clothes we wear, the way we carry ourselves.

Switches expose us. They also reveal us. That's because switching isn't only about logistics, it's also about identity. In making a switch, we start to let go of one version of ourselves and begin to try on another. We feel uncertain. We feel excited. We wonder: will I fit in? Will I be recognised? Will I still feel like *me*?

Let me share one of my own switching stories. It's a story not just about changing jobs but about learning how much work it takes to become someone new.

A Story of a Girl in a Peruvian skirt – British Airways, 1982

I am here at British Airways, working as an occupational psychologist. I've been recruited to redesign the way aircrew are selected. After navigating what seemed like a never-ending selection process, I get the job. I have an office, a monthly pay cheque, my own desk and, for the first time ever – a manager.

But I'm completely bewildered. Who are all these people milling about the office, carrying folders and looking busy, and what do the acronyms on their office doors signify? These provide no real clues about my job and what is expected of me. There's a large folder on my desk with two wire baskets – one marked

'Out Tray' and the other (predictably) 'In Tray'. I'm guessing I must move the stuff in the large folder from one tray to another - but at this stage it's only a guess.

Schooled in the work of anthropologist Margaret Mead and her observations of tribal life in Papua New Guinea, I decided to treat the experience like fieldwork.[1] I became an observer of office life – a newcomer in an unfamiliar village.

And I looked the part of an anthropologist. On my first day, I turn up wearing a long, hand-knitted Peruvian skirt, a pair of blue embroidered cowboy boots and an antelope skin jacket from Morocco. These prized possessions seem a perfect choice for the first day of work, yet I notice other women wear the dark suits and pussy-bow blouses that signify the corporate woman. I brazen it out for a week, then drop my idiosyncratic look and take a more conventional route to office attire.

That weekend, I pull out my *Vogue* pattern book, searching for a suit pattern that fits with the attire of others, is within my budget, and matches my sewing competence. I find the perfect style – a simple collarless jacket and a well-fitting skirt. Over the weekend, I stitch five yards of inexpensive and what I judge to be functional grey wool into a suit with neither a collar nor buttonholes. I am aware of the limits of my stitching mastery.

By the following week the 'hippy academic' is beginning to disappear. I've shed the clothes and (at least some) of the identity of an earlier 'self' and replaced it with a 'self' that I judge will fit in more easily and importantly – attract less attention. I'm no longer 'that hippy chick who has just finished her doctorate studying Maslow's Hierarchy of Needs', I am becoming a 'corporate woman'.

For me, this memory first brought back the joy of making my first suit (and wonderment at my lost sewing skills). Reflecting more deeply, I see a memory of changing identity – of who I was and who I was becoming. I was replacing the long-knitted skirt with a sensible, on-the-knee grey woollen skirt. At the time, it felt like a costume change but underneath that, something more profound was happening.

Your Story: About Switching

Over to you: Do you have a story of when you made a switch in your working life? Did you switch country, company or function? Were you as perplexed as I was? Did you change the clothes you wore, the language you used? Did you feel your identity shifting? Ask yourself: *What does this story reveal about my values, strengths and possibilities?*

My story was one of the first times I experienced how strongly work could shape identity. I noticed my vocabulary changing. I began to speak in the language of 'strategy', 'performance', 'deliverables' and 'timelines' – words I hadn't used before. With every conversation and every new habit, I was reinforcing this new identity and yet, I didn't entirely let go of the old one.

In your story of switching can you compare the initial identity and your later identity?

Switching might feel like shedding one identity for another. Yet most of us don't fully discard the old. Instead, we layer new identities over old ones, and we carry many at once. So we carry multiple selves – different versions of who we are, who we used to be and who we might become. Even at work, we show up differently in different situations. We may be confident and directive in a meeting, but quiet and reflective with a mentee. These shifts are not inauthentic; they reflect how we bring different parts of ourselves into different moments.

Of course, living with multiple selves can sometimes create tension.[2] The self that wants stability may clash with the one that craves adventure. The self who thrives at work may struggle to find space for creativity or care. But noticing and naming these selves helps us make wiser choices. It allows us to ask: *Which self needs more space right now? Which one am I growing into?*

Let me explain... It was possible for me to be *both* a graduate student *and* a business manager. Over time, I overlaid this first self with another. For while I was shedding the skin of one self – the graduate student – I kept some of it inside. That other self was activated when at the weekends I left London, or in the holidays when (enabled in part by BA's generous employee flight benefits), I travelled back to South America and later to Asia – the adventurer was still there.

You may have similar reflections on your multiple selves. Do you notice that as you changed jobs, your working style accommodated new circumstances; while also shaping the way you performed your job?

Over time, you've likely created an array of identities – each with its own language, uniform and norms. Sometimes in harmony with each other, occasionally creating conflict across boundaries. Your multiple selves are important because they are made up of parts of what you have been – but also parts of what you *could* be.

Of course, however complex and intriguing you feel you are, to the observer it is often the dominant identity they see. I recall a drawing by my younger son Dominic, aged about four years old. Asked by his teacher to 'draw a picture of Mummy and Daddy', he drew me as a stick-woman carrying a briefcase. In his eyes, it was 'corporate woman' he saw.

I remember looking at that picture and feeling sad and misunderstood. Perhaps I'd prefer he drew what I would at his age– a picture of my mummy holding a cake. Or better still, an adventurer pushing through a thick forest. He did, by the way, for one of my later birthdays, gift me a glorious book of women adventurers in the nineteenth century with a sweet inscription referencing my travels – he later saw that aspect of my multiple identity.

The multiple selves we build are not final. They layer over time – sometimes hidden, sometimes prominent – but always available for renewal. We are shaped and reshaped across the whole of our lives – the longer you have been working, the more opportunities for morphing.

SIDE PROJECTS: Make Possibilities Real

Your working identity isn't only shaped by big transitions – a promotion, a relocation, a major career switch. Often, identity shifts happen in the margins – through smaller, informal acts of curiosity, exploration or collaboration. These side projects, while often not part of the formal job description, can shape who we become. They are spaces of possibility – and they often change everything.

Let me share a story of one of my own.

A Story of a Side Project – London, 1981

At British Airways, my job is to redesign the selection methods of cabin crew, cabin directors and training pilots. The traditional method – panel interviews with current managers –

has been shown to be biased, allowing poor performers through while great ones fall at the first hurdle. Senior managers mandate change: make it fairer.

We build a new selection method – an 'assessment centre' that simulates job tasks. For cabin crew directors, this meant designing exercises to test key qualities like staying calm under pressure, creating a schedule for the flight, dealing with difficult passengers and reviewing team performance. Over two years we run about 50 assessment centres worldwide, collecting extensive data

At an academic conference I attend, I discuss this data with Ivan Robertson, a professor from Manchester University. Ivan is excited about my findings. Working outside my formal role, often in the evenings and at weekends, we embark on this side project. We analyse the data together – and discover something surprising. Even in structured, standardised assessments, individual assessors showed bias: some habitually score high, others low. So a candidate's outcome often depended on who had evaluated them.

Together, we work up the data and findings for publication to the academic community. We co-author three articles for academic publication describing what we've found and encourage others to take note of this assessor bias that was creeping into process, like assessment centres that were designed explicitly to be fairer.[3]

None of this was in my job description. No one asked me to do it and there was no performance review tick-box. Yet I found this side project fascinating and exhilarating.

When I reflect on the British Airways role, I see now that the skills I developed enabled me to take a job with a consulting company. But it was the side project with Ivan Robertson that altered the direction of my working life. It opened a door, allowing me a glimpse of another identity: researcher, academic, writer.

The work with Ivan gave me more than an experience, it gave me a mirror. As we collaborated, I saw his world up close: the cadence of university life, the debates among researchers, the long sweep of inquiry. For a time, I wondered – could I belong in a university department of psychology? Could that be me?

It turned out the answer was no. I admired the intellectual depth but missed the practical application. The pace felt slow, the topics too abstract. And – being honest –this was a job that didn't pay enough. Growing up in a long line of women with very limited financial means, I knew what it meant to have choices constrained by income: I wanted more freedom than that life offered. But even in ruling it out, I learned something. This side project clarified what I did want – and also what I didn't. That's the power of side projects: they allow us to test new selves in safe, low-stakes ways. And sometimes, the greatest insight is discovering what doesn't fit.

These side projects aren't distractions, they're laboratories. Spaces where you try out new ideas – and new selves. They offer clues to what energises you, what feels natural, what stretches you in the right way. And sometimes, like my own project, they show you a world that isn't yours – and that's valuable too.

Ben discovered this too. In his mid-career role at a major retail bank, he began helping a friend with a digital marketing side project. It was outside his formal remit, but it unlocked dormant skills and revealed a new kind of energy. Now he's integrating those lessons into his day job and considering a pivot in the future. It's not a leap, it's a weave.

EXPERT VOICES: Herminia Ibarra, Career Expert

Across this book I have sought the counsel of experts. Here, I turn to Herminia Ibarra, Professor at London Business School and author of *Working Identity: Unconventional Strategies for Reinventing Your Career.*[4] (Harvard Business Review Press, 2004). It is one of the most useful books I know and I recommend it to my MBA students – and to you. Herminia is also one of my closest friends, our friendship spanning more than two decades. I talked to her about my BA experience and the power of side projects. Here are her observations:

> It does not surprise me your side project at British Airways opened new vistas and avenues for you. I'm reflecting on the transformative impact of stepping beyond the confines of a linear career path. When our career is linear, moving along a

straight line in a predictable way, we rarely see other possibilities or have a sense of the working lives of others.

Even in these straight lines, as you experienced at British Airways, there are ways to imagine other possibilities. In my own research of when and how people switch careers, it is often engaging in side projects that serves as a catalytic for change. These side project take many forms – some people start a small business on the side, others collaborate on a project with a colleague from different parts of the business, and some, like you, work with someone outside their company.

All these side projects create opportunities to reimagine who we are. They allow us to explore new interests, test ideas and develop skills that may not fit within our primary roles. Through side projects, we gain insights into our preferences and dislikes. It becomes a way of checking what we like and identifying what doesn't work for us. It's a way of experimenting in a relatively low-key way.

Side projects are more than just extracurricular activities – they're pathways to growth and self-discovery. Embrace them as opportunities to expand your horizons and redefine your professional journey.

Your Story: About Side Projects

Do you have a story of a side project? Did you pursue the project outside the formal boundaries of your job? Was it a project you did between roles, or something you did in a not-for-profit, a freelance collaboration, or a growing business? What impact did it have on you? What did you learn? Did it shift how you saw yourself? *How might this story guide the promises you make to your future self?*

Here is what I have learned: You don't need permission to begin, you don't need a master plan, you don't need it to 'count' on your CV either. You might be stepping into something that matters more than you know. Because side projects don't just build skills, they build selves.

MY WORKING IDENTITY: Putting it into Practice

Three Actions to Take Now

1. **Name one switch.**
   Recall a job change, a relocation or a shift in role. Write down what identity you left behind and what identity you stepped into. Notice what you carried forward and what you let go.
2. **Spot a side project.**
   Think of one informal project – past or present – that stretched you beyond your main role. What did it reveal about your interests, strengths or possible future selves?
3. **Sketch your multiple selves.**
   On a page, draw three circles labelled *past self*, *present self* and *emerging self*. Jot a few words in each. See how they overlap and what they might be pointing toward.

Three Promises to My Future Self

1. **I will make space for reinvention.**
   I will welcome the shifts that come with switching roles, seeing them not just as career moves but as opportunities to grow into new versions of myself.
2. **I will nurture side projects.**
   I will give time and energy to experiments that spark curiosity – knowing they may unlock hidden identities and shape unexpected futures.
3. **I will honour my many selves.**
   I will embrace the layers of who I am – past, present and possible – and use them as a resource for wisdom, creativity and resilience across a long working life.

Working identity is never singular. In a 100-Year Life, who you are at work will shift many times – layered through switches, stretched by side projects, reshaped by circumstance and choice. Each new role, experiment or reinvention adds another possible self. By embracing fluidity of your multiple selves, you free yourself to evolve again and again – building a working life that is both resilient and alive with possibility.

CHAPTER 4

WHO AM I? Some Final Thoughts

Through this first Guiding Question – 'Who am I?'– you've begun a way of reflection that you can return to across a 100-Year Life. In a long working life, identity is not fixed: it deepens, expands and shifts as you grow through decades of change.

Reflect on what you have learned from each of these dimensions – heritage, personality, working identity. What is it that you are taking away from this first Guiding Question?

Here's what I have learned and taken away...

MAKE PEACE WITH IMPERMANENCE, KEEP BUILDING RESILIENCE

As I delve deeper into my heritage, I'm struck by the impermanence of our working lives. What feels stable can shift quickly. Just as my mother and grandmother experienced war, displacement and personal sacrifice, we too live in times of rapid change – climate threats, pandemics, political and economic upheaval. Some changes we can see coming, others will take us by surprise. Here, I am reminded of Robert Rowland Smith's observation in his reflections on how to make a good working life:

Develop agency of your own so that when something less advantageous occurs, you can look into your cupboard of personal supplies for dealing with it – and find that it is full and not empty.

I am reflecting on the fabric we weave in our working lives and the productivity and nurture threads that hold this fabric together. There is a lesson here about not letting any single thread become so weak that they fray and lose their permanent strength.

MAKE SELF-KNOWLEDGE YOUR GUIDE, KEEP AGENCY IN YOUR HANDS

I've thought more deeply about the power of personality analysis to bring insight. Just as we are shaped by the forces of history, social norms and fate, so too are we shaped by our personality preferences. As Randall Peterson points out: 'Knowing yourself enhances self-understanding, helping you navigate interactions and decisions.' I've reflected on the power of personal agency – the choices we take and the decisions we make. As a humanistic psychologist – I believe we have personal agency, we can change life course and switch, and a longer life affords more opportunities to switch. Yet, I am also aware that as we have looked at my ancestors, the burden of history and context is heavy.

And I am reminded of our musings on fate and luck. Fate makes us vulnerable, but agency gives us options. We don't get to control everything, but we do get to prepare – by knowing ourselves, building inner resources and weaving lives that can stretch and recover.

WEAVE YOUR IDENTITY, CHERISH MULTIPLE SELVES

I am intrigued by the dynamic interplay between our identity and our work. At times, this connection is stable, creating harmony between our experiences and the stories we tell ourselves about who we are.

Yet, there are moments when our working experiences take unexpected turns – perhaps a missed promotion or the loss of a job. These challenges test our resilience and prompt introspection, leading us to question our capabilities and confront feelings of inadequacy.

Conversely, there are times when our evolving identity leads the change. You may recall moments when you assumed new roles: took a new job, stretched the boundaries, embarked on a side project. In these instances, it is your changing identity that shapes and influences your experiences. Beyond the notion of a singular identity lies our 'multiple selves'. This diversity within us is a point of celebration – our multiple selves bring depth and richness to our lives, offering a tapestry of experiences that may hold the key to future possibilities.

As you reflect on the journey explored in this first Guiding Question, embrace the complexity and richness of your identity. Recognise the interplay between who you are and the work you do, understand how each shape and informs the other. This is the beginning of living the 100-Year Life: learning to recognise the threads that shape you, to strengthen what matters and to return to the question of who you are becoming.

PART TWO:

Weaving a Working Life
Across Decades

HOW AM I WORKING NOW?

Our working life is no longer a single path, it's a fabric we create over time. In a 100-Year Life this fabric must be both strong and flexible. The following chapters will help you assess which threads are thriving – and which ones need care. What I'm asking you to do here isn't easy. Looking back at your past, being honest about your present, imagining your future – it's complex. There are many models and frameworks out there, but I want to offer one that feels intuitive and human.

Imagine your working life as something you are weaving: day by day, choice by choice. Over decades, you shape its texture and pattern. Some threads feel durable, others more fragile. Some sections are vibrant and full of momentum, others are sparse, tentative or still emerging. No two fabrics look alike – and in a long life, the weave isn't fixed. This image of weaving reminds us that a working life is not something done to us – it's something we make, with intention, creativity and care.

THE EIGHT THREADS OF A WORKING LIFE

Let's take a closer look at the threads of productivity and nurture...

Make Sense of the Threads of Productivity

You can recall times when you've been highly productive – I could see this in some of my own stories. These periods of high productivity are crucial: they shape your salary if you work for a company, influence your earnings if you are independent or work as a freelancer and are linked to your dividends if you have built a business. They offer options to switch, ramp up and save resources for future use. These threads are crucial sources of meaning and identity. Here are the four threads of productivity together with the reflective question that captures the thread:

Mastery is the practice and motivation to build a diverse array of skills that enhance productivity. It provides the flexibility to switch jobs and transform your working life. Mastery is fundamental to meaning and identity at work.

Reflect: Am I creating what I love?

Knowing is built through developing deep knowledge, insight and wisdom. It enables you to understand yourself better, to have empathy and awareness of others, and to glimpse the world around you.

Reflect: Am I expanding what I know?

Cooperating involves working effectively with others and building diverse connections. It is essential for productivity as collaboration accelerates value creation and innovation.

Reflect: Do I work deeply with others?

Amplifying is how technology can enhance human endeavour and creativity. For while technology can fragment and distract, it also offers opportunities to extend reach, speed and precision.

Reflect: Can emerging technologies like Generative AI support and enhance my work?

As you think about these four threads – are there any that immediately draw your attention to them – perhaps threads you know have been strong for you, or those you acknowledge are weaker?

Make Sense of the Threads of Nurture

In my four decades of studying working people and of being a working person myself, what is striking is how much activities *beyond* work enhance and detract from our working life. These are the activities that nurture us and those around us, and which are crucial to creating and maintaining harmony in our working lives. As I looked at my own stories and the experience of others, four threads came to the fore:

Friendships can be astonishing sources of happiness and satisfaction. They are powerful antidotes to loneliness, a central challenge in contemporary lives.

Reflect: Am I forging deep, sustaining connections?

Intimacy be they partnerships, family groups or close friendships that sustain us over the course of our life. They can bring great joy and happiness but are susceptible to the stresses and strains of working lives.

Reflect: Am I giving and finding love?

Calm provides an antidote to the frenzy and pressure of work. Moments of calm and reflection are vital for general happiness and wellbeing.

Reflect: Can I slow down?

Adventure brings excitement and interest to life, preventing our working lives from becoming mundane, uninteresting and uninspiring. This thread adds buzz and verve, pivotal in a fulfilling working life.

Reflection: Am I having adventures?

Do you have a sense of which of these four threads of nurture are strongest for you? Are there threads which you know to be weak?

You might like to go to *The Living the 100-Year Life Assessment: Thread Strength Test* a free, online tool to assess the strength of these eight threads. You will find it at www.livingthehundredyearlife.com. Then download *The Living the 100-Year Life Workbook: Life Design Guide.* And if right now you feel it's time to really get to work on this – consider purchasing *The Living the 100-Year Life Journal: Reflect, Reimagine, Renew.*

We will look at each thread in more detail and through research, theoretical models and conversations with experts, explore how each thread shows up in your working life. For those threads that are weak or weakening, we will consider the actions you can take now and the promises you can make to your future self.

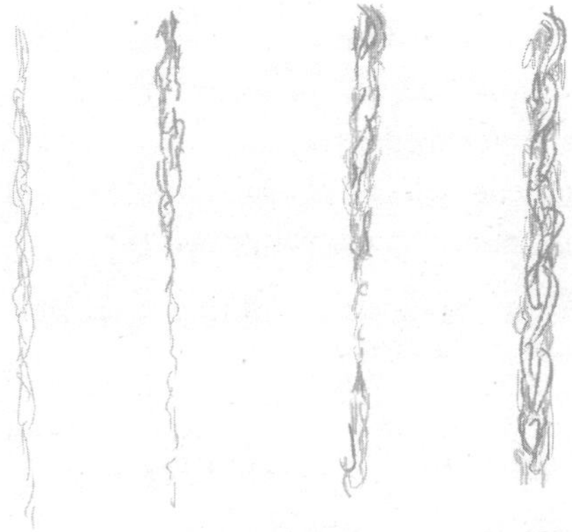

The State of Threads – From Weak to Strong

Each thread tells a story and poses a challenge to be solved. As you learn more about the strength of each thread – you will have an opportunity to assess them – from weak, to weakening, to strengthening and to strong. You may return to these threads many times across your life. In your thirties, adventure may feel urgent whereas in your sixties, calm or cooperation may rise in importance. In a long life, these threads aren't one-time questions, they're lifelong resources.

Weave the Balance: Productivity and Nurture

The hope, of course, is that all eight threads remain strong throughout your working life. But that's rarely how life unfolds. Time, energy and attention are finite. So, we make choices, often unconsciously, about which threads we strengthen, and which ones are left to fray.

This can create tensions. For example, there are times when productivity dominates. In a classic 1980s study, Paul Evans and Fernando Bartolome discovered that while senior executives may appear impressive at work, many privately admitted to broken relationships, loneliness and exhaustion.[1] They had invested heavily in the productivity threads of mastery, knowing and cooperating, but neglected the threads of intimacy, friendship and calm.

Ben saw this in his father, a man whose dedication brought financial security but created distance at home. Now a parent himself, Ben reflects on that trade-off: deep gratitude for the stability his father provided, but also a desire to weave his own life differently.

You don't fix this tension – there is no perfect balance between productivity and nurture. Life shifts. Priorities change. You live with this tension. The more clearly you see your threads, the more intentionally you can choose which to strengthen next.

There will be moments when opportunities to strengthen the threads of productivity arise. Unanticipated chances that beckon – perhaps a new job in a country you've longed to work in, offering collaboration with top-tier professionals. Faced with such opportunities, you may wisely choose to re-focus your resources, your time, energy, skills, on seizing this opportunity. These experiences strengthen the productive threads as you capitalise on emergent possibilities.

There will be other times when the threads of nurture need focus – a new intimate relationship awakens, a much-valued friendship needs care and attention, small children want your attention, ageing parents need support.

Mira has worked part time since her children were born, focusing on her nurture threads. She imagined there would be time later to return to full-time work and strengthen her productivity threads. But now divorced and struggling to find a role, she recognises that her productivity threads, mastery and knowing, need immediate attention.

The *Assessment* tool and our shared analysis and reflection will help you to illuminate those weakening threads, supporting you to choose whether to take action to strengthen them or accept the consequences of their frailty. In other words, this is a lesson in intentionality. There is no universal formula for allocating resources – your time, attention and skills are yours to strengthen the threads that hold meaning for you. It is a choice you must make, relatively often, and it is a choice best made intentionally. In a 100-Year Life, all of these threads are yours to shape – and reshape.

Now that you've seen the full weave – the eight threads of productivity and nurture – it's time to explore each one in depth. We'll begin with Mastery, one of the core productivity threads. Mastery is about developing your skills, growing your competence and pursuing excellence in what you do. It's foundational not only for your career trajectory but also for your sense of purpose and momentum. Whether you've invested in mastery for years, or feel like it's frayed in recent times, this thread offers a powerful place to begin. Let's take a closer look at what it means to build, and rebuild, Mastery across a lifetime.

CHAPTER 5

THE THREAD OF MASTERY: Am I Creating What I Love?

In a long life, mastery matters more than ever – not just to earn a living, but to keep feeling alive. As the world changes, your ability to grow and refine your skills, to pivot to new emerging opportunities becomes one of your greatest sources of dynamic resilience.

Perhaps the word 'mastery' sounds old-fashioned to you – like something carved in stone after years of monk-like repetition. But mastery today looks different. It's agile, deeply personal, additive and enables you to pivot.

As you reflect on your working life, the thread of mastery is one you will often be aware of strengthening – or leaving to weaken. We judge ourselves – and others – in part by the skills we possess, the value we bring to working situations, our capacity for resilience. And we use our sense of mastery as a foundation for naming our working identity, shaping how we describe ourselves to others. My suggestion is to start by first building mastery around something you are naturally inclined to excel at and enjoy – even love. Because mastery, at its heart, is not about prestige or perfection, it's about creating meaning through building skills that feels deeply connected to who you are.

Yet across a long productive life, you will do more than master just one thing forever. Expect some skills to deepen, others to shift, new ones to be added. It is this adaptability that enables you to pivot as circumstances change. That's why the question *'Am I creating what I love?'* is the opening enquiry. You can sense this in how you feel at the end of a working day and what you share with others. When you are building mastery in something you love, you feel excited about the next day.

I've seen people build mastery in diverse areas: writing software programs, preparing reports, working with complex business data, coaching others, turning around failing businesses, strategic planning, writing code, teaching children. The list of possible areas of mastery is long and I invite you to think about your journey to mastery and how you can expand from what you have already mastered.

WHAT MASTERY MAKES POSSIBLE

Mastery Builds Value. When you can, for example, negotiate convoluted deals, coach someone who needs support, build a website, lead an international team – you have a set of skills that others value and are prepared to pay for. Mastery enables you to widen your working options: become a full-time employee, a freelancer selling your skills in the external market, an entrepreneur building a business. In any of these situations, your deep expertise brings you value and potentially differentiates you from others. It is this body of mastery that builds a reputation that lands you the next job.

It Expresses Who You Are. While some of the mastery skills are foundational – anyone building mastery in that area will need them – others are special to you. They reflect who you are, what you care about.

It Opens Opportunities. Mastery and the skills you create can enable you to pivot into new possibilities – new work opportunities, new projects, new connections, new ways to explore who you are and adapt to your evolving interests

It Supports Your Wellbeing. It is that good feeling at the end of a working day as you anticipate the next day – feeling in the flow, immersing yourself, getting better, or finding purpose. This positive outlook can spill over into other aspects of your life, enhancing your overall wellbeing. Ultimately, mastery contributes to a rewarding and satisfying working life, where your passions align with your professional pursuits.

HOW TO STRENGTHEN THE THREADS OF MASTERY

Imagine mastery as a thread made up of many strands – over time your hope is to keep the thread strong, yet also to keep it flexible as your life changes. In this chapter you will learn more about how to spin, strengthen, make it your own and rebraid.

→ **Start Spinning.** This is where your mastery begins. You spin both *foundational strands* – skills shared by many – and *golden strands* – unique fibres drawn from your personality, heritage and lived experience. Together, these become the raw material for the work you love.

→ **Keep Strengthening.** Once spun, strands grow stronger through practice, insight and the lessons of failure.

→ **Make It Your Own.** Once your strands are strong, this is the stage where you shape them into something unmistakably yours. It's about visibility, voice and pattern – how your mastery is recognised, valued and remembered by others.

→ **Rebraid and Reuse.** Over time, you can take your existing strands and braid in new ones – adding, recombining and exploring adjacent skills. This is the art of transformation, creating fresh possibilities while staying true to the weave that makes your work your own.

→ **Explore and Focus.** Over your career, you'll shift between exploring widely and focusing deeply.

→ **Imagine What Comes Next.** Stepping back, you can see the whole fabric you've woven and imagine what is possible. Mastery opens unexpected doors, sparks new adventures, and ripples in ways you never planned – shaping not only your work, but your legacy.

START SPINNING

This is where your mastery begins. You spin both *foundational strands* – skills shared by many – and *golden strands* – unique fibres drawn from your personality, heritage and lived experience. Together, these become the raw material for the work you love. It is this combination that makes your threads of mastery so uniquely you. Let me tell you a story that for me captures this sense of uniqueness. It's the story of a weaving community who live on the shores of Lake Ilya in northern Myanmar, Southeast Asia.

A Story of a Water Lily Weaver – Lake Ilya, Myanmar, Spring 2021

I watch as the weaver picks a freshwater lily stem from the basket of stems harvested from the shallow edges of Lake Ilya. Wielding her sharpened knife, she slices through the tender flesh. The white opaque liquid dropping slowly from the stem quickly changes form into a long, thin fragile strand.

Working with purpose and precision, the weaver holds the fragile strand and lays it gently on the table beside her. This is one of the most exquisite raw materials, unique to this lake and finer than cashmere. Yet so delicate and fragile it cannot be spun on its own – it would quickly disintegrate. To strengthen the thread, the weaver intertwines the fragile water lily strands with strands of stronger cotton and luminous silk.

I have in my cupboard a beautiful scarf woven by the Lake Ilya weavers – incredibly fine and yet durable and beautiful. Your threads of mastery are woven from many types of strands. Like the water lily strands, there are some that are unique to you, drawn from your personality, heritage and lived experience. They reflect not just what you've learned, but who you are. I think of these as *Golden Strands.*

Then, there are other strands, shared by many. Think of them as being like the strands of linen and cotton. These are the *Foundational Strands.* Though they may not feel as personal, they're just as essential – they give your working life structure and strength. Here is how I imagine the thread of mastery:

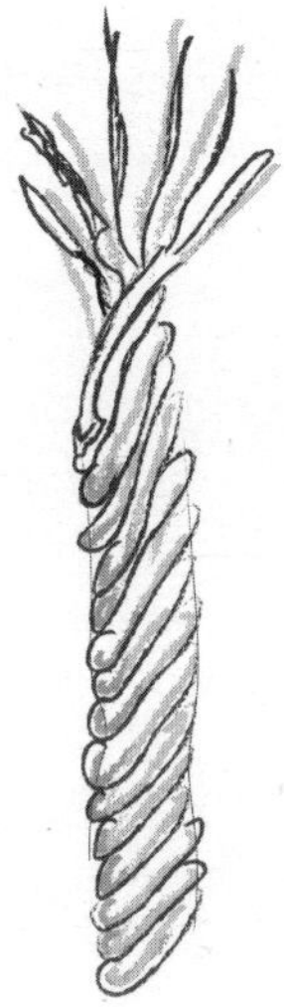

Now, let's take a closer look at a time when your own mastery was on show...

Your Story: Of Mastery

Tell me a story of what you have mastered. Moments of mastery reveal not just what you can do, but who you are becoming. Perhaps this is an easy story for you to tell – and you are way down the path of mastery? Perhaps it's harder for you to think about a time of mastery? Yet we have all been masterful at a time at work, and I'd like you to pick one example of when you practice your mastery.

To illustrate this, let me share a couple of stories of mastery with you – first my own, and then Ben's story. Mine is a story of teaching an MBA class, Ben's is leading a complex generative-AI transformation project.

My Mastery in Teaching

Here's mine: Spring 2023, a one-hour class with about 75 MBA students from London Business School and partner schools. It is part of my 12-lecture elective called The Future of Work. Teaching is intense for me. I prepare hard and care deeply. Most days it goes well, some days it doesn't, but it's part of who I am. Here's how the hour unfolds and woven through this story are what I consider to be my Golden Strands.

A Story of Teaching an MBA Class – London Business School, 2023

I arrive in the classroom early, taking a moment to stroll around the whole amphitheatre to greet those who have arrived– from students sitting on the back seats right to those arrayed on the front seats. I'm facing around 75 students who represent about 40 nationalities with no dominant nationality. This is an extraordinary group of young people to be teaching, and I love the opportunity to spend the next couple of hours with them.

At 8.45 precisely, I open with an overview of the lesson flow. I am using a simple though crucial Golden Strand – let's call it *Keeping Time*. If I feel the class becoming restless, I ask each student to turn to their fellow student for three minutes and discuss their major learning points from the class so far – and the questions on their mind. I am *Managing the Tempo*. As the students describe their learnings, I note them on the whiteboard at the front of the class, elaborating on each one and providing another couple of ideas, or asking the whole class for their perspective and experience. These early key learnings will become the framing for the systems model I create over the course of the lecture. I am *Creating a Systems Map* – a Golden Strand I use on many occasions.

Now, 15 minutes into the lecture, I stand back, take a deep breath and project to the back of the lecture room. I'm using my *Big Voice*, a capability that's been years in development. I review the major theoretical models of the lecture series, take a closer look at motivational theory and consider factors such as personal autonomy and work satisfaction. I am using a Golden Strand a fellow professor calls *Owning the Room*. I want my presence to be felt, especially in a space this large. I'm showing I'm not intimidated by the scale or the numbers.

As the class moves along, I listen carefully to students from different countries – aware of their norms and sensitivities. Slowing down, avoiding idioms, creating a space for different voices. I'm using a Golden Strand, *Inter-Cultural Sensitivity*.

As I move around the large amphitheatre, I'm looking at every student and watching their response. The class is now deep in conversation and I'm bringing antidotes and stories, drawing from a whole portfolio of stories – this is *Storytelling*.

This story might bring back memories from your own education – do you remember sitting in such a class? *Do any of these Golden Strands resonate with you? Are any of them woven into your story of mastery?*

In *The Living the 100-Year Life Workbook: Life Design Guide* you will find space to reflect on and name your Golden Strands. If you'd like to take this further – *The Living the 100-Year Life Journal: Reflect, Reimagine, Renew* is there to support you more deeply on a journey.

Threaded through my story are what I think of as *Foundational Strands* – those important, but more generic skills that every teacher develops. These blend pedagogical, interpersonal and cognitive capabilities. The foundational strands are likely to have featured in development programmes, training sessions or performance reviews. They may appear in course evaluations or be built into institutional frameworks. These are the strands that form the baseline of professional mastery – the expectations that allow your distinctive golden strands to emerge.

Which foundational strands have supported your mastery – and which ones deserve renewed attention in this next chapter of your working life?

Here's the story of Ben's mastery. How he leads a one-hour meeting, bringing together the major stakeholders of a digital transformation project:

Ben's Mastery, Managing a High-Stakes Project Meeting

Ben's mastery story is from a very different arena to mine. He is leading a one-hour meeting on a high-stakes generative AI project in the bank he's employed by. The outcome will affect the daily work of over 15,000 employees and potentially millions of customers.

Ben arrives early, arranging the room so everyone – from IT, Customer Services, Finance and Strategy – sits in a circle. He is using a Golden Strand he would call *Setting the Stage*, signalling that each voice matters. When the meeting begins, Ben shares the bad news. He's come prepared with data and delivers the facts without embellishment: the project is three weeks behind schedule. Then he outlines what needs to be achieved in the hour ahead.

As discussion opens, Ben is *Holding the Room's Mind.* He's listening intently, capturing key points, connecting ideas and testing for shared understanding. Old tensions surface, departments begin blaming each other. Now, Ben draws on his natural composure, *Cooling the Heat* by slowing the conversation, asking clarifying questions and keeping the focus on the shared goal.

He notices the more vocal technical leaders edging into dominance. This is his cue for *Opening the Circle.* He's inviting quieter participants in, ensuring finance and customer services are heard. The tone of the meeting begins to shift as contributions balance out.

When it's time to decide, Ben is *Curating the Evidence.* He's using data he has prepared in advance to show Finance why additional investment is necessary and convincing IT to commit more resources. By the close of the hour, the group has agreed on two critical next steps and a shared plan to move forward.

Behind Ben's golden strands such as Setting the Stage or Opening the Circle, are a set of foundational strands – these include, for example Clarity of Communication, Conflict Navigation and Influence without Authority. These are the well-worn, essential fibres in the weave of stakeholder leadership. They don't define what makes someone exceptional, but they are what makes mastery possible.

As you look at the Golden and Foundational Strands woven into Ben's master are there any that resonate with you?

Tracing the Strands

Your golden strands are not random. They're rooted in who you are, shaped by what you've experienced, and expressed through the work you've done. Let's take a closer look at the Golden Strands you use – perhaps from the Mastery story you remembered earlier. Which of your strands began with heritage? Which come from your personality? Which have been most shaped by your work? As you reflect, notice how these strands weave together. Let's take a closer look at these three dimensions:

What role did heritage play – the values, traditions and influences of the context you grew up in. Perhaps a golden strand was sparked by a family trade, a cultural practice or a formative role model. My strand of *Storytelling*, for example, began as a childhood fascination and deepened through my doctoral research.

What about your personality – the qualities and tendencies that come naturally to you. A calm temperament might give rise to a strand like Ben's *Cooling the Heat*. My *Inter-Cultural Sensitivity* grew from a natural openness to experience – an instinct to notice and adapt to differences.

And perhaps your jobs and the contexts you've worked in have drawn out your strengths over time. Some strands emerge because a role demands them, others strengthen because a particular environment allows them to flourish. My *Systems Mapping* grew during consulting work that required me to see across functions and connect complexity.

To trace your strands, try mapping them.

First draw a vertical line to represent the years of your working life. Then along this timeline, mark significant experiences, projects, transitions or environments that stand out.

Here is how I drew my timeline. On the vertical axis I've shown the years of my working life and some of the major activities that contributed to developing my Golden Threads – being a doctoral student, working at British Airways, consulting at PA, teaching at London Business School, launching my advisory practice HSM and becoming an international speaker. Then I have shown the period when I felt one of these Golden Strands was developed

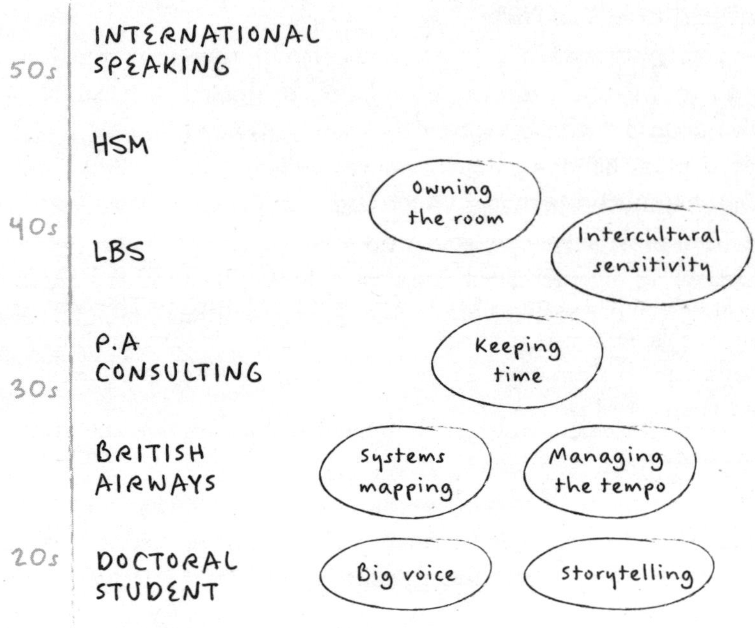

Then, as you look at your timeline, consider:

- → Where did the golden strands first appear? Were they shaped by your heritage, your personality or your working identity?
- → What supported the development of these golden strands – where there times when they faded?

Early Traces: My Path to the Big Voice

My timeline begins in my twenties as a doctoral student. This experience marks the very beginning of the Golden Strand that became *Big Voice*.

A Story of a Slow Train – Liverpool, 1973

I sit in a slow train, my shaking hands holding pages of rustling notes I am intensely reading and re-reading. It is not an unusually hot day, yet I feel perspiration pouring down my face. I've been preparing for weeks and my anxiety and fear are palpable – signalled in my short breath and shaking hands.

I slept badly the previous night and the dark circles under my eyes are a testament.

In 30 short minutes I will be delivering my first lecture to 50 young students – eager, I hope, to hear my wisdom on the psychology of adult learning. Later, as I climb the stairs to the podium and look over those expectant faces, my heart races, my breath becomes shallow and my vocal cords tense. In what I assume is a very small voice, I deliver my lecture from the prepared notes, answering the students' questions the best way I can. Relieved, after an hour I leave the lectern and hurry back on the train. Then I repeat the same journey every week for the rest of the term.

I didn't know it then, but these anxious beginnings were the first traces of my *Big Voice*, a strand that decades later would help me speak to hundreds.

Fast Forward to Summer 2014. Decades after those nervous first steps, I stand on stage at the Royal Festival Hall, receiving the Teacher of the Year Award, my family looking on. The arc from trembling beginnings to that moment of pride reminds me: mastery rarely starts with confidence. It grows from showing up, reflecting and being willing to begin.

Early Traces: Ben's Path to Stakeholder Mastery

Ben's first golden strands began far from the boardroom. As a teenager, he became absorbed in video games like *SimCity*, losing hours to the challenge of building worlds and working out intricate sequences. Looking back, he sees the beginnings of *Holding the Room's Mind* – the capacity to gather, synthesise and understand complex systems.

In high school, he joined the theatre group as a stage manager. Three years backstage taught him how to shape outcomes without taking the spotlight and how to *Set the Stage* for others to succeed. Watching rehearsals, he first saw the power of arranging people in a circle to encourage open dialogue – the seeds of *Opening the Circle*.

Beneath these early experiences lies Ben's personality: a quiet, observant style that favours reflection over performance. The strands were there from the start – they simply needed time, practice and the right context to be woven into mastery.

KEEP STRENGTHENING

We've considered the very beginnings of the strands of mastery – those stories of being nervous, self-conscious and awkward. What happens after these initial stories – what are the pathways to mastery? Three kinds of experiences stand out: the steady rhythm of practice, the clarity that comes with moments of intense insight and the hard-won wisdom that follows failure. Let's take a look at each one in turn...

The Rhythm of Practice

When I look back at my own timeline of developing mastery in teaching, what strikes me most is the rhythm of repetition. It began with teaching as a doctoral student, then deepened as I found my voice in research and speaking and eventually matured through storytelling in the classroom. You may notice similar rhythms in your own life – patterns of skill that return, deepen and slowly become part of who you are.

Mastery takes time. But how much time? For years, the idea that it takes 10,000 hours to become highly skilled shaped the way we thought about practice – whether learning an instrument, becoming a surgeon or writing a book.[1] I was sceptical at first. Four hours a day for ten years? That's a daunting commitment. Does it really work that way? Then I remembered the cello player who lived next door to us. From the age of four, she practised three hours a day. Through the thin walls of our homes, I could hear the early scratch and scrape of practice – awkward, persistent. Years later, her home was filled with the soaring lines of Elgar and Bach. Something had happened: practice had worked.

I also think of my son Dominic, training to be a doctor. The long shifts, the constant rotations, the steep learning curve of medical internships. In just five years, he built a level of skill that would be unthinkable without repetition, reflection and responsibility. But few are training in medicine or music. For most of us, mastery comes more gradually: woven through our working lives, across different jobs, projects and experiences.

Yet when I started counting my own hours of practice I was surprised. Teaching evening classes during my doctoral studies. Later, a part-time job at a college of further education – about eight hours a week. Then corporate training sessions at British Airways and PA Consulting. By the time I joined London Business School, I had already built over 1,000 hours of teaching and presenting. That's when the real intensity began – lectures each week, serious preparation, live feedback. Over time, the hours accumulated. I wasn't aiming for 10,000 – but I got there all the same.

You might want to try this for yourself: *As you think about your own areas of mastery – how have you been practicing. Can you see repetition in your own story?*

For Ben, his mastery in project management didn't begin in his current role in the bank. It started with long hours spent playing *SimCity*, then three years working backstage as a theatre director before volunteering for a food delivery charity – where he quickly found himself planning routes, systems and logistics. Later, project roles in construction, then in retail banking. For Ben, as for me, mastery was laid down over time. Each project, each rehearsal, each repetition added another layer to the thread.

The 10,000-hour rule has been debated – and rightly so.[2] (take a look at the end note if you want to think more about this debate). But an underlying truth remains: mastery builds through practice, strand by strand. And in a 100-Year Life, we have time to do this more than once.

Moments of Intense Insight

Hours of practice matter, but some aspects of mastery don't emerge slowly – they begin with a sudden, intense moment of clarity. A flash of insight. An encounter with excellence. A new way of seeing.

Take the skill of systems mapping, which I now use regularly in the MBA classroom. Yes, it's something I've practised over time but the real breakthrough – the moment that shaped the Golden Strand – came much earlier. I remember it vividly.

I was at British Airways, part of a team exploring the company's customer culture. Into this came Richard Pascale, a master systems thinker and mapper, brought in to help senior leaders better understand the underlying dynamics of their organisation.[3] I watched, transfixed, as Richard sketched on a flipchart. In real time, he created a map – linking behaviours, mindsets, communication loops, incentive structures. It was a living picture of how the organisation functioned beneath the surface.

I could feel the excitement, the power of seeing a system – not just its separate parts, but the whole pattern. And looking at the systems map Richard had drawn I began to understand that behind the symptoms he was describing were the causes. This was not a tool, it was a way of thinking that I found really resonated with me.

After that meeting, I wanted to learn as much as possible. I read systems thinkers such as Peter Senge, Chris Argyris and Russell Ackoff.

Their work helped me understand the architecture behind what Pascale had drawn. I began experimenting with systems mapping in my own teaching, writing and consulting. It became one of my Golden Strands – visible, enduring, mine.

Sometimes a Golden Strand begins with years of repetition, other times it begins with a moment: an insight, a model, a person. And that moment stays with you.

Have you had these times of intense insight? Think about moments where you've observed mastery up close, read something that shifted your view, or been drawn into a conversation that changed your trajectory.

Wisdom from Failure

Mastery isn't just about practice and insight, it's also about risk – how you fail and what you learn in the process.

Failure, especially when mirrored back as tough feedback, can be brutal. I remember, early in my career as a young assistant professor – one of the few women on the faculty – receiving a particularly bruising set of course evaluations. That night, I drafted my resignation letter and yet, the following week, I stood in front of my students and did it all over again. Even now, after decades of teaching, writing and advising, I still receive feedback that stings. Some students find my slides unclear or my examples outdated. Readers of my newspaper column can be blunt. Some books take off, others sink.

Yet mastery demands a feedback loop. Without it, even 10,000 hours of practice leads only to repetition, not growth. For the ancient master craftsmen like glass blowers and goldsmiths the feedback was baked into the process itself. An error was immediately visible in the luminosity of the glass or the shine of the gold.[4] Now, for many of us, our work is cognitive and knowledge-based and the natural feedback loops can be slow or non-existent. This means we must seek it out intentionally. My guess is that you have some of the same experiences – of exhilaration and failure. Daring to fail evinces a certain strength; that you are willing to wrestle with why things don't or do work. And once you have this mindset, this diminishes the fear of making future mistakes.

What are your experiences of failure? How did you feel at the time and can you see how they created opportunities for you to learn more deeply?

YOUR PATH – APPRENTICE, JOURNEYMAN, MASTER?

As you think about how you've strengthened your mastery, you may have reflected on where you are on the path. A linear way of thinking about this are the three ascending tiers of classical mastery: apprentice, journeyman and master. These might seem like ancient craft pathways, but the paths have relevance today, whether you're learning to code, launching a podcast or becoming a skilled therapist. Here is a way to think about this:

Apprentice: Here, you are building foundational knowledge and basic skills, often by observing and imitating a mentor. It's a period of high dependency and repetition. Think of a new designer shadowing team leads, or a barista mastering the perfect espresso shot. Your confidence may be fragile, but your curiosity fuels learning.

Journeyman: Now, you are applying your skills more independently, solving problems creatively, refining your approach through hands-on experience. Think of a software engineer confidently debugging code, a freelance writer developing their own voice, or a teacher designing curriculum with minimal oversight. Your autonomy is growing, confidence strengthening.

Mastery: This emerges with focused practice, reflection and adaptation. Now you are operating with intuitive fluency, drawing on a vast well of experience. When you observe a master in action, their work often seems effortless, whether a startup founder who anticipates market shifts, a surgeon navigating high-stakes procedures with calm precision or a chef improvising with instinctive flair.

As you think about your own pathway, don't be deterred if it doesn't seem linear – it rarely is. You may move back and forth between stages as you take on new challenges or shift domains. But the apprentice–journeyman–master framework remains a powerful lens for you to understand how expertise is cultivated, sustained and shared.

MAKE IT YOUR OWN

Once your strands are strong, this is the stage where you shape them into something unmistakably yours. It's about visibility, voice and pattern – how your mastery is recognised, valued and remembered by others.

In some professions, this is beautifully straightforward. I am thinking about the renowned Yorkshire carpenter, Robert Thompson, who carves a tiny mouse into every piece of furniture he makes. Hidden under a table, climbing up the leg of a chair, peeking from a drawer – this small carving is his *maker's mark*. It says, *this was created by me*. It's a personal imprint of mastery.

Thompson isn't the first person to make such a mark. Medieval goldsmiths – especially those working alone, outside large studios – understood that reputation was everything. They couldn't rely on marketing or LinkedIn; instead, their guilds, rituals and codes of conduct formed a kind of early brand. Their craftsmanship had to speak for them. These traditions of mastery and visible authority gave them identity, credibility and access.

Today, the idea of the maker's mark still matters – but it looks very different. When the result of your work is tangible – a painting, a line of code, a book – it can speak for you. For me, my books and newspaper columns are visible signals of what I know and care about. In more traditional professions, like medicine or law, the markers are formal: exams passed, titles earned, letters added to your name. These professions are the modern-day heirs of the medieval guilds – carefully managing who gets to claim mastery, and how that mastery is shown.

Inside large organisations, the logic is similar. Job titles, grades and internal reputations act as reputational currency. At British Airways, my starting job title was Selection Methods Officer (SMO). Later, I became a Senior Selection Methods Officer and with that promotion came a change in job grade. That grade was, in essence, my maker's mark within the company – visible proof of progress and skill. But what if you're not in a big company? What if like Lucia, you're shaping a more fluid path or like Nico starting your own business? Now the signals of mastery become far less obvious, you need to make your own mark. Lucia is starting to wrestle with this. She's beginning to build and name her skills. She wants to be seen – and to be seen clearly – but doesn't yet know how to do that in a way that feels authentic.

Today, many people are doing just that – through blogs, podcasts, newsletters, short videos or carefully curated social media. Virtual badges and certificates from companies like Microsoft and Coursera are also being used to showcase skill acquisition. These are today's new guild symbols.

Ben is thinking about this too. After years building his mastery in project management, he's started sharing short videos on how to lead digital transformation. He also writes occasional columns for a project management journal. He's not broadcasting loudly but subtly making his expertise visible – testing how it feels to put his mark in the world.

Of course, it's a balance. Some argue you should actively build your profile across every platform, while others warn that too much promotion can dilute your reputation. But here's what's clear: when you've put the time into building something that's truly yours – those thousands of hours, the unique angle, the personal voice – you want, and need, others to see it. Not to boast, but to connect. When others recognise your mastery, they are more likely to seek you out, open doors and offer new opportunities.

Take a moment to reflect on how your mastery speaks for you – whether directly or indirectly. What are you doing now – and what might you do going forward?

What are you most proud of and where does your work currently live? Is there something you've created – a project, article, design, process or idea – that could serve as a signature of your unique contribution? If someone were to describe what you're known for, what would you hope they'd say? And how visible is that to others who might value it?

Perhaps your mark isn't obvious yet or feels scattered. That's okay. What small step could you take to bring it into focus – by sharing your thinking more openly, naming your skills with confidence, or allowing others to see the patterns in what you do well? You don't need to carve a mouse into a table leg, but you do need a way to say, with conviction: *this is me, and this is what I bring.*

Once your mastery is visible - the next question is how to keep it alive. In a long working life, even the strongest weave can stagnate if it never changes. Markets shift, technologies advance, your own interests evolve. To stay relevant and energised, you may need to reshape what you already have, combine it in fresh ways, or expand into new territory – this is the work of rebraiding.

REBRAID AND REUSE

To stay relevant and keep your work alive, you will need to change direction, expand your repertoire, adapt to new contexts. Rebraiding is the process of taking the strands you already have and weaving them into something different – through new combinations, related expansions or entirely new capabilities.

Recombine: Mix the Strands

Sometimes the breakthrough isn't in adding something entirely new, it's in finding new combinations of what you already have. Recombining is about taking your existing skills, experiences and perspectives and deploying them together in a fresh context or for a different purpose.

When I began around 2013 to build HSM, my research-based advisory practice, I didn't start with new qualifications. Instead, I combined strands I already had – research design, facilitation and storytelling – into a new service model. The novelty came from the mix, not from learning something brand new.

Research into career adaptability shows that the most successful recombinations often emerge from deliberate reflection: mapping your skills, seeking perspectives from outside your current field, placing yourself in situations where your familiar capabilities can be applied in unfamiliar ways. It's a mindset of asking: What else could these skills do? Recombination doesn't require you to step into unknown territory without preparation. Instead, it reframes what you already know so it can travel further, work differently and create value in places you hadn't originally imagined.

If you listed your top skills side by side, what unexpected pairings or groupings could you use to solve a different problem or serve a new audience?

Find Adjacencies: Extend the Strands

Sometimes rebraiding comes through adjacencies. Adjacencies are the skills that sit right next to the ones you already have – close enough that you can step into them quickly, yet different enough to expand what you can do. They build on your current capabilities, making the learning curve shorter and the payoff faster. An experienced accountant, for example, might find it far easier to move into data visualisation or financial modelling than software engineering. A nurse who already leads teams might discover that coaching, mediation or patient education are natural extensions.

Labour economists and workforce platforms like LinkedIn and Burning Glass Technologies have mapped how skills evolve.[5] Their data shows that adding just one or two adjacent skills can dramatically alter a career – opening new roles, expanding professional identity and enabling new forms of contribution. Some adjacencies are obvious: a copywriter might learn UX writing, a teacher could explore instructional design. Others are less linear: an artist may develop facilitation skills and pivot into community engagement, a project manager might train in sustainability and begin shaping climate strategies. The power of adjacencies is that they don't pull you away from who you are – they extend you. Over time, strategically adding them creates *compound advantage*: the ability to adapt quickly, combine skills in unique ways and make yourself harder to replace.

Which skills sit just beyond your current capability set – close enough to learn quickly, but different enough to stretch you into new opportunities?

Add New Capabilities: Expand the Weave

Sometimes mastery grows by adding a completely new capability to the skills you already have. This is the biggest leap – venturing into territory that is not naturally connected to your current expertise. Done well, it can open fresh directions, create new opportunities and significantly expand your options.

Ben, for example, had already developed strong capabilities in project management, stakeholder navigation and organisational change. These gave him a solid platform. By adding new capabilities in pitching and relationship-building, he could move into client development – or even build a portfolio career. If he combined his existing expertise with new knowledge in climate strategy or energy transition, he could enter a sector at the frontier of transformation.

For Nico, the addition came after a difficult moment. He had built deep capabilities in sales and product marketing at a global tech firm – listening to customer pain points, navigating complexities and translating across functions. When his first startup failed, he gained unexpected new capabilities: making meaning from failure. This insight reshaped how he approached his second venture, now focused on the fast-moving terrain of AI and human behaviour.

What skills could you add that would broaden your choices, extend your reach, or even take you into new territory?

Rebraiding keeps your mastery alive. By recombining what you already have, stepping into adjacent skills, or adding entirely new capabilities, you build resilience, originality and future-fit strength. Over time, these choices compound – making you harder to replace, more distinct and better able to navigate change.

But mastery doesn't only evolve through the skills you hold, it also shifts in rhythm: sometimes you work broadly, casting your net wide; other times, you focus deeply on one area. Over a long career, these phases of exploration and focus both matter – and knowing when to move between them can be as powerful as rebraiding itself.

EXPLORE AND FOCUS

Over a long working life, your skills will also develop through periods of broad exploration and intense focus.

Research into creative and scientific careers shows a recurring pattern: people often spend years experimenting and exploring widely before narrowing and focusing their efforts into a concentrated phase where they produce their most significant work.[6]

The *exploration* phase is all about range – experimenting, testing boundaries, playing with new ideas and stretching beyond what you already know. It's a time of curiosity and diversity, where the focus is on breadth rather than depth. By contrast, when *focus narrows*: you double down on a particular area, deepen your expertise and begin to build a reputation around it. It's the shift from searching widely to working intensively.

Crucially, the research shows it's not just the presence of both phases that matters – it's the *sequence.* The most productive and innovative periods begin with exploration. It's through this wide-ranging search that people discover the area in which they can later excel. Focus is when creativity is channelled into sustained work and output. Interestingly, during exploration, people often work in smaller, more agile teams where there's space for disruption and fresh thinking. In the focus phase, networks tend to expand – people collaborate more broadly, often with those who help sharpen and scale what's already been discovered.

So how does this land with you? Does it resonate with your own experience? Which phase do you think you're in right now – and can you sense what the next phase might be?

If your career currently feels diffuse or experimental, this research offers reassurance: exploration is not a detour from mastery, it's the essential starting point. And if you're in a focused period of deep work, it may be worth asking: what was the journey that led you here – and where might the next wave of exploration take me?

Take Lucia, for example. Since returning from a year volunteering in Ethiopia, she's worked for a series of consultancy firms on a variety of projects. It hasn't unfolded quite as she'd hoped – some assignments are underwhelming and the structure lacks the mentorship she's craving. She's begun volunteering with a not-for-profit environmental group, helping co-ordinate grass-roots initiatives on land use and conservation. In the process she's gaining skills in facilitation, stakeholder engagement and cross-cultural communication and yet she feels uncertain – *diffuse*, as she puts it – not sure where all of this is going.

Her oldest friend Nico is in a different phase. After early roles in sales and product marketing at global tech firms, he took a risk – leaving to launch a startup. The first attempt failed, but the experience was catalytic. It forced him to reflect, recalibrate and start again. Now deep into his second venture, he's applying what he learned – about customers, teams and complexity – and adding new capabilities in leadership and product development. He's still evolving, but his direction has sharpened. His work has focus, not because the path was linear, but because the *experimentation led him here.*

Together, they reflect the two phases at the heart of mastery. Lucia is exploring – building range, trying contexts, stretching her identity. Nico is focusing – doubling down, deepening his craft, shaping something lasting. Lucia is searching, Nico consolidating – both makes sense to them.

Stepping back, you can see the whole cloth you've woven and imagine its journey beyond you. Mastery can open unexpected doors, spark new adventures and ripple into places you never planned – shaping not only your work, but your legacy too.

IMAGINE WHAT COMES NEXT

Mastery doesn't end where you are now. The skills you've spun, strengthened, made your own and evolved through rebraiding will continue to open doors, sometimes in ways you can't yet imagine. Opportunities can appear unexpectedly: an invitation from someone who has seen your work, a collaboration sparked by a shared interest, a chance to contribute to a project or place you never anticipated. Looking forward is about holding space for that uncertainty – trusting that the integrity and distinctiveness of your mastery will carry into new roles, relationships and arenas you may not yet see.

Ben discovered this early in his career. Before joining the bank, he was contacted by a project team in a South American city who had read an article he'd written on the challenges of digital transformation. They invited him to spend three weeks helping a young team design a city-wide digital strategy. It took some juggling to make it possible, but he describes it as one of the most exciting and meaningful periods of his working life – an experience he could never have planned, but which emerged directly from his mastery.

I've had my own unexpected opening...

A Story of the Prime Minister's Council – Tokyo, 2022

I'm sitting at the dining table, casually scanning my emails, when one subject line draws my attention: *From the Office of Prime Minister Shinzo Abe*. The message is short and formal. It informs me that Prime Minister Abe has read my book, *The 100-Year Life*, and is inviting me to join a newly formed advisory group: the Council for Designing 100-Year Life Society. As I reread the email, it begins to sink in. This isn't a standard policy consultation – it's a direct invitation from the Prime Minister of Japan to help shape the country's approach to living longer, healthier, more purposeful lives.

Soon, I'm sitting in council meetings in Tokyo, alongside a remarkable group: the ministers for education and employment, the president of Tokyo University, a digital entrepreneur in her eighties, a sports innovator focused on active ageing. I am struck by the energy, the seriousness and the diversity of perspectives in the room. On two occasions Prime Minister Abe and I meet in private. We sit together, talking intensely and directly about the future of work, the role of government and how to help people learn and adapt throughout long lives.

I begin to see, first-hand, the complexity of change at the national level and the challenges governments face in making policy. The Council concludes there is no single solution. If people are to flourish across a 100-Year Life, the government must begin by looking at everything – from family policy to workplace norms. It's a systems problem – and it demands a systems response.

Looking back, what amazes me is the power of mastery. You create something with care and depth and sometimes it travels further than you ever imagined. It finds people you will never meet. It opens doors you didn't even know existed. And when that happens, it's not just a moment of pride – it's a moment of purpose. A reminder that what we craft with integrity and intention can ripple far beyond us.

In the years that followed, the ripples continued. The book was adapted into a manga then reimagined for Japanese schoolchildren. Just weeks ago, I led a virtual session with some of these schoolchildren – bright-eyed, thoughtful and full of questions about their future.

Through it all, Japan has come to live in me – not just as a professional connection, but as a place of stories and meaning. Without *The 100-Year Life*, perhaps none of this would have happened. I might have visited as a curious tourist. Instead, because of the mastery invested in something I cared about, I now feel deeply connected to the country. Later in 2025, I took more than 80 London Business School MBA students to Tokyo for an immersive week, learning about its business and traditions – a continuing legacy.

Jobs will change. Technologies will evolve. You may change fields multiple times. That's not failure – it's adaptation. The thread of mastery weaves through it all, giving you resilience as the world moves around you.

When you invest deeply in something you care about, when you make it truly your own, the world often responds in ways you cannot predict. What follows are some actions you can take now and promises you may make to your future self as you continue your own journey towards mastery.

MASTERY:
Putting it into Practice

Three Actions to Take Now

1. **Spot and name three Golden Strands you've strengthened.**
Mastery grows quietly, often without fanfare. Think back over the past year: what skills or qualities have deepened? Write them down and trace their roots – where did each begin and what's helped it grow?
2. **Protect space for growth, not just output.**
Your mastery will shape your future only if you keep tending it. This week, look at your calendar and ring-fence time for learning, reflection or deliberate practice. Even an hour a week signals: I'm still growing.
3. **Choose one action that makes your mastery visible.**
Opportunities often come because others can see what you bring. Post an insight, share a case study, publish a short piece or contribute to a discussion where your mastery can shine.

Three Promises to My Future Self

1. **I will keep investing in what matters, even when results are slow.**
Mastery is a long game. I will stay curious and patient – trusting that small, steady improvements compound over time.
2. **I will honour the skills that make me distinct.**
In a 100-Year Life, my strengths may evolve, but they will also anchor me. I will recognise and refine my golden strands – and put them to work in ways that matter.
3. **I will be open to the invitations mastery brings.**
What I create with care and intention may travel further than I can imagine. I will step through the doors it opens – ready for the people, places and possibilities that mastery makes possible.

Mastery is never finished. Over decades, what you've mastered will evolve – and so will you. In a 100-Year Life, it's your capacity to build, adapt and renew your mastery that keeps you moving forward with confidence, opening unexpected possibilities and shaping a life rich in purpose, connection and opportunity.

CHAPTER 6

THE THREAD OF COOPERATION: Do I Work Deeply With Others?

Long lives are not meant to be lived alone. As your working life stretches across decades, the ability to build meaningful collaborations and strong networks will be a constant source of strength.

When you have invested in the thread of mastery, you are setting the scene to boost your productivity – to use the Golden Strands that will bring value to your work and enable you to switch to meet the ever-changing needs of your working life. The mastery stories I told of myself and Ben focus on us – our motivation, our skills, our capability. Indeed, much of our working life demands this individual focus. But if you look more closely at your day – or your week – you'll notice how much of your work happens with others: in partnerships, teams or wider communities. This shared effort can become the most energising, creative and productive part of our working lives. That's why cooperation is one of the most vital threads we can weave through a long and resilient career. In this chapter we're going to take a closer look at why cooperation matters and what it takes to strengthen your thread of cooperation, but first – what you gain when this thread is strong...

WHAT COOPERATION MAKES POSSIBLE

Cooperation Boosts Your Wellbeing: Working with others can create some of the most wonderful, innovative and exciting moments in your working life. These collaborative experiences are often playful and creative, contributing to a positive sense of wellbeing and satisfaction.

It Enhances Your Performance: When you work productively with others, you have the opportunity to enhance your performance. Colleagues can introduce you to new ideas, share tips and provide valuable feedback, enhancing your skills and effectiveness.

It Helps You Solve Tough Problems: Cooperating with others to tackle challenges increases the likelihood of finding better solutions than if you worked alone. These diverse perspectives and expertise can significantly enhance problem-solving.

It Fuels Your Creativity: When it comes to cooperating, building wide and diverse networks will be crucial for your development in the coming decades. These networks can provide future role models, fresh ideas and varied perspectives. When you are cooperative and open to others, you are more likely to build these networks, fostering an environment where creativity thrives and dynamic projects succeed.

HOW TO STRENGTHEN THE THREAD OF COOPERATION

This chapter is about how to understand the thread of cooperation and the actions you can take now and promises to your future self that will strengthen this thread. Here are ideas and exercises to help you do this:

→ **Make Sense of the Three Elements of Cooperation.** Here, I will share with you how highly cooperative teams and individuals actually work and ask you to reflect on how you go about each of these three elements. Then we will take a closer look at each of these elements.

- **Discover an Igniting Purpose.** In this first element we will consider what draws us together and take a closer look at what happens when purpose fails and the power of great conversations to catalyse cooperation.
- **Cultivate a Cooperative Mindset.** In this second element we take a closer look at how it feels to be cooperative. We will explore your own feelings of cooperation and what it takes to enhance and cultivate a cooperative mindset.
- **Embrace Diverse Perspectives.** In this final element, we take a deeper dive into your networks and connections to discover the extent to which they are amplifying or hindering innovation and creativity. I will tell a story to illustrate the unexpected strength of diverse perspectives.

I will show how important cooperation can be – particularly at a time of advancing technology, and I'll share ideas about how to weave forward.

Your Story: Of Cooperating Deeply

Take a moment to reflect on the strength of your thread of cooperation. Stories of cooperation highlight how deeply we can work with others, and what emerges from shared effort. Can you remember a time when you really cooperated deeply with others? *What does this story show you about the ways you weave with others?*

Ben remembers a time when he worked with teams that just seemed to click – where there was a shared sense of purpose – and an ease in how people worked together.

Cooperation, for Mira, has always been quiet and grounded. She doesn't speak first in meetings, she doesn't dominate agendas. But when she joins a team that works well something powerful happens, she listens carefully, synthesises ideas and offers stability. She often thinks back to her volunteer work with a local mental health helpline. Despite the emotionally intense nature of the work, the volunteers shared a sense of purpose that made the environment feel alive. They were committed to holding space for strangers in crisis – and equally committed to supporting one another.

Here is an example of when cooperation became a significant factor in my productivity:

A Story of a Plane Ride from Hong Kong to Shanghai, 2015

I'm at a meeting in Hong Kong, sharing insights from my latest research. I'm covering the forces shaping the future of work: technological disruption, evolving family structures, climate change – and the growing significance of demographic shifts. Longer lives, I suggested, would fundamentally alter how we think about education, work and retirement.

With me is my London Business School colleague Andrew Scott, who talks about the macroeconomic trends that would reshape global systems. He's also interested in demography – how ageing populations will strain public finances and disrupt established models of economic growth. He's concerned about the sustainability of pension systems if people continued to retire in their late fifties or early sixties.

We meet later on a three-hour flight from Hong Kong to Shanghai and talk deeply about a single provocative question: *What happens when everyone lives to 100?* The pressures this would place on the traditional three-stage working life and the fiscal implications for governments. I am a psychologist, Andrew a macroeconomist, so we come at the topic from different disciplines, but the exchange is energising – an unexpected fusion of ideas. In Shanghai, we went our separate ways: I was off to meet prospective students, Andrew had a full day with recruiters. We didn't cross paths again that trip, but something had been set in motion.

Over the following five years, Andrew and I worked cooperatively together on what was to become a major initiative. Together, we explored the impact of longer lives on individual working lives and the policies and practices of companies and nation states. [1]

Does this resonate with your story of cooperation – was yours like mine, based primarily on the connection with one other person – or was it cooperation on a larger scale, connecting and cooperating with many?

Success May Seem Individual – It Rarely Is

When I reflect on the power of cooperation to connect our lives, I'm reminded of a seminal study by Boris Groysberg, a professor at Harvard Business School, who explored the performance of investment analysts.[2]

The common narrative in that world is that success is all about individual brilliance. Investment firms prize star performers – analysts known for processing vast amounts of information and turning it into sharp, persuasive recommendations. But is it really all about individual endeavour?

Groysberg put this to the test. He explored what happens when top analysts move from one firm to another. If performance were purely a matter of personal talent, you'd expect it to stay the same. But that's not what he found.

In reality, many analysts saw their performance drop after the move. Over time, most did recover – but it took a while. Why the initial decline? Because success wasn't just about their personal skill. It was about the broader web of colleagues they had relied on – people who shared tips, sparked ideas, challenged their thinking, or gave honest feedback. When analysts changed firms, they lost that cooperative invisible support system – and their performance dipped.

This research reveals something important: even jobs that seem solitary are often underpinned by cooperation. The analyst may appear to work alone, but their success is built on a network of connection. You don't have to be in investment banking to recognise this. What really opened Ben's eyes to the power of cooperation was the time he was part of a team tasked with redesigning the emergency response systems at a major airport. On paper, his role was highly technical – focused on data, protocols and operational flow. It looked highly individual and one where his mastery was at the forefront. But Ben later realised that what made the project successful wasn't just his expertise. It was the team around him: a diverse group with different strengths, who trusted each other, communicated openly and pulled together under pressure.

In both cases – whether it's a high-flying analyst or a ground-level emergency team – the lesson is the same. Jobs that look individual often depend on cooperation. And it's those shared, often unseen, efforts that spin the threads of productivity. Sure, there are times when focus is the source of mastery – as it has been for me in some of my endeavours. But when I think about productive outcomes like the book, *The 100-Year Life*, co-written with Andrew J. Scott; the innovative executive program Global Business Consortium co-designed with Sumantra Ghoshal, or the award-winning articles in partnership with Diane Gherson;[3] I realise that often productivity comes through cooperating. Like the Wall Street analysts, the job of a professor might seem highly individual, but like many of these jobs, success comes in part from working cooperatively with others.

MAKE SENSE OF THE THREE ELEMENTS OF COOPERATION

So, what's going on when we cooperate deeply with others? This is a question that's been at the heart of my research for decades. Back in 1995, my colleague Sumantra Ghoshal and I began studying some of the world's most successful companies, including British Petroleum, Goldman Sachs, Nokia and OgilvyOne. Over the course of more than five years we explored these companies and saw first-hand how a cooperative culture could boost productivity – while competitive teams often hoarded information, the most effective ones resolved conflicts and rallied around a shared purpose.[4]

Later in 2003, I launched the *Cooperative Advantage Research Group,* supported by the UK government's Advanced Institute of Management. This expanded our work to 17 companies and 42 teams across the US, Europe and Asia – an extraordinary collaboration that generated valuable insights, later shared in my books, *Hot Spots* and *Glow*.[5]

The bottom line is clear: cooperation is vital for productivity and wise work, yet it can be challenging. It's easy to fall into conflict, competition or 'pseudo cooperation' – speaking the language of cooperation without following through with actions. Our research uncovered that cooperative energy and productivity hinge on three essential elements:

An Igniting Purpose – the compelling force that draws people together, even amid distractions and the busyness of work. This shared purpose acts as a beacon, guiding collaborative efforts and ensuring alignment.

A Cooperative Mindset – that fosters trust and support among team members – encouraging people to believe in each other's intentions and to feel confident their colleagues are committed to mutual success. Trust is the foundation upon which effective cooperation is built.

Diverse Perspectives – in mindset or experience are crucial for innovation and out-of-the-box thinking. Without diverse perspectives, teams may struggle to find unexpected solutions or new ways of understanding problems. Diversity enriches the collaborative process, bringing novel skills and insights into the mix.

Over the years, I've come to see cooperation not just as an act but a system of relationships. Here's the model I use to understand it:

As you reflect on the cooperative story you told earlier, can you see any of these elements? Or, if you are struggling to tell a cooperative story, does this model help you to understand why?

In my first story, I see how sometimes a spark of cooperation happens in the most unlikely places. For me, this was a flight from Hong Kong to Shanghai.

That plane ride with Andrew captures all three elements of the cooperation model. The *igniting purpose* was immediate – our shared curiosity about what happens when everyone lives to 100 sparked a sense of urgency and meaning. It wasn't a casual chat, it felt important. A *cooperative mindset* emerged naturally. Despite coming from different disciplines, we listened deeply, built on each other's thinking and approached the conversation not to compete but to explore. And it was our *diverse perspectives* that made the exchange so rich – Andrew brought a macroeconomic lens focusing on Gross Domestic Product (GDP), pensions and the economic view of life, while I came from a behavioural and organisational perspective, thinking about work, identity and life stages. The combination was energising and the initial conversation, though brief, was foundational.

In the next part of this chapter, we'll look more closely at the three elements that make this possible: igniting purpose, a cooperative mindset and the power of diverse thinking. Each plays a vital role and together, they create the conditions for meaningful and effective cooperation.

DISCOVER AN IGNITING PURPOSE

Lucia felt an igniting purpose most strongly in her time in Ethiopia. Immersed in the intensity of work far from home, often exhausted and stretched, it was this clarity of a shared purpose that bounded her to her fellow volunteers.

Has there been a time when something you really cared about became the ignition that created something truly powerful?

Nico admits he was naive when he launched his first company. He'd trusted a colleague's promises of partnership and funding – neither materialised. This time, his approach is anchored in purpose. He has partnered with a long-time friend he trusts completely, united by a shared vision for what they want to build and how they want to work. Around them, he's created a small circle of fellow founders – people driven by their own missions – meeting each month to share progress, setbacks and hard-won lessons. For Nico, this is more than support – it's a community bound by the energy of building something that matters.

These stories show the many forms an *igniting purpose* can take.

Sometimes it starts with a *question* – something that sparks curiosity and refuses to go away. For me and Andrew, it was a simple but powerful one: *What happens when everyone lives to 100?* That question sat quietly for a while, simmering beneath the surface, until we found the space and energy to return to it.

What about you? Are there ideas or questions you've pushed to the back burner because life is simply too full? Perhaps now is the time to bring one forward – and see who else might be intrigued enough to join you.

At other times, it's the *task* itself that ignites. Nico and his co- founder had a tough task ahead of them: meeting each month to share progress, setbacks and hard-won lessons. It was the sheer momentum of what they created that kept them cooperating.

Have you ever been part of something like that, where the task itself has been the point of ignition? Looking ahead, are there projects that could spark that kind of shared energy in your own work?

And sometimes, it's a *vision* that does the igniting – a picture of what could be. For Lucia, it was the belief that children in Ethiopia deserved a chance to learn and thrive.

Do you have a vision that moves you? Could it be the catalyst for deeper cooperation with others?

When Purpose Fails

Your memories of a cooperative endeavour may also include times when the purpose failed – how did that feel, why did it happen?

My research on cooperation revealed a striking difference between teams with a shared purpose – and those without. When a team lacks a compelling question or a real challenge to work on together, the energy fades quickly. Without that spark, there's nothing to bind people meaningfully. The group becomes subdued, complacent, even stagnant. Conversations start to feel scripted, ritualised – everyone knows what to say, but nothing fresh is ever revealed.

Have you ever been part of a team like that? Lucia has. She'd experienced the buzz of purpose during her time in Ethiopia – every day brought challenges that mattered, and she felt completely engaged in the work. When she returned home and took her first job in a small consulting practice run by a family friend, she had high hopes. She imagined being part of a close-knit team doing interesting, thoughtful work – but it didn't turn out that way. The team drifted from one client to another with no real thread connecting the work. There was no shared ambition, no animating question. Meetings were polite but empty. People said the right things, but nothing truly happened. Lucia soon realised the work lacked not just energy, but direction. She showed up, but she didn't *care*. And that absence of purpose – the contrast with what she'd known before – has left her feeling surprisingly flat.

What a contrast to moments when cooperation feels alive. When there's a buzz in the room, when you find yourself looking forward to the next meeting, not out of obligation, but from genuine interest. You want to hear what others are thinking and you can't wait to share your own ideas.

Great Conversations as a Catalyst

Cooperation may seem natural when everything flows – when energy is high, ideas align and the team clicks. But in reality, meaningful cooperation is often hard-won. It takes time, attention and above all, great conversation.[6] Not the hurried, surface-level exchanges that dominate many workdays, but real conversation – the kind that builds trust, explores difference and makes space for uncertainty.

Do you remember when you last had a great conversation? When you really connected with someone and listened deeply, when you were able to understand them and where they are coming from.

Great conversations often flow around a topic that excites you – helping you make sense of how the other sees the world, their models and assumptions, and what's important to them.

Sometimes they happen in a particular setting. Here, I am thinking about a friend who always has 'walking meetings' when they want to have a real conversation. Looking forward, weaving these times for conversation could be crucial to keeping you energised.

CULTIVATE A COOPERATIVE MINDSET

Cooperation is a mindset – a way of thinking that values generosity over self-interest, sharing over hoarding and collective gain over individual advantage. You've likely worked with people who keep knowledge to themselves, who rarely acknowledge others, who treat work as a zero-sum game. And perhaps you've found yourself in environments where competition is intense and trust is thin. It's hard to cooperate in places like that.

In the earlier section 'Who am I?', we looked more closely at the multiplicity of factors that shape our attitudes and belief – some of these are about the mindset of cooperation.

The Personal Side

Cooperation is never one-size-fits-all. Each of us brings a distinctive style to the table – shaped by our personality, our experiences and the golden strands we've strengthened over time. Take Ben. He's always valued working with others – but not in the way you might expect. He's not the life and soul of the room or the loudest voice in the group. Earlier, we saw two of his golden strands in action – *Holding the Room's Mind* and *Opening the Circle* – during his stakeholder meeting. These aren't just skills, they're at the heart of his cooperative style. Ben listens deeply, notices the subtle shifts in group dynamics and builds trust through steady, dependable presence. His cooperation is less about visibility and more about creating the conditions for others to thrive – spaces where people feel safe enough to share openly and contribute fully.

Mira's style is different again. High in conscientiousness, she brings precision, structure and calm to her collaborations. One of her golden strands is *Bringing Order*. When people work with Mira, they know she will deliver exactly what she promised – and remain composed even when things get messy. Her presence is reassuring; in cooperative settings, she's the one who steadies the ship and keeps everyone aligned.

As for me, I'm introverted, so my cooperation usually happens in smaller groups or one-to-one conversations. Large group settings can leave me drained, so most of my cooperation stories are about working closely with one other person. My golden strands shape this preference: *Systems Mapping* – I love learning how others see the world, spotting the connections between ideas and making sense of complexity – and *Storytelling* – I thrive when exchanging stories, weaving my own experiences with others to build deeper understanding. For me, cooperation is about entering into that shared narrative, where both sides walk away seeing the world a little differently.

When you know your character and your golden strands, you can begin to see your own cooperative style more clearly. Are you the connector who opens the circle? The organiser who brings order? The storyteller who draws out meaning? Knowing your cooperative style doesn't just help you play to your strengths, it also helps you choose when and how to engage so your cooperation is both effective and energising.

The Social Side

A cooperative mindset is not just personal, it's also social. It's shaped by the company you keep. If you're part of a team where collaboration is the norm, you're more likely to cooperate too. Like many social behaviours, cooperation is contagious. But don't be fooled by slogans. In my research, I've often seen companies loudly proclaim their commitment to teamwork: 'We're one team working together on a shared mission' – only to find, just beneath the surface, a culture where everyone's out for themselves.

Mira learned this the hard way. After years of meaningful front-line work, she moved into a role that looked on paper like a natural next step. The organisation spoke often about collaboration, but in practice, it was siloed and status driven. Early on, Mira offered to share insights from her experience – small things that might have helped others – but no one showed much interest. Meetings were formal, carefully controlled and strangely hollow. Eventually, she stopped trying to contribute beyond what was expected.

Earlier, when I recounted my story of joining British Airways, I recalled how I began to 'think like an anthropologist' – observing closely the norms, expectations and the unwritten rules of the game. You will need this anthropologist mindset if you are to understand the cooperative norms of a workplace. Observe how senior leaders behave: are they collaborative or quietly competitive? Look at who gets rewarded: are the highest performers those who share and support, or the ones who climb over others? Culture isn't defined by values on the wall, it's shaped by what's recognised, rewarded and repeated.

I've spent time in places where cooperation didn't stand a chance. People hoarded ideas, played politics and acted solely in their own interests. I've even found myself adapting to those norms. My advice? If you choose to stay in that kind of environment, acknowledge the cost – it may gradually reshape your own behaviour. But if you can, move on. Seek out a workplace where cooperation is lived, not just spoken. Where learning, sharing and mutual success are genuinely valued.

Across a long working life, a cooperative mindset can become one of your most vital assets. Yes, there will be moments when it's tested – when others take more than they give, or when the shared purpose simply isn't there. But when it works – when you find the right people and the right conditions – cooperation fuels not only productivity, but joy. And that, over time, is what makes the journey worthwhile.

If mindset lays the foundation, diversity gives it stretch and dimension.

EMBRACE DIVERSE PERSPECTIVES

Your character and mindset form the mindset that strengthen your thread of cooperation. It is your connections and networks that bring the diverse perspective that fuels creativity. Diversity in thinking is at the heart of effective cooperation. When you cooperate with people with different experiences, perspectives and ways of thinking, you see more, imagine more and solve problems in richer ways. It's not always easy – diverse views can lead to friction – but handled well, that friction sparks insight. And for this kind of thinking to thrive, you need connections. Ideas don't travel far in isolation. They grow and gain strength through networks – formal and informal, local and global – that link people across boundaries. Cooperation flourishes not just through who's in the room, but who's within reach.

As you reflect on your story or stories of cooperation, who were you connecting with? – what was their connection with you? – what did they bring?

We all inhabit our unique networks of connections. As you think about the connections in your story of cooperation, consider the network diagram I've illustrated below:

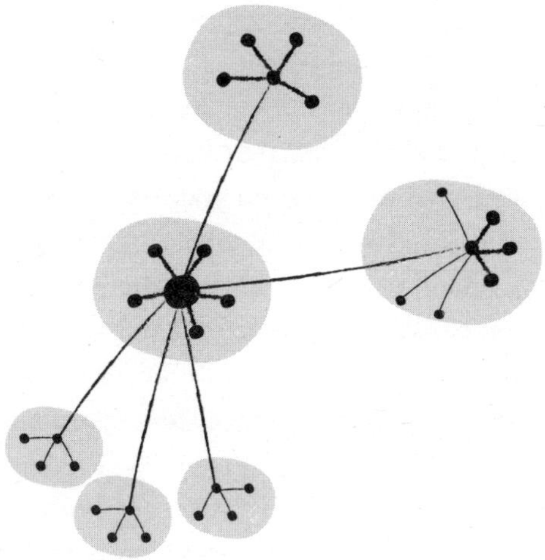

A Network Diagram of Strong and Weak Connections

At the centre of the network is you – you are the dot in the circle at the centre. Surrounding you are people in your network, each playing a different role in how you learn, grow and collaborate. Each person is shown with dot. I've shown a network of five people in your immediate group – then connections with five other groups whose members range from four to seven.

The lines in the network signify the depth of the connections between you all. Darker lines signify strong connections, while lighter lines signify weak connections. Let's take a closer look at these connections and what they mean to cooperation.[7]

The Power of Strong Connections

Closest to you are the people you know well: your immediate team, trusted colleagues, maybe even friends at work. You likely speak to them often, share tasks and support each other. These strong connections are powerful. They're the ones who can give you honest feedback, challenge you directly and support your learning – especially in the early stages of building mastery.

There are some strong connections beyond your immediate group – people in other departments, or from earlier phases of your career. You might not see them every day, but there's a bond of trust and mutual respect. These connections are especially valuable when they bring something different – skills you haven't mastered, experiences outside your own. They can introduce new perspectives and help you build the skills and mastery that make you adaptable and innovative.

The Potential of Weak Connections

On the outer edges of your network are your weaker connections – people you've met briefly, interacted with occasionally, or follow from afar. You may only know them by name or face. But here's the power: because there are so many of them, and because they span different worlds, they dramatically expand what you can see and imagine. In this diverse crowd may be someone whose path sparks a new idea, or whose role becomes a model for where you might head next.

Each layer of connection plays a role. Strong bonds help you go deep; strong but different ties help you stretch. And loose, wide connections help you see what's possible. All three support cooperation – not just through what you already know, but by revealing what you could know next.

Take a few minutes to sketch your own network. Who is in your network? – what are the strong connections and the weak ones? Can you begin to see the benefits these strong and weak connections have brought to you?

Start with yourself at the centre, then look at the people you're closest to: your inner circle. Now think about those you trust but don't see every day, your strong connections across boundaries. Finally, consider the looser connections at the edge, people you barely know, but whose work or perspective you find interesting.

Earlier, I shared a story of cooperating in a situation where the connection was strong (working with Andrew Scott on a book), now let's bring this diversity into perspective by grounding cooperation at a time when the connection is weak.

Your Story: Of Cooperation across Boundaries

Has there been an occasion when you met a stranger who then became important to you – someone you went on to cooperate with? These moments of unexpected collaboration can shift the direction of our work and our lives. What drew you together? How did the cooperation develop? What did you achieve together? *As you reflect, ask yourself what this story reveals about your capacity to build trust and shared purpose.*

Here's a story from my own experience that reminds me just how powerful these unexpected connections can be. This playful collaboration became a vivid metaphor for the joy of cross-boundary cooperation.

A Story of Hot Spots Flavoured Chocolates – Sitges, Spring 2007

I'm in Sitges, the small Spanish coastal town where I have a sea-facing apartment – perfect for solitude, reflection and writing. The town has a particular magic – tapas bars buzzing with light-hearted conversation, people strolling with no rush and a curious mix of characters seemingly blown in from every corner of the world. Here, I become what Baudelaire called a *flâneur* – a wanderer without destination, led by nothing more than interest and instinct.[8]

This morning, strolling through the narrow streets I bump into a friend who invites me to join her for yet another coffee (an essential part of any *flâneur*'s day). One of the people at the table is Oriol Balaguer, a chocolatier from Barcelona, already gaining a reputation as one of the most creative chocolate makers in Europe.

My mind is filled with the book I am writing, *Hot Spots,* and I'm imagining the book cover: vibrant circles of orange and yellow, swirling with energy. I mention this to Oriol and something sparks. 'What if,' he says, 'we created a box of *Hot Spots* chocolates?' The box would look like the cover of the book – and when opened, each chocolate would reflect a principle of cooperation: the warmth of a cooperative mindset (flavoured with vanilla), the surprise of jumping across boundaries (flavoured with sea salt), the ignition of energy (with a hit of wasabi mustard). And one final chocolate – the *Hot Spot* – that explodes in your mouth.

This is a story of two strangers, worlds apart, who happened upon a shared spark. What followed was a joyful collaboration – planning bespoke boxes of *Hot Spots* chocolates. I still remember the thrill of opening that first box and delight of inviting people to taste and imagine. It was a true Willy Wonka moment. Of course, the chocolates were more whimsical than practical, and it would be ludicrous to report the creation of a box of flavoured chocolates was a life-changing event– for me, or indeed for those who ate the chocolates. Yet that's not the point – it was so much fun.

Take a moment to think about the people on the outer edges of your network.

Your strong connections – those you trust and interact with regularly – are few, perhaps 10 to 20 at most. They matter deeply, but they're bounded by time and energy. By contrast, your peripheral network can stretch far and wide. And within that larger pool lies variety: people from other sectors, with different life experiences, alternative ways of thinking. This is where new ideas and surprising insights often come from – not your inner circle, but the unexpected edges.

That's where novelty often lives – not in refining what we already know, but in the spark that flies when different experiences, perspectives and ways of thinking collide. This is the magic of diverse cooperation: the possibility of creating something truly new, not through expertise alone but through *combination.*

The Value of Combining What You Know

What's happening when you are cooperating with someone who has a different perspective from you?

Let's explore this question through the earlier story of the Hot Spots chocolates. In terms of networks and connections, Oriol and I had never met. In fact, I didn't know anyone who works in chocolate – aside from a brief stint as a student packing chocolates on a production line (a story I will tell later). But here was Oriol: a chocolatier from Barcelona, someone who had spent tens of thousands of hours crafting, tasting and imagining chocolate. A master craftsman with a thread of mastery strengthened over his working life.

What made our collaboration so productive wasn't just our interest in each other's work, it was that we each brought a very different set of *heuristics.* Let me explain: A heuristic is a kind of mental shortcut, built up through experience. It's not formal knowledge – it's the stuff you just *know* from years of doing. As Daniel Kahneman and his collaborators showed, these mental shortcuts are powerful ways we simplify decisions – though they can sometimes bias us as much as they guide us.[9]

For me, my heuristics come from decades of researching organisations and the ways that people within them cooperate and compete. Because of this, I have a feel for how teams form energy, how ideas move through networks, how different mindsets collide and fuse. These are my heuristics – they are what I know.

Oriol, too, had his own set of heuristics – only his were built through smell, taste, touch and time. He can predict how a particular spice will behave in ganache, or how sea salt might land on the tongue when balanced against dark chocolate. These are not guesses, they are fast, instinctive judgements borne of years of immersion in his craft: these are his heuristics. It's this combination of two distinct sets of heuristics that created the unexpected – my heuristics about the elements of a Hot Spot – and Oriol's heuristics about how to flavour chocolates in a way that captured the essence of these elements.

These moments of creativity, of genuine innovation, often come from just this kind of meeting: people with different histories, different heuristics and a shared willingness to play. Over your long working life, these opportunities will arise, and when they do, remember it's in the novel combinations – in the mix of different minds, experiences and ways of knowing – that something new and truly human is born.

Ben was leading a project on digital infrastructure when he was paired with Amina, a sociologist specialising in community resilience – someone whose world was, at first glance, far from his own. Ben's heuristic was of systems and logic; Amina brought heuristics about how people respond to change. Initially, their approaches clashed – he sought efficiency, she sought empathy – but over time, their differences became their strength. Together, they co-designed a platform that not only worked technically but was shaped around the real behaviours of the people who'd use it. The result was smarter, more inclusive – and something neither could have built alone.

Take a moment to think about the heuristics you have developed over time. What do you just know how to do, often without needing to think it through? We will have a chance in the next chapter – Knowing – to get more deeply into this question.

Now think about someone you've worked with who approaches the world very differently. What do *they* seem to know instinctively that you don't? What are *their* heuristics? And what might happen if you brought your ways of knowing together?

Is there someone in your wider network – or outside of it entirely – whose thinking might challenge yours and whose skills could combine with your own to spark something new?

TOGETHER, WE FLOURISH

Yes, there are occasions when cooperation is – and must be – serious and task oriented. Yet there are also times when cooperation should – and indeed must be – frivolous and fun. And I sense in this story it was not simply about the production of the chocolates – it was also about the process of cooperating itself: the pure joy of working with someone you trust and like, in the service of creating something you love (or at least love to eat).

I feel this especially now, at a time when so many of us are concerned about the impact of machines on our work. As AI and automation advance, there's a fear that what makes our work meaningful – our creativity, our ability to imagine, to connect and to co-create – might be diminished or even replaced. This fear reveals something essential: that the joy of cooperation lies not just in *what* we produce, but in *how* we work together.

The work that sustains us is rarely just about outcomes. It's about the energy that flows between people, the sense of shared discovery, the unexpected moments of laughter and insight. These are the experiences that help us keep learning, adapting and feeling alive in our work. They're also the very things machines can't replicate – because they arise from relationship, from differences, from being fully human in the presence of others.

Cooperative work, when done well, doesn't just deliver results – it builds resilience. It gives us emotional nourishment, fresh perspectives and the deep satisfaction of being part of something larger than ourselves. And in a world that will ask us to reinvent ourselves more than once across a lifetime, those qualities will matter more than ever.

When I look back at my working life – and you look at yours – my guess is we see glistening in the raw material of our working lives those astonishing times when we cooperate deeply. For me, I think it's fair to say that much of the important work I've done has been in cooperation with others. That's not to say those intense times of cooperation happen all the time. They only come every couple of years and there have been long periods when I've been more solo, cooperating in large communities, rather than in intense partnerships. But when they do occur, they can be magical experiences: ignited by a question that entices, fuelled by working with someone I trust and admire – and made more whole by knowing someone fundamentally different from me.

If you feel your thread of cooperation is weak or weakening, here are some ideas about actions to take now and promises you can make to your future self...

COOPERATION: Putting it into Practice

Three Actions to Take Now

1. **Identify your cooperative style.**
   How do you show up when you work with others? For example, do you connect, organise, story tell, spot patterns? Name your cooperative style and share it with a trusted collaborator.
2. **Spark an igniting purpose.**
   Choose one project or conversation this month where you can invite others into something you truly care about. Share the 'why' – and ask for their perspective to create shared energy.
3. **Stretch your network.**
   Reach out to someone beyond your usual circle – a weak connection – and propose a short, low-stakes collaboration. Notice what new perspectives they bring.

Three Promises to My Future Self

1. **I will build relationships that last.**
   I will invest in people I trust, respect and enjoy working with – even when there's no immediate project – knowing they are my cooperative foundation.
2. **I will keep my circle diverse.**
   I will seek out voices unlike my own – different backgrounds, skills and viewpoints – because difference is where the sparks of innovation can fly.
3. **I will show up generously.**
   I will contribute openly, share credit and make space for others, knowing that the quality of my cooperation will shape the quality of my work and my legacy.

In a 100-Year Life, cooperation isn't just a skill, it's a lifelong asset. The relationships you nurture, the trust you build and the diverse circles you create will sustain you through changing jobs, shifting roles and unexpected challenges. They will give you purpose, broaden your perspective and keep your working life rich with connection and possibility. Over decades, it's not only what you accomplish that matters, but who you accomplish it with – and how those shared moments of cooperation shape the story of your life.

CHAPTER 7

THE THREAD OF KNOWING: Am I Expanding What I Know?

In a 100-Year Life, your knowledge can't stay still. You'll need to keep learning – not just new tools and trends, but deeper wisdom about yourself, others and the world you're a part of.

I imagine the mastery thread spun from multiple strands, and the thread of cooperation constructed from our networks, connections and an igniting purpose. All understandable and relatively easy to observe and describe. This third thread – the thread of knowing – is more elusive. In contrast to mastery or cooperation, it is almost translucent – woven from easily observed training and learning activities yet also created from fleeting glimpses of another's world that burns deep into your memory, or from acknowledging when we learn to know ourselves, it is not always what we expect.

Let me explain... Much of my own knowledge is shallow – I know something about how a combustion engine works, how the COVID vaccine was developed, how to plant a tree in an autumn garden – yet I don't have the deep knowledge to make me an engineer, a vaccine developer or a master gardener. And I expect I never will. We each choose what we are motivated to know more deeply – shaped by our circumstances, our aptitudes and talents, the role models we've observed, the opportunities opened to us.

When we know something deeply – when we know what it takes to run a complex project, or know a question that will ignite others, or know something deeply about ourselves – the impact can be extraordinary. Here are some of the benefits for your working life...

WHAT KNOWING MAKES POSSIBLE

Knowing Strengthens Mastery and Cooperation. Your knowledge isn't static, it's shaped by self-directed learning, sparked by curiosity, deep focus and a desire to understand more. Learning to learn is central to a long working life.

It Sharpens Wisdom and Judgement. Knowing ourselves and others sharpens your decision-making. As adults, we grow through our learning behaviours. When you understand your values and recognise your patterns, you hone your judgement and make better decisions.

It Creates Meaning and Empathy. Wisdom adds context to knowledge – it helps you discern what matters, what can wait and what you should stand for. In a world full of noise and speed, wisdom slows you down just enough to act with purpose, empathy and impact.

HOW TO STRENGTHEN THE THREAD OF KNOWING

As you think about how you learn and come to know more deeply, where does this thread feel strongest for you? Perhaps it has been woven tightly in the past but now is becoming fragile, perhaps it has always been frail. In this chapter, we'll explore how to strengthen this thread:

→ **Lay Strong Foundations.** When you lay strong foundations of knowledge you build long term resilience. We will reflect on times when structured study and repetition shaped what you know and how these foundations can long-term deeper knowing.

- → **Actively Learn From Experience.** Experience can be a teacher as insights emerge from close observation and reflection. Here we will reflect on how experiences shape who you are and what you could become.
- → **Deepen Empathy.** When you step into another's world you expand and deepen your empathy. This becomes a vital form of knowing for a wise working life.
- → **Learn Through Challenges.** Moments of loss, disruption or challenge reveal our values and strengthen our resilience. Here we will consider your crucible experiences and how they have shaped you and what you could become.
- → **Sustain Curiosity for Life.** Learning evolves with age, and the barriers we face as adult learners are very different from those we faced as children. Here we consider the practices that can keep our curiosity alive across a long life.

LAY STRONG FOUNDATIONS

Often the journey of knowing starts with explicit knowledge – that is written down for all to see, and then goes deeper into something more intuitive and implicit. This is a story my son Dominic told me. It is a time when he is a medical student at University College London (UCL), going through an early examination process designed to test his knowledge.

Dominic's Story: Understanding Anatomy – London, October 2013

The classes take place in the university's grand, red-brick Victorian buildings in central London – structures designed to reflect the seriousness of the profession Dominic is entering. Groups of 20 medical students are led into a large rectangular room with 10 tables, each holding five objects – 50 in total. Chairs were set up between the tables so students could sit and observe.

On entering, each student is handed a clipboard with space to write a short description of each object. They are divided into small groups, tasked with examining and describing the five objects with as much accuracy and detail as possible. Standing in the centre of the room is a facilitator in a white coat, stopwatch in hand. The exercise begins and at five-minute intervals each group moves to the next table – they have roughly one minute per object to observe, analyse and record their thoughts.

The objects are not simple classroom props – they are medical specimens: cross-sections of organs, fragments of bone, dissected muscle. The task demanded is not just observation, but careful thought and scientific precision, even under pressure.

This story is a fine example of how knowledge accumulates. The teachers at UCL know what they are doing, it's one of the Top 10 medical schools in the world – they've been training medical students since 1820.

These students are taking the first steps of an eight-year journey to *know* about the human body. At this early stage, the tasks are simply of repetition and observation. Using the mastery terminology, they are at the 'apprentice' stage. Eventually they will *know* by simply glancing at an organ, a bone or a muscle – they will become 'masters'. Later, when Dominic sits his final fellowship examinations as a radiologist, in one test he's given 30 minutes to comment on 30 X-rays – a similar test of intuition and speed he's been practicing for ten years since October 2013.

The second story is about Mira. Recall that Mira, now in her mid-fifties, is looking back and realising that *knowing* about numbers has been a constant thread in her life. Here is her story:

Mira's Story: Knowing about Numbers

Mira began to 'know' about numbers when she joined a small local firm as an accounts assistant straight out of college – not because she knew she wanted to be an accountant, but because she liked order, logic and making things balance. It began with a battered ledger book and her supervisor explaining the logic of double-entry book-keeping. Later, Mira began to know about Microsoft Excel, at first typing in numbers, checking formulas, then gradually understanding its power: how to build automated sheets, link multiple tabs and run basic macros. She started to feel like she could not just record numbers, but *understand* what they meant – spotting patterns, catching errors, forecasting trends.

Bit by bit, through hands-on practice and the coaching by her colleagues, Mira moved from simply entering data to grasping the story behind the numbers. She began to think like an accountant – not just knowing what to do, but why it mattered. And with each spreadsheet she built and each set of books she balanced, her knowing grew deeper.

Mira was knowing through watching and practicing – building her knowledge of numbers in a way that helped her master accounts.

EXPERT VOICES:
Selin Kesebir, Psychologist

Across this book I have sought the counsel of experts. Here, I turn to Selin Kesebir, a psychologist whose research explores meaning, identity and how we come to know ourselves. Selin has written widely on the psychology of the self and the role that values, culture and belonging play in shaping our identity.[1] Here she talks about explicit knowledge and deeper knowledge:

> There is a profound difference between memorising facts and truly knowing something. Deep knowledge isn't about reciting capitals or wine years – AI can do that in a second. It's about integrating what we've learned so deeply that it changes how we live.

ACTIVELY LEARN FROM EXPERIENCE

Knowledge gained through study and repetition lays the groundwork, but it is experience that turns knowledge into something deeper. We come to truly *know* when lessons move from the page into our lives – when observation, practice and reflection sharpen into insight. This kind of knowing is often hard-won: it emerges from setbacks, encounters and the slow accumulation of wisdom over time.

Your Story: Of Knowing Deeply

Think back to a time when you knew something – not because you were taught it in a classroom, but because your experience deepened your understanding. These stories of knowing often mark the moment when wisdom begins to form. What was the experience? What insight did it give you? How did it change the way you saw yourself, others, or the world? *What does this story suggest about the wisdom you are gathering for the decades ahead?*

Let me share three stories – about what Lucia, Nico and I came to know, not through formal learning, but through observation, reflection and time.

Lucia's Story: Embracing Collective Responsibility

Lucia spent a year volunteering with a small education non-governmental organisation (NGO) in a rural Ethiopian town, far from the capital. Over time, she began to *know* what it was like to be there – dusty roads, frequent power outages, unreliable internet. But more important than the surface realities were the transformations that took place over shared meals, long walks and hours spent listening more than speaking.

She watched her mentor – a teacher at the local primary school – manage a classroom of 50 children with ease and navigate the community with low-key authority. Lucia began to understand without judgement. At first, she noticed what was different – how meetings never started on time, how decisions unfolded in circles rather than straight lines – but gradually, her attention shifted. She began to see what she hadn't seen before: the depth of collective responsibility. A neighbour's child was everyone's concern. Generosity wasn't measured in money, but time and presence. This wasn't knowledge she could have learned from a book – this was *knowing*, and it's stayed with her ever since.

Lucia often shares this experience with Nico. And in return, Nico tells his own story of learning – not in a classroom, but in the meeting rooms of his firm.

Nico's Story: Listening for Friction

When Nico launched his first startup, he thought success would come from pitching a clever product. He worked hard on features, slide decks and roadmaps – believing that if he built enough, customers would recognise the value. But he soon discovered that what people say they want and what they actually want are rarely the same.

In conversations, customers would ask for features. Nico dutifully noted them down, convinced each new request would unlock growth. But the product never quite landed. Looking back, he realised he had been listening to the surface, not the substance. What mattered wasn't the feature list – it was the friction. The pauses when people hesitated. The frustration in their voice when they described a daily task. The inefficiencies they worked around but never questioned.

That shift – from hearing words to noticing pain points – was a form of knowing he hadn't learned in any classroom. It was borne from frustration, failure and reflection. Now, in his second venture, Nico begins every conversation differently. He asks less about what customers want and more about where they struggle. He listens for friction. And in those moments of discomfort, he finds the insights that guide what to build next.

Lynda's Story: The Power of Context

Here is my story. As a student of psychology, like my son Dominic at medical school, or Mira learning about numbers, I had learned the important facts. I had read books and manuals and understood the key psychology frameworks. Yet my most vivid memories of this time are not what I read or learned in a university lecture room, but what I experienced. Here, I have been studying child psychology as part of my second year of a psychology degree:

A Story of a Kibbutz – Israel, 1980

I've journeyed to a kibbutz in the eastern most point of Israel. As my final degree thesis, I'm trying to understand something I'm deeply curious about – how different groups and societies bring up their children.

I've come here because this community of kibbutzniks have decided to bring their children up communally. This communal mindset is apparent in many of the daily life decisions: picking clothes from a communal pile every morning; communally cooking and eating food; working together in the nearby orange groves. They explain to me that this deep belief in the value of communal living is the reason they believe children are best nurtured by the whole community rather than their parents.

This is not my only exploration of child rearing practices. The previous year I volunteered at a children's home – where children are housed because their parents are no longer able to care for them. They, like the kibbutz children, are brought up communally yet inevitably, the experience for these two groups of children is dissimilar.

The theoretical model I'm exploring is based on the studies of psychologist John Bowlby. He believes that the most crucial element of a child's positive emotional development is being brought up by someone who loves them deeply. What is less important is whether this person is the child's birth parents. Clearly, the two situations I'm looking at (the kibbutz and the children's home) are not comparable yet they each have insights about the experiences of these children.

What are your reflections on this story? Does it surprise you, have you experienced anything like this? – what does it show you about the world?

Reflecting on my time at the kibbutz, what has stayed with me is knowing more about the power of context. On the surface, in both the kibbutz and the children's home, children are separated from their parents. Yet the emotional experience was utterly different. In the kibbutz, communal care was a choice, rooted in equality and shared responsibility, whereas in the children's home, it was a response to absence and loss.

I had gone in with John Bowlby's theory in mind – that what matters most for a child's development is being raised by someone who loves them deeply, not necessarily a biological parent.[2] Seeing both settings helped me understand the truth of that idea, but also its complexities. Real life is messier than models. More than anything, I came to see that deep knowing comes from watching closely, listening carefully and staying open to what the experience is really showing you – not just what you expect to find.

Did you see this in your own memory of knowing deeply? Did the circumstance you reflected on have meaning for you – a time perhaps when you were particularly attuned to understanding something more deeply?

This is a good moment to return to the first Guiding Question: 'Who am I?' For when we are open to knowing, it often reflects something deep in our history.

For me, my own curiosity about children, and about separation from parents, began as a teenager, when I saw my mother foster new-born babies. She was caring for them in that fragile gap between separation from their birth mothers and adoption into a new family. At this time in the mid-1960s, the adoption of newborns was not uncommon – many young, unmarried women gave up their babies in secret to avoid the social stigma. I remember wondering what these early disruptions could mean for the babies as they grew. Years later, as a psychology student, I was able to explore those questions more deeply during my time on the children's home and the kibbutz.

Writing my dissertation helped me form a perspective on what it means to be a child separated from their parents and the role of community in their development. I was holding onto a question that had ignited my curiosity all those years back.

And what about you? Can you trace your own curiosity back to an early experience – something small, perhaps overlooked at the time, that still shapes how you see the world today?

Our earliest curiosities often turn us inward, helping us to see more clearly who we are. But knowing isn't only about self-reflection. It is also about stepping outward – knowing the lives of others. That's the next strand we'll explore – empathy – and what it means to see the world through another's eyes.

DEEPEN EMPATHY

Your Story: Of Empathy

Can you think of a time when you learned more deeply about the lives of others – and from that became more empathic? Such stories remind us how understanding grows through connection. What did you see or hear? How did you feel in that moment? What shifted in how you respond to others? *Notice how this story deepens your awareness of others, and how that awareness shapes your understanding of yourself.*

Empathy – seeing the world through another's eyes – is a form of knowing that matures into wisdom. I asked the expert Selin Kesebir to tell me more about her take on knowing ourselves and wisdom:

> There is also knowing and wisdom that comes from knowing ourselves. It's about the relationship we have to ourselves. And as we know more, we are more compassionate to ourselves. We have a shared humility – not beating ourselves up, being kind to ourselves. But this kind of self-understanding doesn't happen in isolation, it grows in dialogue with others.

The question I am exploring is: *How do we come to truly know the lives of others?* Here is a story from Mira:

Mira's Story: Listening Without Judgement

Mira's day job is as an accountant – hers is a world of figures and spreadsheets – yet she also volunteers as a counsellor for a local mental health helpline. She began volunteering in her forties. One evening a week, she sat in a booth with a headset, ready to answer calls from strangers in crisis. At first, she worried she wouldn't know what to say but she soon discovered that it wasn't about having the answers, it was about *being there,* listening without judgement, holding space for whatever someone needed to share.

Some calls lasted five minutes. Others, much longer. Over time, Mira began to understand what it meant to really hear someone – to feel the shape of their silence, the weight behind their words. She learned that empathy didn't require knowing a person's whole story – just the willingness to be fully present in a moment of vulnerability. And that changed how she saw others, and how she saw herself.

Here's my story about how I began to know more about the lives of others:

A Story of a Housing Estate – Liverpool, 1978

I'm walking through one of Liverpool's poorest inner-city housing estates. The old back-to-back terraces are gone, replaced by post-war housing now crumbling with age – mould creeping around windows, broken guttering streaking water down the walls and flimsy doors barely holding together. But what stayed with me wasn't the buildings – it was a girl named Tracey.

I'm here for my doctoral research, knocking on doors, asking residents if they'd be willing to talk. One house stands out in my memory. The door opens directly into a bare room – no carpet, just raw concrete. Two large Alsatian dogs lie silently and nearby a toddler sits on what looks like a pile of dirty rags. Against the wall, are two stained mattresses.

The young woman who greets me invites me in. She tells me she lives here with her father, who's unemployed, like generations before him. Her child's father is gone. Her story is one of deep loss, limited options and resignation. She introduces me to her younger sister, Tracey, aged 13. Tracey tells me about school; about the fear she feels walking past the local gangs. I decide to spend more time with her, to offer some support if I can. Over the following months, we meet up. One day, I take her to the city centre – just a short walk from her home. She's never been on an escalator. I watch her, nervous but determined, as she steps onto it for the first time. In that moment, I begin to know just how profoundly her world has been shaped by isolation – and how limited her chances to know anything different have been.

As you think about your own story of knowing another, perhaps like me you are reflecting on the perspective they are taking.

That experience stayed with me because it forced me to imagine life from Tracey's perspective. What did the world look like through her eyes – poverty behind closed doors, fear of gangs on the way to school, so few chances to imagine anything different? It was a glimpse into a life very far from my own.

The experience stayed with me for another reason – it echoed parts of my own story. I'd been walking the same streets where my grandmother Anne once lived. Her terrace house had been bulldozed in the 1950s, replaced by the damp, crumbling estate where Tracey now lived. I couldn't help but compare their lives. Anne lost her father young, and her husband disappeared during five years of war. Yet as a bright, determined girl, she became a nurse. Her daughter – my mother Barbara – had a thirst for learning and all four of her children earned university degrees. It was a path of upward mobility, with education as the bridge. Yet here was Tracey: three generations of unemployment behind her, growing up in poverty, afraid to walk to school. What chance did she have?

I've thought about her often – especially about how easily her life could have been mine. If I'd been born into a family shaped by instability, addiction or despair, who would I have become?

Looking Behind the Curtain

The question of empathy isn't just about feeling for others, it's about imagining life as if you were them. This is something the philosopher John Rawls captured in his famous thought experiment, the *veil of ignorance*. Here was his question: what kind of society would you design if you had no idea who you would be in it?[3]

When I use this thought experiment with my MBA students, I ask them to picture stepping from behind a curtain where their identity is unknown – they could be born into wealth or poverty, privilege or disadvantage, safety or danger. From that place, they are asked: what kind of world would you want?

Psychologists call this ability *perspective-taking* – the cognitive side of empathy. Neuroscience shows that when we imagine the life of another, different parts of our brain activate than when we simply recognise information. It requires imagination, humility and moral reasoning. And unlike data or pattern recognition – which AI already performs better than us – this kind of imaginative empathy remains a profoundly human skill. That's why Rawls' exercise is so powerful. It forces us to step outside the narrow lens of our own identity and privilege. It stretches our moral imagination: our capacity to imagine justice, fairness and care from perspectives other than our own.

So, when I ask my students to do this, it isn't just a classroom exercise. It's training for one of the most essential human capabilities in a 100-Year Life: the ability to know others not through statistics or prediction, but through empathy.

In Selin's view, empathy and wisdom require something even deeper: cognitive humility:

> A consequence of going beyond ourselves is developing what I think of as *cognitive humility*. That's the realisation that we don't know everything and must be wrong about some things. We begin to realise that the world is bigger and more complex than we imagined and that takes us beyond our limited perspective. And because we better appreciate the complexity

and ambiguity of the world around us, we no longer have trite or superficial answers or judgements.

Cognitive humility also makes us more resilient because we understand that our perspectives are just one perspective out of many. Once we open ourselves to the possibility of different perspectives, any difficulty may be met with a shift towards a more constructive perspective. When disappointed and unhappy, we may consider our lives will change and we don't know what's ahead, or we may come to accept that we are all subject to forces we can't control. We may begin to notice that we are expecting more from life than what it can offer to us.

There is also wisdom that comes from knowing and accepting ourselves. This is about the quality of the relationship we have to ourselves. As we accept ourselves more, we are more compassionate to ourselves. We develop a sense of shared humanity, seeing our suffering as part of the human experience rather than beating ourselves up on every occasion.

And that's why empathy matters so much: in a future where machines can analyse faster than us, it is our ability to imagine another's life – and to care – that will remain uniquely human.

LEARN THROUGH CHALLENGES

How do you know who you are, how do you gain self-knowledge? How do we learn about ourselves? I've been reflecting on the moments in my life when I've come to know myself more deeply and I invite you to do the same.

Your Story: Of Self-Discovery

Tell me a story of a time when you learnt about yourself – about the world you inhabit and how you move in that world. Self-discovery moments often come as surprises, sudden glimpses of who we are becoming. What did you realise? What provoked it? How has it shaped you since? *As you reflect, ask: what new possibilities did this moment open for you?*

Self-knowledge isn't something you acquire all at once – it's something you earn, often through difficult or disorienting experiences. This kind of knowing matters because, over the course of a long working life, there will be moments that shake you. Moments that confront you with what it means to be human – not just in the abstract, but in the raw, personal sense of what it means to live *your* life, in *your* skin, with *your* choices. These aren't always grand epiphanies. Often, they are moments of failure, disappointment or vulnerability – when something you wanted doesn't happen, or when life doesn't go according to plan.

Sometimes these are professional setbacks – failing to get the job, losing a role you valued, or facing a project that crumbles. But equally, they can be moments when you surprise yourself: when you respond with unexpected resilience, or, perhaps, realise you've reached your limit. These experiences can be painful, but they can also reveal something essential. They strip away pretence and offer a clearer view of who you are – what drives you, where you find meaning and how you deal with uncertainty.

My story is a story of loss and what I learned about myself. I think it's an important story because most of us will, at some point, be forced to reckon with events beyond our control that test our values, our strength and our perspective.

A Story of Loss – London, 2004

My story begins on the terrible day when my dear friend Sumantra Ghoshal became very ill while I was with him. He had a catastrophic bleed in his brain. He was rushed to the intensive care unit of the local hospital where he stayed and after 12 days passed away – he never regained consciousness. Looking back, I realise the residual grief of losing one of my dearest friends stayed with me for years. Sumantra was 55 when he died and considered by many to be one of the greatest business strategy thinkers of his time. I was fortunate indeed to have the chance to be his colleague and friend. I was dealing with the emotion of losing a colleague and also the trauma of being with someone as they became very ill.

For me this was a time of 'knowing' what it means to be human. I was 'knowing' what grief feels like, and I was 'knowing' what it means to be me and to be tested so profoundly. If you've experienced the death of a close friend or relative, it's a feeling you will have empathy for.

Over the months that followed Sumantra's death, I began to know more about the nature of resilience – first seeking the calm of places that consoled me, then reaching out to friends. When we face something catastrophic – grief, loss or profound disruption – often we reach instinctively for people or ideas that bring solace. For me, it was the Jungian analyst James Hollis, whose book, *The Swamplands of the Soul*, helped me navigate those dark days after Sumantra's death.[4] James Hollis draws on the metaphor of Carl Jung, the Swiss psychiatrist and founder of analytical psychology, of grief as a swampland: heavy, damp, threatening, a place we would rather avoid. But to skirt around it is to deny our own humanity. To be human, Carl Jung wrote, is to walk through the swampland.

Jung's metaphor is both simple and profound. Walking into the swamplands of sorrow or despair is a universal part of the human condition. But it's our *imagination* – our ability to look beyond the present pain – that allows us to emerge changed. We are not the same people when we come out the other side. The journey through grief reshapes us. It softens our expectations, deepens our compassion and transforms the way we see both ourselves and others.

That idea – that walking through pain is not only necessary but also generative – has stayed with me. It reminds me that avoiding discomfort might feel easier in the short term, but only by stepping into it do we grow. And it is often in those bleak, uncertain places that we come to know ourselves – and life – more honestly.

I learned this to be true. Sitting in the Intensive Care Unit, watching the life of my dear friend slip away, I came to know grief not as an abstraction but as a terrain I had to cross. Walking through it reshaped me. It softened my expectations, deepened my compassion and altered the way I see both myself and others.

My friend Warren Bennis, who studied leadership for decades, noticed something striking. When leaders spoke of truly *knowing* themselves more deeply, they often described defining moments that resembled crucible experiences.[5]

The metaphor comes from chemistry: a crucible is a small bowl placed over a Bunsen burner to expose its contents to intense heat. Under that intense temperature, substances like mercury or magnesium are transformed – their very nature altered by the experience. Warren Bennis saw this same pattern in people's lives. The heat of the moment – whether trauma, failure, prejudice, illness or a demanding mentor – acted as a catalyst. These events pushed people into deep self-reflection, challenging their values, assumptions and identity. And while painful, they often emerged stronger and clearer on the other side.

This was true for me in grief – and years earlier on the Liverpool estate. I didn't go there seeking transformation, I went to collect data. But those encounters, like loss, became crucibles. They pushed me beyond comfort into moments where I could no longer look away – and in doing so, they changed me.

And what about you? Have you faced a crucible moment – grief, failure or disruption – that stripped things back and left you knowing yourself more clearly? What did it change in you?

SUSTAIN CURIOSITY FOR LIFE

Before we turn to Actions and Promises, I'd like to pause on a profound question: how is learning as a child different from learning as an adult? As children, learning is our default state – curious, playful, unselfconscious and woven into daily life. As children we learn by trying, by imitating, by experimenting without fear of failure. Now adults, learning often becomes more deliberate and constrained, shaped by goals, roles and the fear of mistakes. Returning to this question matters because the way we learned as children holds clues for how we might reawaken curiosity, resilience and openness later in life. At the end of this chapter on Knowing, it invites us to see learning not only as skill acquisition, but as a way of staying alive to the world.

I am fascinated in how we learn and in 2016 I joined a global consortium on learning.[6] We began with a simple exercise: tell a story of when, as a child, you learned something. Stories poured out – tying shoelaces, baking cakes, stumbling through a grandparent's language. Childhood learning felt playful, immersive, often free of pressure. Yet as we remembered, it wasn't always easy – shoelaces tangled, cakes collapsed. Struggle was part of the process, but as children, we accepted it.

As adults, the picture changes. Learning no longer sits at the centre of life – it competes with deadlines, identity, habits and the fear of failure. It can feel slower, more effortful. But that contrast – the playful immersion of childhood and the cautious effort of adulthood – holds important clues for how we continue to grow across a 100-Year Life. And yet, it's still possible – especially when we create space, stay open and allow ourselves to get a little lost again. Here are three ideas we explored...

Make Space to Learn

We all recognised *time squeeze*. In our fast-paced lives, there's barely enough time to meet our responsibilities, let alone make room for curiosity or reflection. Knowing and learning requires time, but that kind of sustained attention is often eroded by digital distractions and the pressure to stay constantly productive. As one member of the group put it, 'I know learning matters – but sometimes scrolling Instagram feels easier than sitting with something difficult.' I'm sure this comment resonates with you – it certainly resonates with me. *Here a point of reflection is 'how can I make space to learn?'*

Face the Fear of Failure

This was a concept the neuroscientists in the group described as a real cognitive barrier. They explained the deep anxiety many of us feel about getting things wrong – especially in public or professional settings. This fear of failure can quite literally block the brain's ability to form new connections. For adults, learning isn't just cognitive; it's personal.

Think of the first time you stepped into a new role, spoke a language you hadn't mastered, or tried to learn a new technology in front of colleagues. The thought of 'getting it wrong' can be paralysing. Yet those who persist often discover that learning doesn't depend on having every answer in advance – it comes from reframing the experience, lowering the expectation of perfection, and staying present long enough for new patterns to emerge.

Practice Unlearning

This struck many of us as the most profound insight that our community discussed. As children, we reflected how we built our knowledge layer by layer. But as adults, real learning sometimes requires us to dismantle what we thought we knew.

I see this sharply in my conversations and writings with Diane Gherson, previously chief human resources officer at IBM. We came together through a mutual interest in the role of managers. The question that intrigued us was: 'why is it so hard for managers to do a great job?' One profound insight was that the role of the manager has changed significantly over the last decade. It used to be a job involving setting tasks, working in a hierarchy, leading and delegating. That's changed and now the manager is expected to coach, collaborate and lead with empathy.

The challenge is this: for many managers, this shift isn't about adding new tools but *letting go* of old skills and habits – of hierarchical delegating, of telling people what to do. What Diane and I learned was that managers must let go as much as add new capabilities.[7]

As you reflect on your current working life, are there aspects – behaviours, habits – that are no longer serving you and which you should be unlearning?

Let's complete this thread by taking a close look at the actions you can take now to strengthen your thread of knowing – and the promises you can make to your future self.

KNOWING: Putting it into Practice

Three Actions to Take Now

1. **Notice a moment of deep knowing.**
   This week, pay attention to one situation where you move beyond information into insight – perhaps a conversation, an observation or a moment of reflection. Capture what made it feel different.
2. **Practice perspective-taking.**
   Choose one person in your life and imagine their world for a moment. Ask yourself: how might this situation look and feel through their eyes? What shifts when you see it from their perspective?
3. **Make space for learning.**
   Block out one hour to focus on learning – reading, listening or experimenting – without distraction. Notice how it feels to carve out deliberate space for curiosity.

Three Promises to My Future Self

1. **I will stay curious.**
   I will nurture a lifelong habit of asking questions and seeking new understanding, knowing that curiosity is fuel for reinvention.
2. **I will deepen, not just accumulate.**
   I will move beyond surface facts to cultivate wisdom – integrating knowledge into judgement, empathy and action.
3. **I will learn from experience.**
   I will treat both success and failure as teachers, trusting that the lessons of lived experience will guide me through each decade of my long life.

Longevity offers us time – but it is knowing that gives that time depth. A 100-Year Life becomes more than a stretch of years only when it is filled with learning, empathy and self-understanding. To keep knowing is to keep becoming.

CHAPTER 8

THE THREAD OF AMPLIFYING: Can AI Extend My Reach?

In the decades ahead, technology will evolve faster than we can imagine. To thrive in a long life, you need to learn how to partner with it – not fear it, or be ruled by it, but use it to extend what you care about most – and to become more human.

Most of us are asking: What is it to be human in a period of astonishing technological development, and what is it to building a working life possibly stretching into 2065 – as Lucia and Nico could well be doing? I am reflecting on the launch of generative AI tools like ChatGPT in November 2022, which amazed, delighted and horrified us – often all at once. Throughout your long working life, technologies both familiar (like ChatGPT) and as-yet-unimagined are certain to shape your experience of work in profound, unexpected and unanticipated ways. These technologies are not just tools, they blur the line between human and machine. They forced us to ask: where is my unique value?

The rise of AI is a mirror. It doesn't only show us what machines can do – it forces us to ask what makes us distinct. That question is central to this thread of Amplification.

Of all the threads in this book, Amplification is the most dynamic, shaped by inventions stretching back centuries, and with a future that remains unknowable. Technology can create time– to shift pace, nurture relationships and make life more liveable. But it can also fragment our attention, displace our job and drain our energy.

To navigate a long life, it will not be enough to passively follow the arc of innovation. You'll need to make deliberate, thoughtful choices about how you use technology: to boost your performance, to protect your time and autonomy, and above all to clarify what makes you human.

WHAT AMPLIFICATION MAKES POSSIBLE

Amplification Boosts Your Performance. For many cognitive tasks, AI extends your reach, speeds up your rate of work and sharpens precision. And in the coming decades there will be ever more boosting technologies.

It Extends Your Opportunities. Technological fluency opens doors. From remote jobs and freelance gigs to leadership roles and entrepreneurial ventures. When you are tech-savvy you can work globally, adapt quickly and stand out in competitive environments.

It Enhances Creativity. These technologies have the potential to provide freedom to experiment, prototype, build, design and express your ideas in new ways – whether it's editing videos, prototyping apps, starting a blog or launching an online business. It's a tool for self-direction and personal innovation.

It (Potentially) Gives You Time. One of the early wins of AI was its capacity to automate time-consuming routine tasks. It has the potential to free you up to engage in more meaningful and creative tasks – if you have the courage to seize that time.

It Improves Decision-Making. AI can analyse vast data sets and generate insights, helping you make faster and more confident choices. It reduces uncertainty, keeps you learning through digital tools and builds confidence in solving problems independently while staying ahead in a changing world.

HOW TO STRENGTHEN THE THREAD OF AMPLIFICATION

This is a thread that has shown up in working lives for centuries – and is impacting work now more than at any other time in the history of mankind. What is the shape of this thread for you? Is it strong, you feel you're making the best of these emerging technologies and are confident this thread will remain strong in the coming decades? Perhaps you thought you understood technologies and work, but this new array of generative technologies has left you confused and frightened; this is a thread that has been strong in the past but is now beginning to fray. Or, as you think about how you work with technologies, you realise this has never been a strong thread in the fabric of your working life – you've always tried to avoid getting too close to technologies – they make you feel anxious and helpless.

This chapter is about how to understand the thread of amplification and the actions you can take now and promises to your future self that will strengthen this thread. Here are some ideas and exercises to help you do this:

→ **Tell Your Technology Story.** Our history of how we have used technology – from childhood, adolescence and adulthood – shapes our expectations, insights and habits. I will ask you to tell some of your stories and share mine.

→ **Understand How Technology Shapes Work.** Technology rarely replaces a whole job at once – it transforms the tasks inside it. I'll share an exercise that helps you see which parts of your work may be automated, which may be amplified and what that means for your future.

→ **Adapt and Thrive.** Once you've seen how technology shapes your tasks, the next step is to decide how you'll respond. In this part of the chapter we'll explore your options and how to thrive as new tools emerge.

→ **Becoming More Human.** As technology grows more powerful, the real challenge is not just to keep up – but to stay true to what makes you distinctively human. Here, we'll explore the qualities that machines can't replicate and find out how to cultivate them in your working life.

TELL YOUR TECHNOLOGY STORY

Our history of technology is shaped by the year we were born, the region we grew up in and our family's attitude to technology. As we entered work, technology inevitably played a role in how we worked and our expectations. Now, technology – particularly those of Large Language Models like ChatGPT, is changing the flow of work – often in what seems like every day.

Your Story: How You Use Technology

Technology stories capture how tools shape our choices and identities. How has technology shaped the way you live and work? Can you tell two or three stories of this? What role did technology play in your childhood, then later as a young adult? How has it influenced your working life? *What do these stories tell you about how you want to use technology in the years ahead?*

This is how technology showed up in my childhood. Born in the UK in 1955, I recall as a child my family gathering around a black-and-white television in the living room. It had two channels and the whole house had to tune in together. On a side table in the hallway sat the household phone. Here, I stood impatiently waiting for the dialling tone that would connect me to an outside line. Then I slowly dialled the number, my parents shouting for me to get off the phone to my friends when we had been on too long. Long-distance calls were rare and expensive – something for special occasions. Then in school, calculations were done by hand and only those in the top set had calculators.

When I looked through my pile of stories, there are no standout childhood memories of technology. Technology was in the background – it hardly figured. The major impact of technology was its absence (no easy connections, no online games), of what I did not have – not what I had. It's only later in my adolescence and early adulthood that stories of technology emerged. Here are three little stories of me and technology:

A Story of an Assembly Line: Terry's of York, Summer 1971

It's the summer before my final year of school and I've taken a job at Terry's chocolate factory in York, packing Black Magic chocolates. Every morning, I cycle to the towering brick building, the air thick with the rich, sweet scent of chocolate.

Inside, the production floor hums with mechanical energy with the assembly line at the centre – a long, motorised conveyor belt that moves with unrelenting precision, carrying rows of chocolate boxes past the workers, each assigned a single, repetitive task.

At first glance, the job seems simple: pick up two chocolates from a tray and place them in half-filled boxes. But there's a catch – the tray stays still, but the boxes glide past on the moving conveyer belt. I struggle to match the rhythm. At first, the supervisor slows down the line for us newcomers and I manage. But the period of grace ends quickly. The machine picks up speed, indifferent to my panic. I find myself racing up and down the belt, trying to fill the gaps I've missed.

Music blares from the loudspeakers– Rod Stewart's 'Maggie May', Lennon's 'Imagine'– but it's the mechanical tempo of the line that dictates our pace. The belt moves, whether I'm ready or not. My feet are aching from hours on the concrete floor in my thin gym shoes. My hands cramp from the repetition. By the end of each shift, I limp home, exhausted. In bed, I still hear the hum and clatter of the line. It drones in my head – a relentless reminder that this machine isn't built for people, but for efficiency.

What were your first remembered encounters with a technology – how did you feel about this technology?

For me, even as I remember it – 50 years later – I can still feel my thumb and first finger move to pick up the two chocolates and place them in the moving chocolate box. I was experiencing automated work, my first feeling of working with a machine. Chocolates had been (and indeed can still be) made by hand in a crafted way, as I had seen Oriol the Sitges master chocolate maker. But this was not mastery. This was work brought to its most unskilled element. The repetitive work of women (this was considered a female occupation) factory workers packing chocolates on a moving conveyer belt. Never stopping, ever demanding, totally brutal in the demands it made on the women serving it.

Mira was born in 1970 – about the same time I am packing chocolates. Yet Mira's world and mine – even across a 20-year gap – is still largely analogue. Like me – she used rotary phones and watched television on a set with only a few channels. At school, she had no access to computers and typing was taught as a skill on manual typewriters. Ask Mira her first standout memory and she'll tell you about her much-loved cassette player: listening to her favourite music on cassette tapes, sitting for hours waiting to record songs off the radio – finger poised over the 'play' and 'record' buttons.

If you were born before 1980, for you, technology was moving at a relatively slow rate.

Fast forward, and by the 1980s, technology had begun to speed up. For me, now aged 25, this was the year of my first encounter with a computer.

A Story of a University Computer – Liverpool, 1980

I've completed most of my doctoral research – collected data from surveys, structured interviews and observations. Now the real challenge begins: making sense of it all. While the calculations can be done manually, like most doctoral students using quantitative methods, I rely on the university's mainframe computer. It's the size of a small car, housed in a temperature-controlled room, and must be booked weeks in advance.

Before my scheduled session, I carefully input my survey results onto hundreds of punch cards. I arrive clutching my neatly ordered stack then feed each card precisely into the machine. Even a slight bend or misfeed can crash the process – something I learn the hard way, more than once.

Once the punch cards are successfully loaded, I leave the machine to work overnight. Returning the next morning, I hold my breath and press the flashing green button. Out churns ream after ream of continuous paper, neatly folded as it emerges. Thirty long pages of basic correlations and matrixes spill out – my statistical treasure, if only I can decipher it. Now comes the real work: What patterns matter? Have I missed a key variable? Do the results support my hypothesis – or the null? The machine has done its job. Now it's up to me to find the meaning.

How old were you when you first encountered a computer – how did you feel about it?

If, like Lucia and Nico, you were born after 1990, you'll have many childhood memories of technologies. They remember watching *The Lion King* on a VHS; the Tamagotchi cyber-pet they became obsessed with – until it beeped one too many times in the middle of the night and Lucia's mum took the batteries out. At 10, Lucia was given her first mobile phone – a chunky Nokia with *Snakes*, which she played constantly. Later, Nico upgraded to a flip phone with texting and a camera that barely worked. Later still, they set up their first email, got on MSN Messenger to chat with friends after school and even later, joined Bebo and early Facebook for social networking. CDs turned into MP3s and suddenly there was YouTube, where for hours they watched music videos and funny clips.

Anyone born in a developed country in the 1990s was experiencing an in-between era – bridging the world of analogue and digital, learning to play, communicate and create through evolving tech. Now, technology was not just part of a childhood – it *shaped* a child. These generational stories reveal how quickly technology has shifted from occasional tool to constant companion. Each shift demands a new kind of adaptability.

Fast forward again to November 2022 when the frenzy about ChatGPT began in a big way:

A Story of ChatGPT – Geneva, 2022

Preparing for a late-afternoon flight back to Heathrow from Geneva, I settle into the lounge at the airport. With the flight take-off imminent, I briefly scroll through my emails. There is a message from a friend: 'I've just looked at this new program ChatGPT. It's really interesting – like to hear your views.'

Looking at the message, I see a flight delay warning flashing on the departure screen. We will be lucky if the flight leaves before 10 p.m. I've four clear hours ahead of me so I do what hundreds of thousands of other people did that week – I go to the Open AI website and start to play with ChatGPT.

I begin by asking the machine a question I am an expert in: 'What is the future of learning?'. Then over the next hour, I ask eight follow-up questions (like 'Can learning be personalised?', 'Are there examples of upskilling?'). For some questions I asked the machine 'to write in the style of Lynda Gratton'. Within the hour I had created, let's call it an essay, of over a thousand words of the standard of a middle-level university student.

I then asked the machine the same question with other requests: 'In the style of a Shakespeare sonnet'; 'As an Old Testament parable'; 'Written by a person obsessed with making jam'. Honestly, on a bleak Geneva evening in an airport lounge, I am laughing out loud. This machine is a crack-up.

By 2022, technology was no longer seen as a tool, it was becoming an extension of how we thought, created and connected.

Perhaps your day looks something like this. You started your day with a smartwatch, tracking your sleep and heart rate; later at work, you used AI-powered tools to streamline research, summarise meetings and draft reports. Then you collaborated with colleagues globally through platforms like Slack, Notion and Zoom. You managed your finances through budgeting apps and invest in cryptocurrency and digital assets using real-time analytics. In your downtime, you listened to personalised podcast playlists, read e-books on your Kindle and explored emerging tech trends in virtual and augmented reality.

And if you are reading this book in 2030 – your day is going to look different still – in ways that are hard to imagine as I write this in 2025.

These long trajectories of technological development will be especially extraordinary for our children. Imagine if they live 100 years – what will life in 2125 look like for them? We can already see how their lives have been shaped. Ben has two young children. He watches his two-year-old daughter, sitting cross-legged, clutching a tablet almost as big as her lap. She's swiping through colourful icons until she finds her favourite app – a cheerful alphabet game that sings each letter as she taps it. She doesn't read yet, but she knows the rhythm of the buttons, the jingle of the intro music and exactly how to get to her favourite videos on YouTube Kids.

Ben watches his 10-year-old son engrossed in *Minecraft*, building a digital treehouse while chatting through a headset. He's using Google Classroom to check his homework and watches short YouTube tutorials. He knows how to type, copy-paste and use voice-to-text. Already he's started experimenting with Scratch, a beginner coding platform, and proudly shows Ben the little game he's built – a bouncing cat that meows on command.

Ben's young children treat technology as second nature, as much a part of their world as books or toys once were for their parents. For them, screens aren't just devices – they're playgrounds, classrooms and stages for imagination. Ben wonders how they will live and work – will Gen AI, as some are saying, destroy their future work, break apart societies, create ever-greater gaps between the rich and the poor?

Do you share Ben's concerns? How has technology changed your life, how will it in the future and how best can you prepare? These are the questions I'd like us to turn to now.

Faster, Embedded, Fearful

What stands out as I look at these technology stories – is how the speed of change has accelerated dramatically. Contrast me or Mira, who experienced long stretches with the same tools, with Ben's 10-year-old son whose digital environment evolves every year – apps, platforms and expectations shifting constantly. This rapid pace demands a new kind of resilience and adaptability, not just in how we use technology, but in how we raise, teach and guide those growing up with it.

It's not just speed – technology has moved from being an occasional, external tool to a constant, *embedded companion*, woven into the fabric of everyday life. And that means that each generation faces a different learning curve: Mira had to adapt to technology introduced later in life; Lucia and Nico grew up learning as technology evolved; and Ben's children are native to it, though not always aware of its risks.

Ben fears his kids spend too many hours on screens – especially when playtime or outdoor activity gets pushed aside. He wonders what might sitting and staring mean for their attention spans, sleep and physical health? Will this constant digital engagement affect their ability to interact face-to-face, will they struggle to hold a real conversation and to learn to read emotions beyond emojis and video filters? And speed is becoming part of their life. Ben notices how quickly his children expect responses – from games, videos, even him. When a loading screen takes more than a few seconds, frustration flares. He worries they're getting used to a world where everything is instant and patience is a dying art.

What's happening here – how can we make sense of how technology shapes work?

UNDERSTAND HOW TECHNOLOGY SHAPES WORK

We are all wondering how technology will impact our work – what will we do, what will be left?

I teach a class at London Business School about technology and work. I use an exercise with my students – you might find it helpful. Here are the steps...

First, note down the *tasks* that you perform in a normal day or week at work. Most of us have about 30 tasks we perform as part of our current job. It is important we focus on tasks because technology rarely replaces all the tasks in a job, it replaces some of them. You need to figure out which tasks these will be. To do so, you need to move to step two:

Now look at each of these tasks and ask of each task, is it routine or non-routine?; and is it manual or cognitive? Let's take a closer look:

Is the Task Routine or Non-Routine?

You will discover some of your tasks are *routine* (you could describe them to someone with ease). If I look at my current job then a routine task is marking the scripts of my students, completing a performance review of my team, writing a report from data. Look at your list of tasks and make a mark against any that are routine. Others are *non-routine* (they are more complex and not easily described or done). In my current job, a non-routine task is writing a book, working creatively with a senior team on their strategy. Look at your list of tasks and make a mark against any that are non-routine.

Is the Task Manual or Cognitive?

The second dimension describes the human nature of the task. Some are *manual* (you use your body muscles to accomplish). If I look at my current job, I can find very few manual tasks – perhaps typing an email, walking students around Tokyo on their global experience week. As I look forward into the next decades of my life, I'd like to perform more manual tasks – like making a pottery vase or painting a picture. Look at your list of tasks and make a mark against any that are manual.

Some tasks are *cognitive* (you use your brain). Much of my current job is cognitive – analysing data, writing reports, teaching a class, thinking through the structure of ideas to write a newspaper article or a book. What are the cognitive tasks you perform?

Now you have put these two dimensions together – you've created four categories of the tasks you perform. Let's take a closer look at each category and the impact on work:

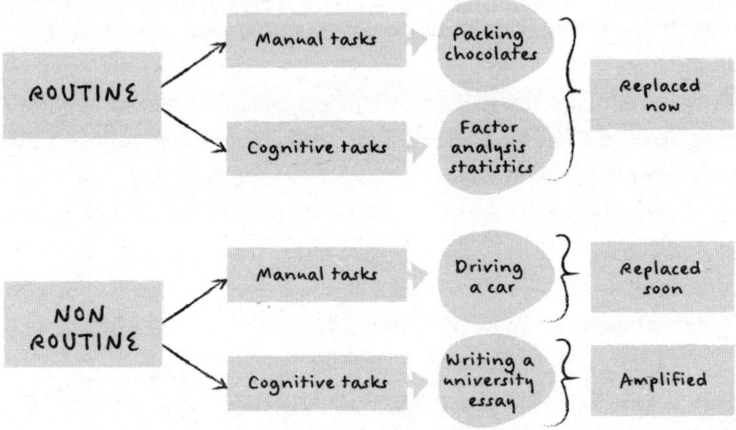

Modelling the Impact of Technology on Work

Routine/Manual Tasks – like packing chocolates
The example I give is of the task I performed in 1970. A manual/routine task – packing chocolates by hand on a moving conveyer belt. Over the 1980s this task became entirely automated. In the following decades, many other routine tasks were automated – packing, metal pressing, welding, even operating forklifts. You can assume that any routine manual tasks you perform will be completely automated in the future.

Routine/Cognitive Tasks – like factor analysis statistics
The example I've used is the factor analysis statistics I performed in 1980 on the university mainframe computer. While this machine looked futuristic – it was essentially performing routine work – in this case, statistical analysis. The output might seem complex, yet any trained statistics student could have followed the same steps manually. The key difference was speed and accuracy: what might have taken me days could now be completed in hours.

The assembly line replaced hands, the computer replaced brains – but only for routine tasks that could be broken into clear, repeatable steps.

And it turns out, there are many such tasks – something discovered by spreadsheet assistants and bank tellers whose roles were later digitised. So, you should expect that any routine/cognitive tasks in your list will be automated and replaced.

Non-Routine/Manual Tasks – like driving a car
Non-routine manual tasks – like driving a car, sorting laundry, or plumbing a house – were once expected to be the frontier of automation. When I wrote in 2010 about the future of work in *The Shift*, the technologists I consulted predicted that by 2025, we'd see fleets of driverless cars and even robotic plumbers.[1]

Yet as I look out of my London window today in autumn 2025, I see no autonomous vehicles cruising the streets and no robot plumbers at my neighbour's door. The rollout of driverless cars has been far slower than expected, slowed by safety regulation and high costs. And those early Boston Dynamics videos of humanoid robots? It turns out most of us don't want full-scale machines wandering our homes – at least, not yet. Household laundry and plumbing, meanwhile, remain stubbornly human: each pile, each home too idiosyncratic for easy automation.

But this is not the whole picture. In San Francisco, you can ride in a driverless Waymo taxi – astonishing at first, then quickly normal. In China and the US, billions are flowing into robotics startups, with companies like Figure 01 building humanoid robots designed for flexible, general-purpose work. Uber and others are experimenting with robotic solutions, betting that today's constraints will give way to breakthroughs.

Predictions are often both wrong and right: slower in some places, faster in others. What looks impossible in one city is already routine in another. That is why technological forecasting is so hard. Some changes creep forward, others arrive suddenly and with force – like social media and generative AI.

Non-Routine/ Cognitive Tasks – like writing a university essay
My third story of ChatGPT showed a technology augmenting and, in some cases, replacing complex, non-routine cognitive tasks like writing a university essay. Unlike earlier technologies that automated predictable, codified processes, this wave – beginning in 2023 – felt startlingly human. It didn't look human, of course, but it could do things we once believed only humans could: write, analyse, summarise, create. This wasn't rule-following anymore. The engine behind it was a Large Language Model,

trained not on fixed logic but the vast ocean of human knowledge and expression.

What struck me most was the moment I realised why ChatGPT could respond to the prompt *'write an essay like Lynda Gratton'*. It could do this because it had ingested much of my writing – books, articles, blogs. Without my permission, but with astonishing fluency. That revelation – that so much of ourselves is already in the machine – was both deeply unsettling and deeply impressive.

And essay-writing was just the start. Very quickly, these tools began to take on roles we once thought uniquely human. In medicine, AI systems were already supporting specialists in areas like radiology – detecting tumours or fractures invisible to the human eye. Algorithms trained on millions of scans could deliver faster and sometimes more accurate diagnoses, shifting how doctors worked and what patients expected. In drug discovery, AI compressed timelines from years to months, scanning chemical possibilities at unimaginable speed.

Equally striking was the rise of AI in counselling and coaching. By 2024, one of the largest reported use cases of generative AI was in therapy and mental health support. People turned to chatbots not because they believed the machine truly cared, but because it was always available, non-judgemental and – ironically – sometimes seemed more empathic than humans. In workplaces, AI 'coaches' were deployed to help employees prepare for performance reviews, to simulate difficult conversations, even to suggest personalised learning paths. Coaching and counselling, once the most human of professions, were suddenly being reshaped.

There's another reason these technologies spread so rapidly: their ease of use. No punch cards, no coding. Just type and go. In that extraordinary month of November 2022, millions of people, myself included, simply plugged in and got started. For many, the barrier to entry was so low, experimentation became irresistible. Overnight, the boundaries of non-routine cognitive work felt porous.

This is the essence of amplification. It is not that machines have taken everything, nor that they will. It is that they amplify human capability.

That leave the crucial question: when these tools take away chunks of what once felt uniquely ours: *what remains?*

What's Left for Humans?

When you step back from these categories – routine and non-routine, manual and cognitive – you see a stark truth: most tasks are, sooner or later, touched by technology. Some are automated quickly. Others take decades. But few remain untouched forever.

That raises the most urgent question: *what's left for humans?*

The answer is not a single skill or occupation, but a stance. The real challenge is to build resilience – the capacity to continually reassess your value as technology advances. In earlier decades, you might have done this once every ten years when a new platform or process appeared. Now the cadence is accelerating. AI models update monthly, sometimes weekly. The ground under your working life is constantly shifting

So, what remains human is not simply the task list, but the practice of reflection. Knowing how to ask: *What do I bring that no tool can? What questions do I ask that others overlook? What perspectives do I hold that machines cannot imitate?*

This is where distinctly human capacities – curiosity, empathy, judgement, imagination – become more important, not less. As machines grow more fluent, our unique value lies not in matching their scale, but in deepening our difference.

ADAPT AND THRIVE

In the face of constant technological innovation, what will you do – how will you adapt?

That's a tough question – and one that depends on many unpredictable variables. Still, we can look to the past for clues about how people respond to technological change.

Economists such as Daron Acemoglu and David Autor[2] have explored this question deeply and identified three consistent pathways.

I can see these three pathways playing out in the subsequent histories of the women packing chocolates in Terry's factory in the 1970s. As robotic assembly lines were introduced into factories such as this, the jobs of the women standing next to me vanished. The machines that replaced them were faster, more reliable – and didn't require breaks, time off for childcare, for holidays. Here's what happened...

Some of these displaced workers were able to *re-skill* and switch to other jobs at the same pay grade – using some of the skills they had and now adding others. They moved into administrative roles – such as typists or clerical assistants. The result was their pay stayed roughly the same and their jobs were more secure – for the time.

Those that took the second pathways *up-skilled* into better-paid roles. These jobs were often created by the emergence of new technologies. As manufacturing jobs declined in the city of York, including those lost when Terry's finally closed in 2005, some workers moved into the city's expanding service sector – such as retail, care and call centres, and some of these jobs were better paid.

There was a third pathway – *down-skill*. Some people, (perhaps 30 per cent) were laid off during the cost-cutting rounds of automation at the factory. They lacked the means, the motivation or the competence to re-skill. As a result, over time they took lower-paid jobs – cleaning or waitressing in cafés and fast-food outlets as York became a tourist hub. These jobs were more precarious, lacked benefits like pensions or sick pay, and paid less than factory work.

These three pathways – *re-skill*, *up-skill* or *down-skill* – are not just historical patterns. They will continue to define our response to automation. If you want to stay in decent work for the decades ahead, you'll need a job strategy, to be proactive, strategic and supported in your efforts to adapt. That's where strengthening the threads of Mastery and Knowing becomes so crucial.

Let's take a closer look at your job strategies. My suggestion is you consider three areas: Imagine new jobs and the path of job creation; Explore options: Collaborate – with technologies, and Explore Options: Hop – from frontier roles.

Imagine New Jobs and the Path of Value Creation

The earlier exercise gave you a sense of the trajectory of the tasks you perform now – or perhaps had thought about performing in the future. From that you imagined the tasks that will be replaced and those that could be amplified. It is those tasks that are amplified that are your path into the future.

Remember, this only a snapshot of now – what are the tasks and jobs that will become valuable in the future and that you should steer towards? Do you know what these are?

These predictions of job creation change over time. Over the next couple of years, the general consensus is that jobs will emerge at the intersection of technology, sustainability and human-centred design. In technology, there will be growing demand for AI trainers, data ethicists and machine learning explainers – roles that help shape and guide intelligent systems. Green economy jobs will expand, including climate analysts, renewable energy technicians and carbon auditors. As we live longer, healthcare and bioinformatics will rise, and as we think more about our health, we will engage digital wellness coaches, learning designers and experience curators.

Yet, while we can have some sense of those jobs likely to be created in the next few years, what of the longer term? Ask yourself: How long do I expect to work? Lucia will likely be working 40 years from now – that's 2065. And Ben's children? Perhaps 2105. What will be their working lives, what can they expect and what should you anticipate? What would you tell a 10-year-old child?

It's a very challenging question – one I've been asked many times. Here's how I think about how to imagine future jobs. It begins with thinking back and a game of imagination ...

Imagine the Year is 1830 and you are living in a northern English town. As you look out of the window of your cottage, you hear the noise and see the smoke of the first railway being built. Later, you see the first train running through your town.

If I asked you then (in 1830) what impact this new technology would have, you might tell me of job destruction. Your family has a horse-drawn wagon; you know the farrier who manages the local stables, the cobbler who shoes the horses, the farmer who grows the grain that feeds the horses, the landlord and waitresses of the post house who serve passing carriages. You will be worried about these jobs, and you'd be right to be concerned – hundreds of thousands of workers depend on horses and over time, many of these jobs will vanish.

But predicting new jobs – of job creation is harder to see. You could watch with thrill and trepidation the first steam train, but it would be difficult to picture who might benefit. And yet, history shows there were many beneficiaries. Market gardeners could now sell beyond their villages; warehouses and transport jobs multiplied; mill workers could take seaside holidays, giving rise to café keepers and boarding houses. And further downstream, the combustion engine would launch the oil industry, reshaping economies and geopolitics.

These second-order effects are almost impossible to imagine at the time, but they remind us that technological change rarely stops at the obvious.

The same will be true now. Some jobs will vanish in ways we can already imagine, others will appear in forms we can barely conceive. That is the nature of technological change: destruction visible, creation harder to picture.

So, in the face of such deep complexity and uncertainty, what can you tell yourself – and what guidance would you offer a 10-year-old child? The answer cannot be certainty. It must be readiness: the willingness to experiment, to move, to renew.

That is why I offer two working options - Collaborate and Hop – not as predictions, but as practices. They are ways of meeting the future with resilience, of staying alert to what is possible and ensuring that even as technologies advance, your distinctly human edge endures.

Explore Options: Collaborate – with Technologies

Right now, the power of technological tools often lies in *partial automation*, rather than taking over whole processes end-to-end. They excel at fragments of work – the drafting, the coding snippet, the statistical check – while leaving the higher-level architecture, system design and judgement to humans.

Take for example the way that medical doctors use AI. A recent insight is that these tools work best not when they replace human expertise, but when they *collaborate* with it. Studies show, for example, that doctors and AI together perform far better than either alone: the human brings judgement, empathy and contextual understanding, while the AI brings scale and pattern recognition.

And this complementarity works most powerfully for experts, who know when to question, refine or override the machine. For beginners, the story is more complex. Without the grounding of experience, there is a tendency to treat AI as an oracle, which can block deeper learning and leave critical thinking undeveloped. Amplification, then, is at its best not when it substitutes for expertise, but when it expands and strengthens it.[3]

So, in your current role, collaborate means more than just adopting a new tool. It means testing what it can do, and – crucially – what only you can do. It's an ongoing experiment and each iteration sharpens your discernment and extends your reach.

As the now well-known saying goes: You will not be replaced by a machine – you will be replaced by a human who knows how to use a machine better than you. Collaborating is how you make sure that human is you.

Explore Options: Hop – from Frontier Roles

Whether you're a software engineer, a teacher, a marketer or a manager, chances are high that in the coming years, you'll find yourself working *in*, *with* or *alongside* AI.

This isn't speculation – it's already happening. Right now the fastest-growing categories of new jobs are emerging inside the AI economy: model training, data labelling, AI operations, machine learning ethics, product alignment, synthetic content, prompt design. These aren't just technical roles. Many are hybrid, drawing on communication, judgement or domain-specific expertise.

You may not plan a career in AI but it's increasingly likely that you'll work within a system that includes it. You'll join projects where AI is your colleague – or your competition. You'll see tasks shift – some disappearing, others emerging in strange, unnamed forms. These are *frontier roles,* and you will need to be prepared to move when the terrain shifts – to *hop*. This is not about restlessness or risk, it's about the ability to re-anchor – to move early, not late; to shift with insight, not just instinct.

Nico knows he must be nimble. He's watched entire job categories rise and fall in real time. In 2023, his friend was working as a prompt engineer – earning well and riding the AI wave. Eighteen months later, this frontier role was declared obsolete. How does it feel to be in a frontier job? Here is an analogy I find compelling

Picture your job as an island. You're standing on that island and the tasks feel solid, your expertise sound. Then you notice the sea level around your island rising. Imagine the sea level representing the increasing power of Generative AI. As the power increases, so the sea level rises – lapping at the edges of your island – reshaping your role, eroding familiar tasks. This is not your failure – it's acceleration: you are in a frontier job that's fast eroding.

Hopping recognises that some jobs are, by nature, temporary. These roles live at the frontier: fast-moving, loosely defined, often experimental. And if you're in one of these roles, you already know it. The pace is high. The tools evolve weekly. The edges of your work keep changing.

Are you in a role that feels close to the edge – where tools shift quickly, definitions change and the future shape of the job is still forming? If so, you may already be in a frontier role.

For people in these roles – prompt engineers, AI ops specialists, digital content creators, synthetic media editors – hopping isn't a response to disruption it *is* the rhythm. You don't move once and settle, you learn to move again and again – between projects, roles, skills and sometimes even industries.

This can be energising. You're close to the edge of what's new; you get to build, test, shape. But it also requires a different kind of mindset.

You need to stay light – carrying what you know, but never assuming it will be enough. You need to invest not just in expertise, but in versatility. And you need to make peace with the fact that your working identity may never feel final.

For many, this period of work is already happening and in a long life, it will become more common for us all to take frontier roles and to be prepared to hop.

What all of this points to is resilience – not as a one-off act, but as a continual practice. In the past, you might have paused every decade or so to reflect on your value and adjust your skills. Now that cadence is collapsing. New models arrive monthly, sometimes weekly. Roles appear, peak and disappear in the space of a few years.

That means your ability to thrive is less about mastering a single tool and more about building the habit of real-time self-assessment: asking, *what is it that I bring that no machine can? What is my unique human edge?* Your analysis of Mastery and the Golden Strands will help you anchor this assessment.

This question of empowerment leads us directly into the next challenge. Because adapting to technology is not only about keeping pace with tools – it is about clarifying what makes us distinct. That's where the thread of amplification ultimately takes us: to the work of becoming more human.

BECOMING MORE HUMAN

The deepest challenge of amplification is not speed or scale: it is humanness.

If the rise of generative AI has brought anything into sharper focus, it's this: staying human is no longer something we can take for granted. As tools become more capable, more persuasive and more embedded in our working lives, we're faced with a challenge – and an opportunity. To use technology not just to do more, but to become more. That's the heart of this thread of amplification and it's something I want to explore further in conversation with someone who's spent years thinking about what makes us distinct.

EXPERT VOICE: Tomas Chamorro-Premuzic, Psychologist

The rise of AI offers a kind of mirror. It doesn't just show us what machines can do – it forces us to ask what makes us distinct. AI is more fluent, more scalable, more consistent. But it lacks depth. It doesn't understand meaning, it doesn't care. So, the question is: do we?

That question runs through much of Tomas Chamorro-Premuzic's work.[4] A psychologist who has written widely about talent, leadership and the future of work, he argues that the greatest danger of AI is not that it will outsmart us, but that we will lower ourselves to meet it – outsourcing thought, flattening curiosity, dulling judgement. We've become obsessed with efficiency and visibility but amplification, he insists, should be about depth, not reach. Here is some of our conversation:

> I'd like to draw your attention to what I call the *paradox of empathy*. At the very moment when AI is incapable of true care, many people describe their interactions with chatbots as more empathic than those they have with humans. Cognitive empathy (understanding how someone thinks or feels) can be simulated. Emotional empathy (mirroring how someone feels) can be approximated. But the third level – caring enough to act on what we feel – remains distinctly human. If we don't cultivate empathy ourselves, we may end up in a world where machines appear more humane than we are.

Tomas describes what he sees as the *80/20 balance*. AI may take 80 per cent of what we do, but the vital 20 per cent – the unexpected, the creative, the surprising – remains ours to renew. To be human is not to be predictable or routine; those patterns can be codified and automated. What distinguishes us is our willingness to argue, to bicker, to show care, to play, to act in ways that are not expected. The danger is that if we let ourselves become standardised – living only by default tendencies – then AI will capture more of us than we realise.

This is why Tomas urges people to invest not only in skills, but in the practice of *being fully human*. That means cultivating self-awareness: knowing your patterns, your defaults, your blind spots and finding the courage to step outside them. It means critical thinking: pausing when fluency tempts you to accept easy answers and asking instead, *Is this true?*

Is this right, here, now? And it means empathy in its fullest sense: noticing, listening, caring and sometimes surprising others with how you respond.

Tomas also reminds us that renewal often requires stepping outside the digital altogether. Here is how he describes it:

> If we reinvest the time AI saves us only in more screen time, we're living without thinking. The challenge is to rediscover analogue adventures: to go into the world, to seek novelty, to surprise ourselves. Paradoxically, this unpredictability – our capacity to do something different each day – is what makes us hardest to replace.

Of course, I am in complete agreement with Tomas and in the final thread *Adventure* – we look at the rediscovery of analogue adventures and how unpredictability fuels resilience.

As we talked, what emerged most clearly is Tomas's belief that amplification must be grounded in character. That who we are shapes how we use the tools – and how the tools, in turn, shape us. 'We don't need to become more like machines,' he told me. 'We need to become more like ourselves.'

So, how do we become more like ourselves?

Tomas reminds us that becoming more human isn't a slogan, it's a practice. It's not about resisting technology or rejecting the tools that now shape our working lives. It's about returning to what we do best and doing it with more attention.

That starts with *knowing yourself.* Not just your skills or preferences, but your patterns – what drives you, what unsettles you, how you respond when things get uncertain. In a world full of prompts and distractions, self-awareness becomes a kind of navigation system. It's no coincidence that 'Who Am I?' is the first Guiding Question in this book. Because without this anchor, amplification can pull us in the wrong direction.

It also means *thinking more critically*. When systems are built for speed and fluency, we can confuse smoothness with truth.

That's where curiosity becomes essential. It's what enables us to step back, to ask better questions and to challenge easy answers. We touched on this in Chapter 6 on Cooperation and will look at it later in the thread of Adventure – how curiosity creates bridges, opens up possibilities and leads us into new terrain. Without it, amplification becomes repetition.

Empathy, too, matters more than ever. Amplifying your impact doesn't just mean scaling your voice – it means tuning in to others. That's where the Nurture threads of Friendship and Intimacy that we will come to offer guidance. They're not only about connection, but about care: about paying attention, listening well and responding with imagination as well as insight. These are the relational muscles that AI can't build, but that we ourselves can – and must.

Amplification isn't just about doing more. It's about doing what matters, more deliberately. And in a long life, that matters more. With more time ahead, the way we choose to show up – as colleagues, as partners, as people – carries real weight. These choices shape how we grow, how we connect and how we bring meaning to our working lives.

So, ask yourself: What are you amplifying – and why? What are you working towards – and who are you becoming in the process? These are not questions an algorithm can answer. They are central to living the 100-Year Life.

Tomas reminded me that amplification begins with self-awareness, curiosity and empathy – capabilities that thread through this book. Yet as we spoke, I found myself thinking about something more specific. In a world where tools are becoming more fluent, more generative and often more convincing, what becomes valuable isn't just what we know, but how we choose. What we notice. What we refine.

This led me to something I hadn't quite named before: a set of human capacities that aren't easily taught but deeply felt. They don't replace tools – but they guide them. That's where I see something emerging. Not a checklist of skills, but a cluster of human capabilities: subtle, interpretive and deeply shaped by experience. They're harder to name and even harder to train, but in the work I see ahead, they matter more than ever – they are the human edge.

THE HUMAN EDGE

One theme that emerges consistently when you talk to those working at the forefront of AI research is this: the more fluent the tools become, the more important human judgement becomes. Leaders in the field – from design theorists to AI ethicists – are increasingly naming a set of human capabilities that remain outside the reach of even the most powerful models. Not technical skills, but interpretive ones. Not speed or volume, but the ability to choose, refine and sense.

Yes, track model updates every morning, but don't build your identity on knowing the tool of the moment. Build something deeper: taste, discernment and nuance – a feel for what matters.

Taste: Recognising Quality

This is not about personal preference or surface style, but something more cultivated: an ability to recognise quality when you see it, even if you can't immediately explain why. Krithika Shankarraman, a former vice-president at OpenAI, put it starkly: 'Taste is going to become a distinguishing factor in the age of AI because there's going to be so much drivel that is generated by AI.' In design, writing, strategy or leadership, taste allows you to make value-based decisions in a world of infinite options.

Taste is what allows you to stop scrolling, prune the unnecessary and elevate what truly matters. And it's not innate. Taste is shaped by what you pay attention to, what you practise, and what you learn to admire.

Recent experiments with AI confirm this. Models can predict what is popular or trending, but they stumble when it comes to genuine discernment. Ask for travel advice and you'll receive the predictable 'Top 10 Destinations.' Ask for music and you'll be offered more of the same songs you already know. What's missing is surprise, subtlety, cultural depth – the hallmarks of human taste.

And this is where taste connects to two other threads in the fabric of a working life. Taste is part of the thread of *Knowing*: not just acquiring facts, but developing the discernment to see what has depth, what has weight, what will last. It's wisdom applied to the choices you make, large and small. And taste also touches the thread of *Adventure*: because recognising quality often means being willing to step off the beaten track, to explore the café hidden down a side street, to take the unexpected left turn, to back the untested idea.

Cultivating taste is therefore more than a matter of style – it's a discipline of attention and curiosity. It's how you avoid the flattening sameness of mass culture and instead build a life that is richer, more textured, more your own. AI can offer volume and speed, but taste – discerning, surprising, deeply human – will remain one of the most valuable capacities you can bring to the decades ahead.

Discernment: Questioning the Logic

Discernment works alongside taste, but in a different register. Where taste identifies potential, discernment tests it. It's the ability to spot weakness in something that looks polished, to question the logic beneath the surface, to notice when something isn't quite right. Discernment is especially important when working with large models or fluent tools. Just because something sounds plausible doesn't mean it's true; just because it's smooth doesn't mean it's useful. When you are discerning, you probe further, ask sharper questions and resist being overly impressed by fluency alone. It draws on your experience – but also on your confidence to pause, reconsider and go deeper.

Machines can generate answers but not always understand why something matters – or whether it aligns with what we value. That's what discernment gives us: a way to bring judgement, context and care to what the machine produces. It's not about dismissing what AI offers, it's about asking: is this the right answer, here, now, for this?

Nuance: Seeing Multiple Perspectives

Then there is nuance – the ability to work with complexity rather than strip it away. Nuance helps us hold competing ideas, see multiple perspectives and adapt to subtle shifts in tone or context. It's what allows someone to reframe a challenge rather than rush to solve; it helps a leader respond to uncertainty without resorting to false clarity.

Nuance isn't vague – it's specific. It notices detail, context, emotion. It draws on what's said, but also on what's implied. And it matters most in situations where there isn't one right answer, but several possible interpretations.

As Fei-Fei Li, one of the leading voices in AI, has pointed out, machines can classify with astonishing accuracy – but they don't understand *why* something matters. 'The computer may be able to describe in simple, literal terms what it "sees" ... But it can't describe the stories behind the pictures.'[5] They can detect patterns but not meaning. They can't sense tone or weigh cultural significance or read the room – that's what humans bring. Nuance allows us to slow the impulse to simplify and instead to stay with the complexity. In a world that often rewards speed and confidence, nuance gives us something else: the ability to respond in ways that are measured, attuned and human.

Tomas Chamorro-Premuzic adds another dimension here: the role of *unpredictability*. If you become too standardised, too routinised, you risk being imitated – and eventually automated. What keeps you distinctly human is not just your sensitivity to context, but your willingness to surprise. To argue when silence is expected, to play when seriousness dominates, to go against your nature now and then. These moments of unpredictability – small acts of disruption in otherwise patterned behaviour – are what machines cannot capture. They remind others (and yourself) that you are more than a set of routines.

These qualities– taste, discernment, nuance and the courage to resist predictability– aren't usually named in job descriptions or career plans. They don't come with certificates or courses. But as work becomes faster, more fluent and more automated, they are coming into sharper focus. They shape how we show up, what we notice, what we let go of and what we stand by. In a long life, they are not only valuable – they are durable. They help us make better choices, form better judgements and build work that holds its shape over time.

Amplify Your Humanity: Curiosity and Stories

I want to finish this chapter on Amplification by reflecting on Curiosity and Stories.

Generative AI is powerful when it comes to processing information – especially the kind stored in books, databases and documents – but it doesn't draw from lived experience. It can't lean on intuition or make sense of ambiguity through memory or emotion. It doesn't know how it feels to try, to fail, to hope, to wonder. The stories you've thought about in this book – my stories, your stories – the stories of Nico, Lucia, Mira, Ben – draw their power from that kind of knowledge. Human knowledge. The kind shaped over time, and through life.

That's why curiosity is the foundation. It's not just about collecting facts or scanning for trends, it's about caring – about how things work, how people behave, what matters to someone else. Machines can process information, but they can't be curious. They don't notice what's unexpected. They don't ask better questions. Curiosity is how we deepen our understanding and how we keep growing – not just professionally, but as people too.

And creativity? This, too, comes from life. From travel, challenge, friendship, failure, joy. From noticing something small. From conversations that stay with you. From moments that change your mind. Machines can generate content but they can't make meaning. They can't tell stories that are rooted in experience or connect one insight to another through memory and emotion. That's something only us humans can do.

If you want to amplify your humanity, stay curious. Keep paying attention. Keep telling stories. That's where your deepest creativity lies – and your most enduring power to shape the long life ahead.

Use the Time You Save

One of the real effects of generative AI is speed. For many tasks – summarising, drafting, researching, coding – it makes work faster. Studies suggest a 30 to 45 per cent productivity gain on typical knowledge tasks. That's a significant shift – not just in how we work, but in how we use our time.

And that raises a question: what happens to that time?

In theory, it should create space. Space for reflection, for deeper work, for the kind of activities we will explore in the Nurture threads. Time for connection, rest, creativity and adventure. This is one of the promises of amplification: that by speeding up what's routine, we make more room for what matters.

But that outcome isn't guaranteed. As the old consulting joke goes, in a cake-eating competition, the prize is... more cake. If we're not careful, time saved becomes time filled. Productivity gains turn into longer to-do lists. More meetings, more deliverables, more output.

That's the deeper challenge of this thread. Amplification isn't just about doing things faster it's about deciding what's worth doing at all – and how to protect the time you reclaim. And as we move into the threads of Nurture – we have a deeper sense of how to spend that created space.

AMPLIFYING: Putting it into Practice

Three Actions to Take Now

1. **Audit your tasks.**
   List the tasks you perform in a typical week and mark which are routine and which are non-routine. Notice where technology could automate, amplify or free you for more creative and human work.

2. **Experiment with a new tool.**
   Pick one emerging technology – an AI app, a creative platform or a digital productivity tool – and try it out on a low-stakes project. Observe not just what it can do, but how it changes the way you think and work.
3. **Name your human edge.**
   Write down one capacity you bring that no machine can replicate – empathy, judgement, humour, imagination. Keep it visible as a reminder of where to focus your energy.

Three Promises to My Future Self

1. **I will adapt with curiosity.**
   I will treat each wave of technology as a chance to learn, experiment and extend my reach – without losing my sense of self.
2. **I will cultivate discernment.**
   I will strengthen my human edge – taste, judgement, nuance – knowing that these qualities guide me through a world of fluency and speed.
3. **I will use time for what matters.**
   When technology saves me time, I will not simply fill it with more output. I will reclaim it for reflection, connection, rest and creativity – the human pursuits that make a long life meaningful.

The thread of Amplification is not only about surviving technological change, it's about weaving a working life that can last for a century. In a 100-Year Life, you will encounter wave after wave of new tools, platforms and possibilities. Some will disappear quickly, others will alter the shape of work for decades. Each time, you will face the same choice: to resist, to drift or to adapt with intention. How you choose to engage with technology will not only shape your career – it will shape the person you become across a century of living.

TRACING THE PRODUCTIVE THREADS SO FAR

We've now reached a pivotal point in this book. So far, we've explored four of the eight threads that shape a wise and enduring working life: *Mastery, Knowing, Cooperating* and *Augmenting.* These are the threads of productivity – the ways you contribute, create value and get things done. Through each of these four threads, I've invited you to reflect: to look closely at how you build mastery, make sense of the world, collaborate with others and engage with technology. Each thread offers a way of being productive, but also a way of being in the world. Now is the time to pause. To take a step back and ask: *What do these threads look like in my life today?*

→ Is your **Mastery** thread strong – built on deep skill and personal motivation? Or has it been side-lined or left underdeveloped?
→ Are you **Cooperating** with others in meaningful ways – building trust, sharing work, achieving more together? Or has that thread grown thin?
→ Does your thread of **Knowing** help you focus, discern and stay grounded in a world of noise? Or is it fraying and overloaded?
→ And how are you engaging with **Augmenting** technologies? Are they enhancing your work, or distracting you from it?

Now is the time to look again at the *Assessment* and consider – which productive threads are strong, which ones may be fraying and how your weave has changed over time. If you are using *The Living the 100-Year Life Journal: Reflect, Reimagine, Renew,* you are already on the journey to strengthen your productivity threads.

You might think back to moments when one of these threads felt especially alive. What made that possible? And equally, where have you noticed one of them starting to wear down? What changed? Weaving isn't static. It's a dynamic, ongoing process. These threads strengthen, weaken and change shape across time. The raw materials you use – your skills, relationships, tools and experiences – are always shifting. That's what makes a working life so personal, and so complex.

Now we turn to the second set of threads – those that don't just support what you do, but sustain *how* you live and work over time. These are the threads of *Nurture*. They speak of connection, energy, resilience and growth. While often less visible than productivity, they are just as essential to a wise and enduring working life.

CHAPTER 9

THE THREADS OF NURTURING

I imagine these threads of nurture as the fibres that protect and sustain us through the inevitable stresses and strains of working life. In my book *The Shift: The Future of Work is Already Here*, I'd described a possible dystopic future of fragmentation, isolation and inequality. These threads of nurture offer an antidote: By making and sustaining friendships that help you flourish and invest in partnerships and family ties that bring resilience and joy. Nurture is also about energy – bringing calm to your life through moments of peace and sanctuary, and welcoming adventure that stirs your curiosity and shapes the story of who you are and who you will become.

These threads of nurture are continuously strengthened – or depleted – by our actions over time and place, both in our home and at work. They are not confined to one space or the other. Instead, they flow between the two, as a circular pattern of emotional exchange:

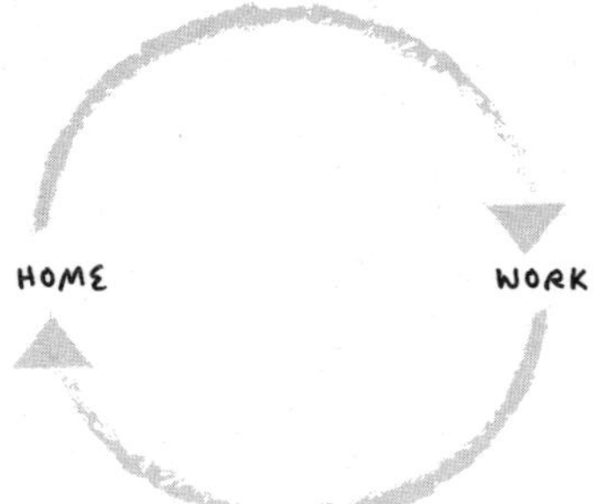

A Circular Pattern – Continuously Connecting Work and Home

This circularity of emotional exchange between work and home/home and work has fascinated me for years. It became the foundation for a series of research studies earlier in my career.[1] Through this research I began to see more clearly how the two places are connected and of course I also experienced this through my own lived experiences.

Here is an opening question – thinking about the last couple of months, can you recall a time when that emotional circle of connection between work and home felt really positive?

Perhaps the positive feelings originated with work. You are thinking about a time when you left work energised by new ideas, strengthened by connections, or clear on your direction. As you made the transition to home, you did so with a sense of purpose and possibility. Or it could have been an example of a positive connection originating from home. You recall leaving home feeling rested, loved, supported. You arrived at work ready to contribute. This is the positive circle of emotions connecting experiences at work and home. But the circle of emotion can also be negative.

Here is another question – thinking about the last couple of months, can you recall a time when that emotional circle of connection between work and home felt really negative?

Perhaps a time when you left work feeling depleted, frustrated or angry – only to arrive home unable to concentrate, short-tempered, not present. Or woke up after a restless night, burdened by guilt or emotional distance from loved ones, and walked into work with no bandwidth for empathy, creativity or care.

What happens at work is never sealed off from what happens at home. When the emotional flow between home and work is positive, the whole fabric of our working life begins to strengthen. When the emotional flow is negative, the whole fabric of our working life begins to weaken.

When I imagine this pattern of a circle between work and home, I remember the weavers of Lake Inle in northern Myanmar that I described earlier. I have in mind the most intriguing motif these weavers create: the ikat pattern. You may have seen an ikat pattern – it's a repeat pattern that has a distinctive feathery edge, with an element of repetition and of the unexpected. It's as if the thread has slipped and the pattern moves. It is the making of the ikat fabric that is most intriguing...

A Story of an Ikat Weaver – Inle Lake, 2021

I'm sitting in a room beside Inle Lake in northern Myanmar, watching a woman at her loom. She sits cross-legged on a cushion, her hands moving swiftly as she threads the warp – the strong vertical threads that will hold the fabric together. With a small shuttle, she begins to pass the horizontal yarn through – back and forth, and I watch as a pattern starts to emerge. The background is gold and layered on it is an iridescent motif – soft-edged, shifting, unmistakably ikat.

I assume she's changing the yarn to create the pattern. But she isn't. She uses the same yarn, the same motion, the same rhythm. And yet the colours shift – from golden brown to dark brown, and back again – and a complex design appears, almost like magic. She catches my eye and gestures to another woman seated nearby, surrounded by clay pots of yellow and brown dye. This is where the real magic happens. I learn that the yarn has been dyed in advance, in precise sequences, so that when it is woven – *only then* – the pattern is revealed. The colour is already in the yarn; the weaver simply brings it into form.

That image has stayed with me. It reminds me that our working lives are woven in much the same way. What we put into the yarn – our experiences, relationships, attention, care – shapes what eventually emerges. The pattern is not always visible in the moment but later, when we step back, we see it was there all along.

For me, the making of the ikat pattern is a metaphor for the repetition and change that is woven into our lives and of the circular pattern connecting work to home and home to work.

In the past, this delicate balance of strengthening the threads of productivity and nurture was achieved within the whole family – one person (often the man) working to strengthen the family's productivity threads, while the other (often the mother) focusing on nurturing. I saw this clearly in my own parents' lives. Today, this delineation within families is no longer clear. Each of us must find a way to strengthen both threads of productivity and threads of nurture.

Managing that balance between strengthening productivity and nurture is rarely easy. There are times when work demands everything – our attention, our time, our energy. These periods can be essential for deepening mastery and building micro skills. But if the focus on productivity becomes relentless, the threads of nurture begin to become fragile. Sleep suffers. Empathy fades. Curiosity flattens. And over time, mental health may begin to falter too. What makes this balance even harder is our human nature itself. In an ideal world, we'd make thoughtful, rational investments in both productivity and nurture based on what we most need. Yet we often favour what gives us immediate results – what feels urgent rather than what truly sustains us. This is the trap: choosing what's immediate over what's enduring. How we focus on what is enduring will be crucial to strengthening these threads of nurture. To summarise, these four threads:

Friendship. These sustaining relationships bring joy, connection and protection against loneliness – one of the defining struggles of modern life. Ask: *Am I forging deep, sustaining connections?*

Intimacy. The close bonds of family and partnership that carry us through life's biggest transitions. These relationships bring meaning, but they are not immune to strain. Ask: *Am I giving and finding love?*

Calm. The moments of stillness that restore us – repetitive rituals, solitary walks, spaces for reflection. Without them, our pace can become unsustainable. Ask: *Can I slow down?*

Adventure. The energy-giving experiences that add colour, vitality and story to our lives. They remind us we are more than our roles or routines. Ask: *Am I having adventures?*

As I look back on my own memories of nurture, these four threads appear many times: friendships that still make me smile, the intensity of lifelong bonds, moments of peaceful ritual and times of boldness and discovery that shaped my sense of self. These are the threads that make a working life not just sustainable, but worth living.

Remember there are resources to support you – *The Living the 100-Year Life Assessment: Thread Strength Test* helps understand which threads are strong, which ones may be fraying and areas to focus on. You will find it at www.livingthehundredyearlife.com And *The Living the 100-Year Life*

Workbook: Life Design Guide is a space to reflect. If the time is right to really get to work on this, *The Living the 100-Year Life Journal: Reflect, Reimagine, Renew* is there to support you on your journey over the coming months.

CHAPTER 10

THE THREAD OF FRIENDSHIPS: Am I Forging Deep, Sustaining Connections?

Over the course of a 100-Year Life, friendships may drift, deepen or renew. What matters is that you tend to them. A longer life will bring more transitions – your friendships can help you stay grounded through them all.

Spend a moment thinking about your friends and friendships – perhaps like me, you smile at these memories of joy, a sense of being understood by another. And perhaps you feel a tinge of regret about friendships that soured, or you let slip away. In the circle of emotion that connects home and work, it is our friendships that can hold both together, creating a pattern that repeats across the whole of our life. Friendship is a wonderful contributor to our happiness and health, and friendships at work are a risk worth taking.

Imagine spending eight hours a day working without friendships – the emotional toll is great. And this emotional toll can become the foundation of loneliness, with all its tremendous costs and negative consequences. This spectre of loneliness casts a shadow over the lives of many people. Let's be sure it does not cast a shadow over your life. Here's why investing your time in friendships (especially at work) can be so valuable...

WHAT FRIENDSHIP MAKES POSSIBLE

Friendship Brings Joy. In tough times at work, a friend shares the burden and makes the day worth staying for. Friends lift you when you feel low, remind you of who you are and make you laugh. Sometimes nothing benefits your health more than time with friends. They bring happiness, vitality and the thrill of being deeply understood.

It Strengthens Human Skills. When you have long friendships, you share the experiences of another – and you share your human experiences and the repetitive patterns of your life. Our friendships remind us there are others who have gone through the same experiences – we empathise with them, and they with us. We strengthen our human skills of listening and empathy.

It Helps Withstand Shocks. We each face turning points, unexpected shocks that will change the course of our lives, times when our lives become chaotic. At these times, friends help you navigate this chaos. Your friends diminish your perception of hardship, help you perceive the adverse events you face as less stressful. They are your 'bright rays of hope'.

HOW TO STRENGTHEN THE THREAD OF FRIENDSHIP

Strengthening friendship isn't about chance encounters alone – it's about being intentional. In a 100-Year Life, friends will come and go, but the practices you develop to nurture, renew and create them will shape the depth of connection you carry across decades. In the chapter ahead, we'll explore why friendship matters so deeply, what helps it flourish, and how you can weave strong friendships into both your personal and working life. Here is how this chapter unfolds:

- → **The Power of Friendship** Friendship has the power to lift us in hard times, bring us joy in good times and shape the course of our lives. In this opening section we explore why friendship matters so deeply – how it supports our wellbeing, sharpens our human skills and offers the rare gift of being truly understood.
- → **Create Friendships that Flourish** Here, we look at friendship through three lenses – the wisdom of an ancient philosopher, the insights of a contemporary psychiatrist and the reflections of a close friend – to explore what helps friendships flourish, what undermines them and why making new friends can sometimes feel so hard.
- → **Make Friends at Work** Workplace friendships are among the most important we form. In this section we focus on how to build and sustain them and set out the actions to take now and the promises to our future self that strengthen this vital thread.

THE POWER OF FRIENDSHIP

More than simple connection, true friendship brings the thrill of being understood by another person. It is both a comfort and a catalyst – reminding us of who we are and helping us to imagine who we might become. Friendship takes many forms. Mira is precise, introverted and not drawn to socialising for its own sake. She prefers a small circle of long-standing friends – relationships grounded in trust, intimacy and predictability. She doesn't network, she cultivates. And though her social world is smaller, it is no less rich.

Lucia made a small group of deep, value-driven friendships in her year in Ethiopia, but in the years since, she's struggled to hold onto them. The time zones, the life shifts – it's all made harder by the fact that, for Lucia, friendship isn't just about connection, it's about shared meaning.

As for me – I am more introverted than extroverted so prefer small gatherings and deeper friendships with a small circle and I look to my friends to bring me calm and to sally forth with my adventures. Yet as I reflect on my thread of friendship, I see that it's frayed at times when work takes all my energy or when family seems all-consuming. That's why I want in the next part of my life to strengthen this thread – perhaps you feel the same.

Your Story: Of Enduring Friendship

Tell me a story about the friends you made earlier in your life and whom you've kept close to. Friendship stories reveal the enduring threads of trust and care. Who were they? How did the friendship begin? How has it lasted? What role does this friendship play in your life today? *What does this story tell you about the friendships you most want to nurture in your 100-year life?*

Here is an early memory of a friendship that has lasted across decades:

A Story of a Café – Keswick, 1970

In the main street of the market town of Keswick, Cumbria, five miles from our family house in the Lorton Valley, is Pillar House – a seated restaurant where fish and chips, buttered white bread and pots of tea are served. As a 15-year-old I cycle from my house in the Lorton Valley to Keswick to spend many of my Saturdays as a waitress in this establishment. My prudent dad has decided that if we children want some money (and we do), then we will need to earn it. As the eldest, I am first into the labour market for the under-16s.

Once I walk through the doors of Pillar House, there is a feel of warmth and homeliness as I am enveloped in the smog of frying chips. Then throughout the day I take orders from customers, clear the plates and cups and feed them into an industrial dishwasher in the washing room. It's a Saturday during the summer peak time, the restaurant inevitably understaffed, turnover fast, the holiday makers hungry and then often fractious.

I am determined to get the mental and physical aspects of these tasks under control as quickly as possible because once mastered, I and my fellow waitress Shirley – a friend from school – have time to get on with the interesting aspect of the day. That's listening in the washing room to the telephone conversations of the senior waitress. For crucially, plugged into a small shelf on the adjacent wall is a public telephone, the conduit between the senior waitress and her Scottish boyfriend.

Three or four years ahead of us at school, she is in our eyes a goddess and piecing together the puzzle, Shirley and I learn that on a recent Scottish holiday with her family, she met a young man. What makes him extraordinary in our eyes is that not only does he come from what she assures us is 'one of the important families of the Scottish Isles', but his father is the clan chief. So, as the eldest son, he too will himself one day become the clan chief. This is magical beyond imagination.

The senior waitress instructs us in a slightly panicked voice: 'He could phone at any time', and instructs us that 'at all times' either Shirley or I must stand by the phone 'in case he rings'. If he does phone, then we are instructed to pick up the phone and engage him in conversation until the senior waitress can complete the customer order and rush back.

I only got one chance to pick up the phone – and the senior waitress rushed back before I had a chance to say much. But even at this distance, me and my friend Shirley could listen in to a love affair which we could only imagine.

That job, that summer and those moments bonded us. Looking back, I can see the shape of a friendship that's lasted more than 50 years. Shirley's life took her to New York, mine to London. We went to separate universities and for a while our paths diverged but years later, when we both had young children, we found each other again.

I remember one trip in particular to New York. I was giving a presentation to a client and brought along my young son, Christian. We stayed with Shirley at her apartment on the Upper West Side. There's a photo of us from that visit – each pushing a buggy, strolling side by side down Fifth Avenue, chatting as if no time had passed. That moment, like many since, reminded me how some friendships stretch, pause and resume – always with a thread intact.

I spoke with Shirley this morning on the phone. I told her about a problem one of my relatives is facing, knowing she would have a fresh perspective. She gave me advice and updated me with a challenge she is facing. And between these commiserations we laugh about a visit she had taken to Keswick last week, enjoying the pies and the ice cream of our youth.

What a joy it is to have a friend. Amazing things can happen when a relationship is nurtured over decades – affection, curiosity, empathy and a willingness to face challenging emotions and problems rather than avoiding them.

EXPERT VOICES: Robert Waldinger, Wellbeing Expert

Across this book I have sought the counsel of experts. Here, I turn to Robert Waldinger, a psychiatrist, Buddhist and a director of the Harvard Study of Adult Development – the longest-running longitudinal study of adult life. He is also co-author, with Marc Schulz, of *The Good Life: Lessons from the World's Longest Scientific Study of Happiness.*[1]

Robert and I first met while serving together on the advisory board of a Swiss investment company. Our friendship has grown through long conversations, often walking beside Lake Geneva. His work – and his personal reflections – have shaped the way I think about friendship. Here is his opening belief:

> 'The clearest message we get from the 84 years of the Harvard Study is this: good relationships keep us happier and healthier. Period.'

Think back to your opening story - were your friendships forged at school, in a university dorm room, at your first job, or standing beside another parent on the first day of school? Perhaps they began through shared routines – walking the same route, sitting next to each other in meetings, or chatting during a run in the park. For, as the studies of Bernice Neugarten,[2] a pioneer in the field of ageing and life stages, show, for many of us our investment follows the natural tempo of our life stages.

Do you recall how, in your adolescence, forming friendships was uppermost in your mind? I can see that in my story of Pillar House, working in a café and creating a strong bond with my lifetime friend Shirley. Often deep friendships are formed in those early years at school or in the first months of college. These are significant transitional times as we move away from family connections and strive to make new friendships. Then, oftentimes in our twenties and thirties, we are building our life independent of our family and creating intimate attachments.

Lucia in her early thirties can feel this time deeply. It's a period when our sense of identity, of who we are, begins to be clearer. This is a time of searching, where a primary challenge becomes finding meaningful work that resonates with our emerging sense of who we are. For some, this is a period when the focus is on getting ahead in the world and becoming more self-sufficient. It's a time when close friends really matter, giving us confidence and providing a space where we can blow off steam.

And Ben, in his forties, is not alone in feeling this can be a life stage of stress: possibly bringing up young children, often continuing to forge a career, sometime caring for parents. As many have found, it's not unusual for the thread of friendship to fray during this period as friendship takes a backseat to other, more pressing responsibilities. It is in our late fifties and beyond sixties when we have more time and a clearer sense of our life priorities, that we again invest in those precious friendships that bring such joy.

These are all catalysts for friendship – some fleeting, others enduring. As you think about your own, ask yourself: What did these friendships mean to you then? What do they mean now?

CREATE FRIENDSHIPS THAT FLOURISH

When we think about friendships that flourish, wisdom about the nature of friendships comes from many places: from ancient philosophers, from contemporary science and from the lived experience of those closest to us. Here, I draw on three voices: Cicero, the Roman philosopher; Robert Waldinger, psychiatrist and director of the Harvard Study of Adult Development; and my friend Shirley, whose reflections bring friendship into everyday life.

Voices on Friendship: Cicero

Cicero, the Roman statesman and philosopher, wrote extensively about friendship more than 2,000 years ago. Yet his reflections remain strikingly relevant today. Of course, Cicero lived in a world very different from ours, with norms and hierarchies we would rightly question today, yet when he writes about friendship, he captures something essential and enduring. In *Laelius de Amicitia* (*Laelius: On Friendship*), written in 44 BC,[3] he offers this exhortation:

> All I, myself, can urge you is to place friendship above all other human concern that can be imagined! Nothing else in the whole world is so completely in harmony with nature, and nothing so utterly right, in prosperity and adversity alike.

I still feel emotional when I read this. So much has changed since those words were written, yet that phrase – *in harmony with nature* – still resonates. When a friendship is going well, when it is mutual and steady and rooted in care, it really does feel like something natural, something aligned with who we are. Yet Cicero also acknowledges what we all know: that friendship is not always easy. He draws a distinction between shallow friendships, built on convenience or shared pleasures, and true friendships, when circumstances change. The latter, though rarer, endure. He also explores how close friends should be – whether it's better to keep emotional distance or share everything. Some, he notes, argue for loose ties, to avoid discomfort or dependence. But Cicero is clear: those looser connections may be easier to manage, but they are unlikely to stand the test of time.

It's a strikingly modern dilemma – how much to open up, how much to hold back. How do you feel about this?

Cicero's reflections remind us that friendship, at its best, involves vulnerability, investment and a willingness to be known. And while his words remind us that friendship has always been a cornerstone of human life, the context has certainly changed. The pressures of modern work, the shifts in how we live and connect, and the loneliness many of us felt during the pandemic have brought new urgency to an old truth: friendship still matters – perhaps now more than ever.

Voices on Friendship: Robert Waldinger

Robert Waldinger, a psychiatrist and director of the Harvard Study of Adult Development, has spent decades studying what makes friendships endure and thrive. As we walked in Geneva one spring morning I asked Robert what had stayed with him most after all that research – what struck him most clearly:

> When you can observe the totality of someone's life – the jobs they did, the money they had, the state of their marriage, their family structure and so on – one factor stands out. The extraordinary impact of friendship on life happiness and vitality. One of the aspects of friendship and happiness that plays such a crucial role in happiness is the affirming nature of generosity. About being deeply curious about the other, listening to your friend's stories, hearing their opinions and feeling the thrill of being understand by another. There is something extraordinary about having someone you care about listen to you deeply and be curious about your life.

Looking again at that conversation, Robert's opening statement stays with me: that of all the things we can do in life – work, achievement, ambition – it is friendship that has the most extraordinary impact on our happiness and vitality.

That's a bold claim. But what about you? Does it ring true? Think of the friendships that have shaped you – the ones that steadied you, challenged you, carried you through. How central have they been to your happiness and vitality?

For me, I think of Shirley. Our 50-year friendship, built across decades of change, geography and growth, is living proof of Robert's observation. When I look back at the most joyful, meaningful and enduring parts of my life, it's often her presence – her care, humour and steadiness – that's woven through them. And I wonder: who might that be for you?

Voices on Friendship: Shirley

Shirley is a close friend whose reflections on friendship are grounded in lived experience, kindness and generosity. To understand the real work of sustaining a friendship, I've looked closely at what Shirley does – because if I'm honest, it's she who has held our friendship together over the past 50 years.

I'm constantly struck by the time and attention she gives to her friends. I see it in small gestures that never feel small: a birthday card every year, knowing my sons' characters, their personal milestones, remembering the dates my parents died. She calls when I'm going through something difficult, listens deeply and gives me her presence as well as her time. As Robert Waldinger puts it, this is the life-affirming nature of generosity. One day I sat with Shirley in her garden and asked her to tell me more about the nature of her friendships:

> My friendships are part of my infrastructure. They're a foundation – something I've built over time. They're not like family or colleagues. Friendship is more equal. My friends choose me, and I choose them.
>
> Every decade of my life has brought new close friends, and those friendships follow the arc of my life. We've been through ups and downs. What holds us is our shared history. There's a richness in those long conversations that evolves with time. You don't have to explain who you are – your friends already understand your hinterland. Even eight minutes can hold more connection than an hour of distracted talk.

Then Shirley told me her story about friendship-making in action – one of her favourite friendship stories from her early twenties in New York. Working in an arts supply store to pay for her studies, she met two American women with whom she clicked instantly – one was an artist, the other an acrobat. The friendships formed quickly. They were all penniless and eager to explore the city:

> We'd walk for hours; share meals we could barely afford. I adored them. And then came the party. I invited my new friends – whom I jokingly called my 'downtown girls' – to meet the friends I'd made on an earlier student exchange. These 'uptown girls' from more established professional circles – a banker, a researcher, an immunologist. I introduced everyone and they hit it off. I loved seeing those different worlds connect. That's friendship too – being a bridge.

Introducing friends to friends, what a great tip for a lifetime of friendship. Shirley puts making and keeping friends at the top of her time distribution equation. Just last month these downtown and uptown girls got together for a trip – still friends after four decades. . .

I've been inspired by this – are there aspects of Shirley's way with friends that inspires you?

Across time and context – ancient Rome, research labs at Harvard, a garden in southern England – I'm struck by how similar the insights are.

Cicero, writing 2,000 years ago, reminded us that friendship is in harmony with nature. Robert, with eight decades of data, shows how central it is to our wellbeing. And then there's Shirley, my friend of 50 years, whose actions – not just her words – have embodied this truth. She hasn't written a treatise or led a study, but she has lived the daily rituals of friendship with dedication.

What Stops Us From Making Friends?

I feel in my own friendships – with Shirley and others – the power of Robert's statement, 'What our research has found is that friendship has an extraordinary impact on life happiness and vitality.' And yet – I know for myself that my thread of friendship has been fragile at times and even now could be stronger.

How do you feel about yourself – how strong is your thread of friendship?

I asked Robert why we don't devote more time (as I have seen Shirley do) to nurturing our friendships, inside or outside of the workplace. This is his response:

> When it comes to our broader lives, we are bad at *affective forecasting*. The result is that we are generally poor at predicting those activities that generate long-term positive benefits. Reaching to schedule another work meeting, assuming that another meeting will be a valuable activity. Each time we do this, we are losing the opportunity to do something that can in the longer term bring profound value – the activity of building and sustaining friendships with others.
>
> By pressing that scheduling button for your next virtual work meeting, you are taking away time from that messy, unpredictable business of making friends. Yet when we engage in that messy, unpredictable business of making friends, we are strengthening our resilience. It seems that whilst our affective forecasting on the value of giving time to friendships might be poor, when we experience friendship, we really feel their value.

As Robert reminds us, investing our time in building and sustaining friendships could be one of the best decisions we make. So, if we confront the fact that we are bad at affective forecasting, what then?

Part of it is about making time for friendship – I am thinking about the time Shirley makes. You might be thinking, *Shirley has the time for friendship – maybe she's not juggling a demanding job.* But that's not the case. Until recently, Shirley was the CEO of a major health charity employing thousands of people. She also serves on the boards of several not-for-profits. Her life is full, but she still makes time for friendship – not because she has that time, but because she chooses to prioritise it.

That realisation gave me pause. Shirley is my only friend from that period of my life who has stayed in close contact, and I can see now it's because she gave our friendship time. I, by contrast, have let some friendships slip away – not through intent, but inattention. Forgotten birthdays, left messages unanswered, was too busy when someone needed support... Perhaps you've had that feeling too – the slow drift of connection and a sense of regret that arrives later.

The question we all face is this: How can we be sure to make more time for friends?

I guess each of us must find our own way. You could promise yourself to reduce the number of virtual work meetings you do. Or lessen the brisk pace of your daily working day so you have more time in a sense to 'breathe'. And the good news is that, like the connection between Shirley and I, you can re-ignite an old friendship at any time. Perhaps there have been (and will be) busy working years when you simply don't have time to reach out. Yet there will still be a link when you do have more time. I am thinking about the time Shirley and I reconnected when our children were babies and how that reconnection became a continuation of the last time. You could give yourself the best gift you can – the gift of time.

Let's now turn to that most valuable and also potentially complex form of friendship – having friends at work.

MAKE FRIENDS AT WORK

Your Story: Work Friends

Think of a story about friendships at work. Work friends often become anchors in our lives – sources of laughter, support or insight. Who was the friend? What drew you together? How did this friendship shape your experience of work? *As you reflect, notice what this story reveals about the role of friendship in your working life.*

Mira has always kept a careful distance from friendships at work. Growing up, her father drilled a clear message into her: *don't get close to the people at work, they can't be trusted.* It was advice she absorbed early and followed faithfully. Over time, she added her own reservations. What if you become more senior? How do you navigate the power imbalance? Would a friend still treat you the same if you were suddenly their boss? And so, while Mira has friends outside of work – people she walks with, reads with, talks to deeply – her professional life remains emotionally contained. She is respected, competent and often relied upon, but rarely confided in. And during those long stretches when work takes up much of her time, the absence of connection leaves her feeling unexpectedly lonely. It's not that she wants more people in her life, it's that she sometimes wishes someone at work really knew her.

Do Mira's feelings about friendship resonate with you? Did your stories of friendship include a close friend at work? And if you don't have close friends at work, what are you missing out on?

I can understand Mira's dilemma – having a friend outside of work, as I have with Shirley, is not the same as having a friend at work. In the circle of our lives, 'Work' for many of us is distinct from 'Home'. Work as a context for friendships can feel more fleeting, possibly highly political, likely to be hierarchical, with the dynamics of promotion and performance also in the mix.

Mira's father thought you cannot have a friend at work – but can you have a true friend at work, and if you have, how does it feel? Here's how it felt to me as I reflect on a friendship at work that lasted more than two decades. It is a story – not of me – but of two work colleagues, Rob and Gareth. This story takes me back to the early stages of my work at London Business School:

A Story of Friends at Work – London, 2007

I'm working hard at my computer, trying to complete a project draft. The door of my office is closed shut – I'm absorbed and want to be undisturbed. Then, barging through the door is Gareth with the apocryphal words 'Come on, Lynd [for he is one of the few people who call me Lynd – in fact, the only one], come out for a quick pint with me and Rob'. I glance up at the clock – it's 6.05, so stopping for the evening seems plausible. 'Okay,' I say – 'See you in five.' I race to get the last sentences complete, throw on my jacket and within the allocated time, I'm ready to sally forth.

Rob, Gareth and me duck out of the building, down the steps to the Regent's Canal, dash along the towpath and emerge at the local pub by 6.30. Moments later, clasping a half-pint of shandy (a local mixture of beer and lemonade) in my hand, and they with a pint in theirs, we dissect our day – I admit it is something of a ritual here.

First, we check in with a quick conversation about a senior member of the group who we all find intolerable – sharing any juicy gossip we have of their latest exploits. Then we turn to our students – what's driving us mad, what we are pleased about. Then it's a quick run-through of our families. Then Gareth tells a couple of jokes – based almost always on his laconic Welsh sense of humour. Finally, Rob glances at his watch with the oft-repeated words, 'I fear it's time for me to catch the train home,' and we disband as quickly as we came together.

This was a friendship ritual repeated over and over again with the three of us. I realise that I was simply an interloper on a friendship that went back decades when first Rob Goffee and Gareth Jones set eyes on each other at the sociology department of Kent University. Since then, they had been what seemed to the casual observer as inseparable. Their families holidayed together, they wrote together and worked with each other as advisors to leadership teams. They sweetly invited me out whenever I was around, but between themselves, they were inseparable. A friendship that, for an observer, was a joy to behold. And also, along the way, the creative energy for four wonderful joint authored books including *Why Should Anyone Be Led By You – What It Takes To Be an Authentic Leader* and *Clever: Leading Your Smartest, Most Creative People*.[4] Tragically, Gareth passed away in January 2021, leaving Rob bereft of his truest friend – though with many, many happy stories.

What a joy it is to have a close friend at work. And if you have a close friend at work, then you probably understand the Gallup (a survey data) consulting company's finding that saying 'yes' to the survey item 'I have a best friend at work' is one of the strongest predictors of whether you (and possibly they) stay in that job and that company.[5] Yet, survey after survey shows that for many people, their working lives are devoid of close friendships. Here is data from December 2020, which found almost three-quarters (76 per cent) of workers said they had difficulty making connections with their work teammates, while 58 per cent described their social relationships at work as 'superficial'. And importantly, the loneliest group are those aged between 16–24, 40 per cent of whom report feeling lonely 'often or very often'.[6]

So, while you might acknowledge the nurturing impact of friendships at work, you may also be wary. I witnessed this wariness when I wrote a column for the *Financial Times* about the positive power of friendships at work.[7] The comments section from the article was revealing, including these sentiments: 'you cannot have a good friend at work', 'people are only friends with you at work because they want something from you', 'it's hard to be a good friend with someone who is more/less senior', 'I cannot trust people at work'.

Looking at these comments, I could not disagree with my readers. These are indeed legitimate concerns. Perhaps Mira's father was right and he is certainly not alone – many people feel wary of making a friend at work.

So, here's the paradox: sometimes we feel lonely at work, yet we are also wary of making the work relationships that could reduce our loneliness. Robert Waldinger and I have talked at length about the nature of friendship at work. Here's how he sees it:

> It is important we acknowledge the potential for complexity of work-based friendships. Take, for example, a close friendship between two people who were peers, but one is now more senior – perhaps even the boss. These friends are now managing dual roles – as a friend and a boss, and as a friend and a subordinate. These power differentials are real and they do create complications. And whilst all relationships are to some extent transactional (think about the relationship between partners), working relationships are more delineated: 'you are my boss, you pay me'.

Our relationships, particularly working relationships, go through a journey of initially being transactions and then slowly morph into friendships as we steadily accumulate personal affection and trust. You become friends with another because over time you are both able to reveal your innermost thoughts and memories. But – and here's the challenge – to reveal yourself to someone at work is potentially dangerous. Might they use this information against you, or even tell others? So first, you must establish trustworthiness...

When you think of how you developed a close friendship with a work colleague, how did it begin?

Build Trust

You get a sense of trustworthiness by paying close attention to the possible friend. Their actions will reveal whether they are trustworthy. Ask yourself: How do they behave when they don't believe they are being observed – for example, in their treatment of subordinates? How do they talk about others, do they show what Robert calls 'sympathetic joy' or are they envious and calculating? How do they deal with confidential information – are they telling you secrets they are not supposed to tell, and do they overshare? For how they speak of others and behave towards others is how they will behave towards you. Of course you don't have to be friends with everyone at work. Each relationship you form has to be considered on its own merits and no situation is identical.

Share Openly

In most work situations, it's possible to do the other harm: sharing confidential information about them, speaking badly of them behind their back. So, there must be a sense that you are willing to take the risk, to lean on each other. That begins with mutual sharing: Perhaps you talk about a challenge you've had that morning with one of your children, or the anxiety you feel about working with a colleague. If it keeps feeling right, you share more and it's now possible to take more risks. And if and when it does not feel right, you move back to a more business-like relationship.

Friendships develop over time, based on incremental actions which are frequent and informal. Saying 'Hi' through an open door, chats over the coffee machine, gradually shifting into a friendship, sharing interests, volunteering information.

Practice Radical Curiosity

This means a deep curiosity about what the other is experiencing, listening to their stories and their opinions. Here, I am thinking about Robert Waldinger's earlier words: 'Hearing an accurate understanding of your own experience coming from another person, articulated in their words can be thrilling.'

As I step back from this reflection on friendships, I turn again to the wise words of Cicero: 'Everyone has an idea of how many goats and sheep he owns, but nobody can say how many friends he possesses. An immense amount of care is devoted to acquiring cattle, but none to choosing friends.'[8]

We could substitute cars and houses for cattle and goats, but I think we can get the point here. Friendships help us to share our times of prosperity and adversity by 'dividing and sharing the burden'. They provide the talking partner, the person to whom we can describe the wonder we see around us. In the words of Cicero, 'Nature abhors solitude and always demands that everything should have some support to rely upon. For any human being, the best support is a good friend.'

FRIENDSHIP: Putting it into Practice

Three Actions to Take Now

1. **Reach out to a friend you've drifted from.**
   Send a short message – something simple and genuine. Reconnection doesn't require a grand gesture, it starts with 'I've been thinking about you.'
2. **Take stock of your friendship network.**
   Ask yourself: Which friendships feel nourishing? Which ones feel neglected? Which need space or renewal? Noticing is the first step towards reweaving.
3. **Make space for one real conversation.**
   Choose one person you trust and suggest a chat with no agenda. Friendship deepens not through productivity, but through presence.

Three Promises to My Future Self

1. **I will invest in friendships, not just when I need them, but while they're strong.**
   I'll nurture connection as an everyday act – not just in crisis or celebration.
2. **I will stay open to new friendships at every age.**
   A longer life brings more chances to connect. I won't assume my friendship circle is fixed, I will stay curious, available and brave enough to reach out.

3. **I will choose people who help me grow.**
   Over time, I'll prioritise friendships that energise me, reflect my values and make me feel more like myself – not less.

Don't wait for connection to happen. Nurture your friendships now and your future self will thank you. In the fabric of a long life, friendship is one of the strongest threads you can weave. It brings joy, resilience and meaning across every decade, shaping how you live your 100-Year Life.

CHAPTER 11

THE THREAD OF INTIMACY: Am I Giving and Finding Love?

In a long life, your intimate relationships will shift – through times of closeness, distance, loss and renewal. But the need to love and be loved remains constant, no matter your age or stage in life.

This has been the hardest thread for me to write. Our intimate relationships are so very deeply personal, so uniquely shaped by time, culture and circumstance. It feels almost impossible to say anything that holds meaning for everyone and yet I believe there is something universal here – something essential to all of us.

In my own life, the thread of intimacy has taken many forms. Periods of marriage, years of being single and now, life in a blended family. I've experienced a full spectrum of emotion: joy, contentment, a sense of being grounded – but also worry, guilt and exhaustion. And through all of it, I've come to see intimacy not just as a relationship status, but as a thread – changing shape, but always present.

When I reflect on this thread, I return to the circular pattern I shared earlier. That continuous flow of energy and emotion between work and home. How our loving, intimate relationships can make us feel truly happy, yet also profoundly sad, deeply angry. And how these emotions inevitably shape how we show up to our work – what we're able to give, how much we can hold, how much we feel seen.

Your intimate relationships matter to your work. And your work matters to your intimate relationships.

To be intimate with someone – to feel loved, cherished, understood – is a life-enhancing experience. That intimacy might come through a formal partnership, with commitments and shared resources. It may also be looser, more flexible. It can be found in the bond between parent and child, in the care we give to nieces, nephews or godchildren. It may exist in friendships so deep, they become a form of chosen family – woven into who they are and what they care about.

This chapter is about how intimacy and working life intertwine – sometimes in harmony, sometimes in tension – and how we might understand and strengthen that thread across decades. When the thread of intimacy is strong, it can support every part of your life. It doesn't eliminate difficulty or prevent pain but changes how you carry it. Here are some of the ways this thread can sustain you...

WHAT INTIMACY MAKES POSSIBLE

Intimacy Builds Emotional Resilience. A close, loving relationship gives you someone to turn to when life gets hard. When you feel safe and seen, you're more able to recover from stress, disappointment or uncertainty. It doesn't make the hard moments go away, but it means you don't go through them alone.

It Creates a Sense of Belonging. To be truly known – and still loved – is one of the most profound experiences you can have. Intimacy helps you feel anchored in the world. It reminds you that you are not just a worker or an achiever – you are also a partner, a parent, a child, a companion.

It Counters Work Pressure. In moments when work feels overwhelming or hollow, an intimate relationship can offer perspective. It reminds you of who you are beyond your role or title, and it gives you somewhere to land and someone to share the weight with.

It Fosters Growth and Reflection. Close relationships invite us to grow. When you love someone over time – when you care deeply and are cared for in return – you learn things about yourself that you wouldn't discover alone. Intimacy is not static, it evolves. And in doing so, it helps you evolve too.

HOW TO STRENGTHEN THE THREAD OF INTIMACY

We each have our own form of intimacy that might change, as mine has, through our life's path. Intimacy is foundational to the nurture we give ourselves and the nurture we are able to give to others. To help you think about this, together we will go through these ideas and exercises:

→ **Understand How Intimacy Transforms** – helps you to bring clarity about how the norms and expectation of families and intimate relationships are transforming and why conversation and negotiation are now central.

→ **Explore Going Solo** – we take a closer look at what it means to be going solo and how for many people (including me), that's a significant part of their life journey.

→ **Navigate Work and Parenting** – we share the joy and challenges – the clock (still) ticking and the sense of time being squeezed.

→ **Sustain Love and Work** – brings the whole thread together as we explore the potential and benefits and reflect on how conversation, learning and experimenting will be key to sustaining and strengthening this thread.

→ **Look Ahead: Structures of Intimacy** – our intimate relationships are shaped by the role models we experience and the social norms that surround us. They are also shaped by the institutions we work with or of which we are members. Here, we explore how these institutions are changing.

Your Story: Of Intimacy

Take a moment to think about the intimate relationships you've observed or experienced – your own, or those of your parents or grandparents. Stories of intimacy show how love, closeness and care weave through our working lives. What did you see? What did it teach you? How has it shaped your view of relationships? *What does this story remind you about the love and connection you want to carry forward?*

Often, our sense of what intimacy means is shaped not just by who we are, but by the era and family we were born into. The social roles and norms we observe growing up leave a mark – sometimes as models to follow and sometimes as patterns we feel compelled to resist.

I've been thinking about this in the case of my own ancestors. There's Lily, my great-grandmother, widowed with seven children, taking in laundry to survive. My grandmother Anne, married but hiding her children from her employer for fear of losing her job. My mother Barbara, raising four children on one income and embodying the traditional role of caregiver. And then there's me – married, divorced, solo, remarried into a blended family, working all my adult life. Here's a story from my childhood that I feel sums up aspects of the family I grew up in during the 1950s and '60s.

A Story of a Family Dinner – Lorton, 1968

We are sitting around the table – the whole family. Mum has made one of her nutritious, homemade pies and there has been some good-natured banter across the table between my parents and us four children – me, my sister and our two brothers. For pudding, Mum has made an apple pudding and it arrives on the table, golden brown and fragrant. But it's the jug of custard that interests me. This is one of my favourite puddings and I get my head down and simply enjoy the taste and the smell.

The meal is nearing the end. Across to the kitchen, the pots and pans have been piling up. Mum is a highly organised cook and washes up as she goes but inevitably, there is a sink full of dirty crockery. As the meal comes to an end and we place our spoons in our pudding bowls, Dad looks contentedly around the table at his four well-fed children. Then, he stands up to leave and says as he leaves: 'The girls will do the washing up.' My sister Heather and I exchange shrugs and make our way to the kitchen to stand at the sink and wash and dry the dishes.

Does this resonate with your childhood experiences? What were the norms and expectations you grew up with?

Of course, at the time, I didn't have the words to describe what I was seeing. I did not question (at that time at least) the assumption that it was girls who did the housework. Yet I was beginning to notice the texture of my parents' partnership. Their roles were clear, unquestioned and shaped by the gendered expectations of the time. That memory has stayed with me as a marker of how invisible norms shape the way we live together. We each have our own unique experiences of intimacy. Perhaps you can see some similarities with the childhood experiences of intimacy of Mira, Ben and Lucia.

Our oldest character Mira, now in her fifties, grew up in a household where order, responsibility and boundaries were paramount. Like mine, Mira's parents had clearly defined roles: her mother handled the home, her father the finances. And like my family, the personalities of our parents played a role beyond era expectations. Around Mira's childhood family table, the talk was about tasks to be achieved, not about intimacy. Her father was a tough, introverted man and Mira wonders if that's impacted her capacity to navigate emotional conversations.

In my family, with a gregarious father and conscientious mother, who'd fallen in love and eloped at the age of 19, it was an emotional warm feeling – with occasional blasts of anger from Dad – frustrated at his undisciplined children.

For Ben, his father – a high achieving but emotionally distant figure – looms large in his background. He's determined to chart a different path in fatherhood – more present and engaged – yet he struggles to balance those aspirations with work demands.

Lucia had a different experience. Born in 1992, she's the daughter of South Americans who emigrated in the late 1980s. Her childhood was a story of contrasts – between cultures, between expectations, between the sacrifices her parents made and the choices now available to her. From early on, she learned how to move between worlds – how to listen, adapt and decode unspoken norms.

These are our stories. Yours will be different still. As you look back on your own experiences – and those of the people who raised you – what patterns do you notice?

UNDERSTAND HOW INTIMACY TRANSFORMS

You will notice that intimacy is being transformed by social norms, roles and identity – and how our intimate relations with others is becoming more negotiated.

Shaped by Social Norms

I don't recall my dad ever asking, 'Who will cook dinner tonight?' or 'Who's going to shop for the children's clothes?' In my childhood home, the roles were clear and rarely questioned. My father worked full-time to earn the income, while my mother managed the household and, where possible, took part-time roles that fitted around caregiving. One partner focused on paid work, the other on home and family. In our house, that meant my sister and I helped in the kitchen, while my brothers did not.

Such arrangements were common in the 1960s. In the US, 65 per cent of families had married parents, with the father employed and the mother staying at home. Mothers averaged 10 hours a week on childcare and 32 on housework; fathers averaged just 2.5 hours on childcare. Those routines didn't just describe behaviour, they shaped beliefs about what was normal and expected. Think back to your own household: who cooked, who earned, who paid the bills? Which roles were quietly assigned, and to whom?

Since then, much has changed. In many countries, fewer people marry, more live alone or in blended families and women are just as likely as men to be in paid work. Yet the social norms we grew up with still influence how we see the world. Sometimes we copy them, sometimes we reject them. I know I still fall into roles I saw my mother take on – especially cooking, which was central to her identity and became part of mine, even when I find it tiring.

What about you? How have your parents' behaviours shaped your sense of role allocation and the boundaries between home and work?

Increasingly Negotiated

Since the 1950s and '60s, intimacy has become far less predictable – and far more personal. The old templates my parents lived by have loosened or disappeared altogether. Rather than following a set script, we're being asked to write our own. This can feel liberating but also demanding. It calls for a different kind of self-awareness and often, more negotiation.

The sociologist Anthony Giddens has written about what he calls *'the transformation of intimacy'* and his 1992 book of the same name has been a touchstone for me – something I've returned to often as I try to make sense of my own experience and what I've seen others navigate.[1] His core argument is this: that the structure of intimate relationships has changed. There are now many varieties of families and partnerships, and the bonds between people are no longer dictated by fixed social expectations. Instead, they are – more often than not – *negotiated*. That means they are built, over time, through conversation, reflection and mutual adjustment. These relationships are less defined by tradition and more shaped by the personal needs and values of the people within them.

If you're in a relationship now, you might recognise this shift. Tasks that were once assigned by gender are increasingly discussed. And that discussion is part of a broader transformation – one where roles, responsibilities and expectations are not fixed, but fluid. We are, many of us, working it out as we go along. The assumption that childcare is primarily a mother's role is being challenged – perhaps even in your own family or your own thinking. This is something Ben is working through right now. He wants to be present but between deadlines, meetings and the culture of constant availability, he sometimes struggles to find a model that fits. He asks himself: How do I show up at home the way I want to, without compromising what I've built at work? It's not about abandoning ambition, it's about trying to rewrite the script in real time.

You've looked back to the patterns of intimacy you grew up with, now let's look forward to consider: What do I want now from an intimate relationship?

This may be a question you've returned to at different points in your life – or perhaps you're asking it now, in real time. If you're in your twenties or early thirties, you're likely just beginning to weave this thread. How are you managing the balance between building a relationship and building a working life?

Chances are your views on intimacy are shaped by a blend of influences. Some are inherited: echoes of what you saw in your parents – whether you admired it or wanted to avoid it. Others come from the norms around you now: the relationships you observe in your peers. And still more belong to your future self – the kind of connection you hope for, even if it doesn't feel possible just yet.

If you'd asked me in my twenties what I wanted from a partnership, I'd probably have said I wanted stability. In other words, the warm structure I grew up with: parental presence, home-cooked meals, a sense of order.

But I also wanted independence. I wanted my own career, my own income and to be with someone who had theirs too. In other words, I wanted it all. Like many others I know – what I got was periods of being married and periods of going solo.

EXPLORE GOING SOLO

What is clear is that the traditional marriage my parents lived is no longer the norm. There is a wide variety of arrangements: couples living together but unmarried, co-parents raising children from separate homes, people choosing not to marry or have children and chosen families that provide the same depth of connection as traditional structures. And within this pluralism, solo life is not an outlier – it is one of many valid ways to build intimacy.

In a long working life, many of us could spend significant stretches of time on our own – by choice, by circumstance, or as a pause between relationships. These periods matter. They are not just gaps between partnerships, they can be chapters of growth, independence and unexpected connection. In Denmark, for example, individuals – not couples – are considered the basic unit of society, reflecting a cultural shift away from the idea that a life alone is incomplete. In my grandmother Anne's generation, her unmarried sisters were labelled 'spinsters', a term heavy with judgement. Today, many reject that framing – single people are often more socially connected, engaged in volunteering and active in community life than their married peers.

Mira is solo now, having emerged from a painful divorce. For her, this is a time to focus on work, friendships and stability. She values the independence, knowing intimacy may come again but not feeling the need to chase it.

Solo life is often framed as something to fix, but it can be a season, or a lifetime, of freedom, clarity and connection. Perhaps you've built strong routines, meaningful work or deep friendships. Maybe you've come to know yourself more fully, to chart your own course without compromise. If you are solo now, ask yourself: What do I value about this way of living? And if you imagine a future where you are solo again, could you see it not as a loss, but another version of a full life?

And perhaps the deeper question is this: if you knew you would spend long periods of your life solo, how would you choose to shape them – so that they nourish you, connect you and leave you feeling deeply alive?

NAVIGATE WORK AND PARENTING

Of course, many people also long to raise children and for those who do, the question becomes: *how can I integrate parenting with a working life?* Whether you're in a partnership or solo, the demands of caregiving bring a new layer to intimacy. They stretch us; they reshape our time, our energy, our priorities.

Your Story: Of Being a Working Parent

If you are a parent, there will be many, many stories you can tell. Choose one that sits at the interface between being a parent and being a worker – when these two parts of your identity came together. What happened? How did you balance the demands? What did you learn about yourself? *What does this story suggest about the legacy you want to create for your family?*

Let me take you back to one of those moments in my own life. Here is a story from 1988 – I am not a parent at this time – I guess I am a 'pre-parent' and its three years before my first child – Christian – is born.

A Story of a Busy Consulting Day – London, 1988

It's another frantically busy day at PA Consulting Group. I'm working through my lunch hour and into the early evening at the firm's office in Belgravia, central London. I've just returned from a client meeting in New York, working for the first time with a corporate board. Watching carefully the senior consultant's interactions – how he times his interventions, watches the room carefully, speaks concisely. I've been asked to become a partner at the firm, ditching my homemade woollen suits for pale grey Armani, and the company car I now drive is a fancy BMW.

But, but… I've reached 33. When I look around, there are no senior women who are mothers. Is this what I want? I come from a large, relatively happy family and my husband would like a family too, but between constant travel and no role models, it's not clear to me how to make this work. I know my biological clock is ticking – how much longer will I be fertile? – and if I am not fertile, how long would the recently developed IVF take to be available to women like me?

The Clock Still Ticks

For those of us who become parents, there is often a moment when we realise: this isn't just about love or identity, it's also about logistics. About how the rhythms of home and the expectations of work collide and sometimes harmonise. And for many – especially women – this moment can come with urgency, with pressure, with tough decisions about timing, fertility and what it means to 'have it all'.

As you think about your stories, does the phrase 'have it all' resonate with you?

Talking to a girlfriend recently about this, she said, 'I thought I could *have* it all. Now I realise that what happened was I *did* it all.' There are occasions when I feel just the same. Looking back, I realise my story begins with wanting to strengthen my productivity threads – become more masterful, then switches to nurture – how to strengthen intimacy. My guess is that often our stories of productivity and nurture are intertwined, sometimes in conflict.

This is also a story of how far back many of us go when we begin to think about becoming a parent – what I called earlier the 'pre-parent phase'. And that's particularly true for women – because while our lives have grown longer, fuller, more flexible in so many ways, our natural window for fertility has remained remarkably unchanged.

Is this something you've faced – or expect to face in the future? It's not an easy issue.

When I was wrestling with these issues in 1988, the average age of first-time motherhood was around 26. I was already seven years older, and I could feel the biological clock ticking. At that time, IVF was still a relatively new technology. Louise Brown, the first 'test-tube baby', had been born a decade earlier, so the idea was known but it wasn't something we talked about and certainly wasn't a 'normal' part of the conversation. I'd calculated the window: if I had a child after establishing my career, I had perhaps nine years – from 26 to 35. After that, I knew the probabilities of conception would start to drop; slowly at first, then rapidly. I had to make a call. It was a watershed moment. Within a year, I left the consultancy firm – along with the salary, the Armani suits, the expense account, the BMW – and joined London Business School – hoping for more autonomy and flexibility.

Much has changed since then but in some ways, the challenge is still the same. Women today experience perimenopause around 45, the same age I did. What has changed is the context: more support, more visibility, more choices. Over ten million children have now been born using IVF. As people marry later, many are having children later too – and, like me, often have fewer children than their parents. Still, the clock ticks. As I speak to younger women and their partners, I hear the tension in their voices. The average age for first-time motherhood has risen to 30, but only 5 per cent of births occur after 40. The window is wider than it was, but it's still narrow.

Diverging Clocks: Lucia and Nico

When they were in their early twenties, Lucia and Nico were in the same rhythm – focused on work, friendships, figuring out who they were. Now, in their early thirties, their rhythms are beginning to diverge.

In their conversations, Lucia wants to talk about intimacy. She's not in a panic – but she does have a growing sense of timing. She doesn't know if she wants children, but she knows the window to decide won't stay open indefinitely. She wonders what kind of partnership could hold the complexity of her life.

Nico, meanwhile, feels no such urgency. He's not avoiding intimacy – but he's not pursuing it either. His days are full; he tells Lucia about the deadlines, meetings, travel, workouts. He's in no hurry, he's got time and imagines settling down in his forties, once things are more stable: career sorted, finances solid, identity clearer.

Neither is wrong, but together, they reveal something important: how intimacy, like work, unfolds along different timelines. And how those timelines are shaped not just by personal preference, but by biology, culture and expectation.

Lucia feels the clock ticking. Nico doesn't hear it yet. And between them is a gap familiar to many people in their thirties. Between urgency and ease, between now and later, between the lives we imagine and the ones we postpone.

Time Gets Squeezed

When you're trying to balance a job and the desire to have a baby, is there ever a 'right time'? For many people, especially in their late twenties and early thirties, this is the period when two trajectories – career and family – are rising at the same time. And that creates a time squeeze. You're trying to launch your professional life while laying the foundation for a family. There's barely enough time for either – let alone for the rest of life: skills, networks, partners, friendships, self-care.

It's a pressure point. And one that deserves our full attention.[2]

Where are you in this story? Are you beginning to think about children? In the thick of it now? Or perhaps looking back at how your life unfolded?

What pressures have shaped your timeline – your work, your choices, your sense of what's possible or expected? Have you felt the weight of time? The need to choose? The desire to wait? The fear of waiting too long? And if you're still navigating these questions, what do you know – deep down – that you want to protect? What matters most, even if it doesn't fit the standard plan?

These choices are never simple but giving yourself the space to name what you hope for, and what you fear, is a powerful act of clarity. For me, these questions weren't abstract – they came to a head in real time, in the midst of a life that already felt full. My son Christian had been born and I was learning to be a mother and trying to return to work. And like so many working parents, I was doing my best to hold both – sometimes with grace, often with exhaustion. Here is a moment I remember vividly, a story that captures just how hard that balance felt for me:

A Story of Tears – London, January 1991

Christian is three months old and I'm trying to reclaim my identity as an academic. I set up my computer on the kitchen table in the small house we're living in, ready to get back to work. I feel the pressure mounting.

Just last week, I returned to teach a class at London Business School. I was deeply embarrassed when patches of breast milk began to seep through my dress, thankfully, I'd worn a jacket. I'd made a mental note: always wear a loose jacket. The lecture itself had been straightforward, but the effort it took left me utterly exhausted. In the afternoon I returned to my office, closed the door and lay down on the floor. Within seconds, I fell asleep on the hard carpet.

Today, I plan to work from home. The task – writing the first draft of a report – shouldn't be difficult. I've written white papers and academic texts before. But now, everything feels harder.

Baby Christian is fretting. With no childcare arranged, I decide to strap him in a baby pouch against my chest, hoping he'll settle. I remember seeing mothers in Zambia carry babies on their backs while working. How hard can this be? I think. With Christian strapped to me and my computer open, I begin to type.

At this point I am aware of two competing emotions. For rather than the clear-sighted alignment between brain and words I'm used to, I'm finding it hard to construct meaningful sentences. It feels like I'm working through a fog and failing to muster the dexterity of thought that's been second nature. The competing emotion is my feelings for my beloved son. For rather than sleeping happily as I had anticipated, Christian is whimpering. Indeed, within five minutes, he's resorted to full-scale tears. I feel frustration and feelings of helplessness well up. Frustration at the slowness of my brain, helpless in the face of my son's need. We sit there, Christian and me – with tears running down our cheeks.

I am not the first working parent to feel the sheer exhaustion of working and bringing up a small child. I recall as a young woman at British Airways, one of my colleagues had recently become a father. Every day he came into the office looking ever more exhausted. He started to tell us about how his newborn had not slept the night; how he and his wife had alternated through the night caring for the baby; how he left the house drained of energy. My colleagues and I (all of us young, none with children) tried to muster sympathy. We said how sorry we felt and how tired he looked but inside we were thinking, 'Come on – it can't be that hard! It's only a two-week-old baby – don't they sleep all the time?'

It's tough. And it's no surprise that in my generation (born in the 1950s and early 1960s), nearly half of women stepped out of the workforce at some point in their careers – most often for family responsibilities. That was three times the rate of men.

If you're a younger, educated man or woman today, you may be entering a career-type job with the intention to work continuously – perhaps hoping to combine work and family, as I tried to do. And in many ways, the opportunities are greater now: there's more support, more flexibility, more visibility around working parents. But that doesn't mean it's easy. You could be asking some hard questions: *What would it take to keep going? What would I have to sacrifice? What am I not yet ready to decide?*

These aren't just personal questions, they're structural ones. And they echo across generations.

What does that look like in real life? Compared to my mother, I certainly didn't devote the same attention to my children that she gave to me. I wasn't there in the afternoons with homemade cakes, as she had been. But of course, there were other things I could offer. I've asked my sons about their experiences of me as a mum. They say, 'You weren't a helicopter mum, always checking up on us,' and 'You took us around the world with you as you worked.' I guess they appreciated the autonomy and the adventures.

Frankly, I'd describe myself – using a phrase made famous by the paediatrician and psychoanalyst Donald Winnicott, as a 'good enough mother'.[3] In his view, the most helpful kind of care begins with being highly attentive to a baby's needs and then allowing small moments of frustration. These moments give children the chance to grow resilience and independence. What mattered, he argued, was not flawless caregiving, but the steady, reliable presence of a parent who is good enough.[3] I'd say as a parent – I was not Great – but Good. By that, I mean I did the best I could. I tried not to dwell on what I couldn't give and instead tried to stay optimistic about the choices I had made. It wasn't perfect, it was a trade-off – time with my children for time with my work. And it was a tough one.

I reflect on this now partly to underline a point that many studies of working parents agree on: it is not straightforward. In my partnership, both of us worked – and I often wonder what it takes to make these kinds of relationships more stable, more satisfying, more supportive.

So, what does it take? How do we build intimate relationships that can survive – and even strengthen – alongside the demands of work? That's the question I've been asking more deliberately, both in my own life and in the lives of others.

SUSTAIN LOVE AND WORK

Your Story: Of Being a Partner

Think of a story about the partnership at the heart of your life – the person you chose, and who chose you. When have you felt most deeply connected to them? Perhaps it was a quiet moment of care, or a time when you stood together in the face of difficulty. Maybe it was laughter shared, or a decision made that shaped the path you walked side by side. As you recall this story, notice how love, trust and companionship weave through it. *What does this story remind you about the bond you and your partner have created, and the connection you most want to nurture in the years ahead?*

There are so many different shapes that intimate partnerships can take today. My hope is that our stories reveal some universal truths – ideas, mindsets or practices – that can help us do it well. This is particularly so for those situations when both partners are working. For a long time, the way we've talked about relationships where both partners work has been shaped by the language of trade-offs. Two people, both with ambitions, both with demanding jobs – *something has to give*, the thinking goes. Underneath that narrative is a deeper assumption: that time, energy and opportunity are fixed resources. That one person's success must come at the cost of the others. In other words, that managing two jobs is a zero-sum game.

But what if it isn't?

EXPERT VOICES:
Stew Friedman, Leadership Scholar

Across this book I have sought the counsel of experts. Here, I turn to Stew Friedman, a long-time colleague and friend. In 1991 he founded and directed both the Leadership Program and the Work/Life Integration Project at The Wharton School in the US.[4] Over the decades, Stew has taught generations of students and studied their lives as they sought to integrate work, family, community and self. When I asked how he sees people making this work in practice, he offered insights drawn from both his teaching and his research:

> I have looked at aspirations for families for more than 40 years now. The traditional perspective is this is a 'zero-sum game', that there is limited time available – so focusing on one part comes at the detriment to another part. And the narrative is one of 'trade-offs' – one part grows whilst the other shrinks and it's all about 'work-life balance'.
>
> My counter-intuitive belief is that work and the rest of life are not a zero-sum game. And it is not 'work-life balance', it's

> about seeking *harmony* across the different parts of life. The challenge is to continually experiment in pursuit of what I call 'four-way wins' – improved performance and greater harmony, in and across the whole of life.
>
> I can see those who figure this harmony out are attending to the most important needs and interests in four domains: their work, their family, their community – and importantly – their self (that is, mind, body and spirit). And this is a mindset shift from a zero-sum game to 'it does not have to be this way'. People with this mindset are interested in the question: 'how can this harmony create value for me and the people about whom I care most?'. These four domains can create mutual gain – it's a powerful shift and creates a greater sense of freedom. How, for example, by being a better parent do you become a better manager, a better friend, a person more at peace with herself? Certainly, you can rarely have it all, all of the time – so the question is creating harmony across a longer timeframe. Not trade-offs but finding mutual benefits.

Aligning Across Time

Our conversation stays with me. Stew's vision – that work, family, community and self don't have to be competing forces but can reinforce one another – feels both hopeful and challenging. His research highlights:

> People who figure out this harmony see life not as a zero-sum game, but as a system of investments and commitments. They ask, 'How can I experiment with ways of living and working that create value for me and my most important people – not just in one area, but across my whole life?'[5]

How do you feel about Stew's vision of 'harmony over time'?

For Ben and Yuki, it's a central question. With Yuki, his partner of ten years, Ben has built something grounded and resilient. Born in Japan, Yuki moved to the UK in her early twenties from Osaka, carrying with her a determination and a deep respect for both independence and care. She teaches part-time at a local school and brings a calm, clear-eyed steadiness to their home. She notices what others overlook. She values small rituals. She believes in making space for feelings, even when they're messy.

In their partnership, where Ben tends towards action, Yuki often brings reflection. Where he pushes through, she pauses. It's not always easy – they move at different speeds, but their differences have become part of the fabric of their partnership. Her presence has softened him, helped him question some of the internal rules he inherited and offered a different kind of strength.

Now the conversations about harmony have become more poignant. Yuki is an only child and over the past few years, her attention has begun turning more often towards her parents in Osaka. They are ageing. Her father's health has declined slightly. Her mother, once fiercely independent, now calls more often, not just for updates but for reassurance too. Ben feels the weight of that shift. It's not a burden – but it is a responsibility, one that he and Yuki are beginning to carry together.

They've started taking evening walks again – no phones, no agenda, just space. At first, the conversations were practical but slowly, deeper threads re-emerged: what they miss about each other, what kind of parents they want to be, what kind of marriage they still want to grow into. It was crucial when Yuki told him, 'You don't have to carry so much alone.' That's a thought that Ben is taking forward.

Take a moment to reflect: What would greater harmony between work and intimacy look like for you – not just today, but over the next few years?

Are there conversations you've been postponing? Options you haven't allowed yourself to consider? Like Ben and Yuki, you may find that what once made perfect sense now needs to evolve. What would it mean to choose not just what works for *you*, but what works for *both of you*, over time?

Stew Friedman's idea – that harmony is something we build intentionally over time – stayed with me. It felt like a powerful counter to the narrative of constant trade-offs. But I also knew it was only part of the picture. What does that look like day to day, especially when both people are ambitious, working hard and trying to stay connected? To explore that question, I turned to someone who's both living and studying this reality.

EXPERT VOICES: Jennifer Petriglieri, Dual Career Expert

Across this book, I have sought the counsel of experts. Here, I turn to Jennifer Petriglieri, Professor at INSEAD business school in France, whose research explores how dual-career couples navigate the challenges of work and life. Jennifer brings both professional insight and personal perspective – her husband, Gianpiero, is also a professor and together, they live the realities she studies.[6]

I wanted to hear how she sees the dual-career journey: not only through her research, but also from inside her own partnership:

> Dual careers, when well-managed, can be a positive resource for both partners. People in dual careers have the possibility of developing a deeper and broader sense of themselves and a stronger professional identity because of their non-work relationships with their spouse and their interactions with them. The benefits are strengthened when each is able to give the other a '*secure base*' through providing support and encouragement for the other's exploratory behaviour. Imagine that both partners are dependable, supportive and encouraging when the other is exploring what they want to do next – taking challenges and risks and making discoveries.
>
> When these two careers are varied and different, I think together they make us richer because they open our eyes to new areas; they give us access to diverse types of people you each know, people that are involved in the arts, people involved in finance or tech, and that makes us together more rounded, more informed, more interesting as people. So, I think our careers enhance us as people.
>
> What I have experienced is the most positive outcome of a dual career, which is that our combination enables us to accrue resources that neither could have accrued alone. Rather than a 'win-lose' experienced by many baby boomer women, this could be a win/win where both achieved more and grew more together than they could have independently.

Create a Secure Base

Jennifer talks about the importance of each partner acting as a secure base – a concept drawn from attachment theory but reimagined in the context of adult partnerships. A secure base is someone who provides not just emotional safety and support, but also encouragement to explore, stretch and take risks. In strong dual-career partnerships, this means your partner doesn't just accept your ambitions, they actively make space for them. They don't just say, *'Do what you need to do,'* they say, *'I've got you – go.'*

A secure base might look like one partner encouraging the other to apply for a job abroad – even if it means a big change at home. Or being the person who takes the emotional load during a period of intense study or travel. Or simply asking the kind of questions that help the other person see their own potential more clearly. These are acts of love, but also of partnership. They say: *your growth matters to me.*

I can see what Jennifer talks about here: a sense of mutual enhancement, both partners become better people as a result of the other's professional life – how it's possible to merge one's professional identities through joint projects. This is a recent story about my own life these days:

A Story of a Quiet Morning – London, April 2021

It's early and we're both at home. We do what we often do on mornings like this – sit with coffee in hand and talk through the day ahead. It's become one of those small, grounding rituals in our marriage – no rush, no agenda, just connection.

I bring up a challenge I'm facing at my consulting company, HSM. One of our core products is an online platform that enables large groups within organisations to have meaningful conversations about emerging issues. It's something we're proud of and it's worked well. But the platform is ageing and now we're at a crossroads: do we redesign it entirely, or continue patching and updating? It's not something we'll solve that morning, but Nigel talks through the options with me – laying out the trade-offs, raising questions I haven't thought of. I leave the conversation with more clarity and some new angles to consider.

Then we switch. Nigel sits on the board of a museum, and he's been thinking about how the institution can evolve in a post-COVID world. It's a topic close to my heart – how people work, how they reconnect – and I share a few ideas from my own research and practice. I agree to speak with the senior team. It's informal, fluid and mutual.

Some context: we've been married for five years. When we met, Nigel was a corporate lawyer. Now, he's stepped away from his partnership to build a portfolio career – made up of profit and not-for-profit roles. He's still busy, but the pace is different. Our children are older. We have more time. Less pressure. And, I suppose, more ease.

It's often said that the sixties and seventies are the happiest decades of our lives. Perhaps conversations like this are part of why this is: the companionship of someone who knows you well, who shares your values and who's willing to help you think more clearly. Not with urgency, but with care.

Learn and Experiment

What strikes me is the nature of learning and experimenting in partnerships – something I heard from both Stew and Jennifer. Here's how Stew describes this:

> It's about actively learning about yourself and your life – asking questions like: who are the most important people to me and why are they important? You need to be prepared to experiment, to innovate and to discover. Partnering with those who are important is crucial – their feedback, involvement – can create a ripple effect. I can see how some couples see change as experiments. They adopt a mindset of trials, assessing, looking for evidence. They are asking 'how does this feel?'. I counsel people to think about their own life as a laboratory, asking each other – could we try this? – then looking for evidence, making small wins and learning from them. To do that takes meaningful conversations and the permission to have these conversations. It also takes self-care – taking better care of yourself – showing up as more present (sleep, exercise, diet, walks, meditation, reading).

As I listen to Stew, I find myself thinking about my own life as a kind of laboratory. I've lived through several phases of partnership – early marriage, a decade as a single mother and now a later marriage with a very different rhythm. In each period, I've tried to create harmony. Sometimes I managed it, sometimes I didn't.

Looking back, I realise how often I avoided the kind of open, searching conversations Stew describes. I carried with me many of the values I'd grown up with – values that were rarely questioned, only enacted. And I didn't always give myself permission to experiment. But what if we saw our lives – especially our intimate partnerships – not as something to get 'right', but something to explore? A series of small experiments. Adjustments. Learning moments. What if we made space to ask, regularly: *Could we try this? Could this work better?* It's a shift in mindset, but a powerful one. And perhaps it's something we all need more of: the freedom to learn our way into better lives.

What if you treated your relationship – or your hopes for one – as a laboratory? Not a place for perfection, but for learning. Is there something you've been holding tightly to, because it feels like the 'right' way? Is there something new you might try if you gave yourself permission to experiment? What small adjustment might bring more harmony – right now, or over time?

And if you're not in a partnership right now, this idea of experimentation still matters. Mira and Lucia are both solo, but that hasn't stopped them from thinking deeply about what intimacy could look like for them – now and in the future. For Mira, close friends have become her sounding board; for Lucia, friendships are where she explores what kind of relationship she might want to build. They may not have a partner beside them right now, but they're still experimenting – with boundaries, values and the kinds of conversations that help us grow. Sometimes a trusted friend is the best kind of talking partner.

LOOKING AHEAD: Structures of Intimacy

How we are intimate with others is in part shaped by our personal values and social norms – what we inherit, what we choose, what we negotiate. It's also shaped by the institutions we work within.

I was one of the first waves of career mothers married to career fathers. We tried to make it work. In the end, we couldn't, and we weren't alone. Data from the 1990s shows that many couples like us eventually shifted course – sometimes one partner stepped into a job rather than a career, sometimes one became a full-time caregiver and sometimes, like us, the relationship ended in divorce.

I'd seen the reason for this earlier in my consulting career. The workplace didn't make parenting easy: Flexibility was rare, remote work was unusual. Time off for caregiving was limited. I left consulting and moved into academia, hoping for more space. But as one of the first professors to become a mother, I quickly realised there were no real norms for how to do that either. I went back to work within weeks of giving birth – not because it felt right, but because I couldn't imagine another option. I didn't yet know there was one.

Over the last two decades, things have changed, and they will continue to do so. In some companies, family-friendly policies are not simply a perk but a strategy to attract and retain talent. When I was a young parent, I couldn't have imagined taking a slower career path for a few years or stepping away and opting back in later without penalty. Now, in some places, that's a real possibility. Yet there is still much to be done. What you want – the support, the leave, the flexibility – *should exist* but doesn't yet. Paternity leave was once like this: unthinkable, then rare, and now – slowly – becoming more available. Many of the policies that will allow intimacy and work to coexist well haven't yet been fully built. But they can be. They will be – as more people ask for them, need them and expect them. So, here's a question to consider: *when it comes to choosing where and how you work, how important are these structures to you? Would you trade a higher salary for more flexibility? Would you choose a slower pace if it gave you more space for family, or recovery, or love?*

There is no right answer – but there is value in being intentional. Some companies still reward constant availability and uninterrupted presence. Others are beginning to rethink what matters. When you choose where to go next, choose with care. The institutions we enter shape not just our work, but our lives too.

INTIMACY: Putting it into Practice

Three Actions to Take Now

1. **Identify one inherited norm you want to keep or change**
   Reflect on the roles and expectations you observed growing up (as in the 'family table' story). Choose one that still shapes your relationships today – and decide whether to keep it or let it go.
2. **Start a conversation you've been postponing**

Like Ben and Yuki's evening walks or Stew Friedman's 'meaningful conversations', open up a dialogue with someone close about how you want to share time, care and responsibility over the next few years.

3. **Protect one connection outside of partnership**
   Inspired by the solo life and friendship stories, commit to deepening one friendship or chosen-family relationship. Put time in your diary for it and treat it as essential to your intimacy thread.

Three Promises to My Future Self

1. **I will keep rewriting the script**
   As life changes – through marriage, parenting, solo seasons or later-life partnership – I will negotiate my relationships consciously, not live by default.
2. **I will see solo periods as part of the story, not a gap**
   If I am on my own, I will use that time for growth, independence and connection with friends, community and myself.
3. **I will work for harmony, not constant trade-offs**
   Like the dual-career couples in the chapter, I will look for ways my work, family, community and self can strengthen one another over time.

Partnerships evolve. Families shape and reshape themselves. Over the course of a long life, the forms of intimacy you create will not stay fixed – they will be rewoven. Yet through all these changes, the effort you make to give and receive love will be among your most enduring investments. In a 100-year life, intimacy is not only a source of joy in the moment, but also a thread that strengthens the whole fabric of your years, binding your story together across time.

CHAPTER 12

THE THREAD OF CALM: Can I Slow Down?

You may live 100 years but that doesn't mean rushing through them. In a long life, the ability to slow down becomes not a luxury, but a skill: one that helps you restore, reflect and recalibrate.

There are times in our working life when calm feels almost out of reach. Times when work is tough, distracting, all-consuming or simply overwhelming. Times of personal upset, when friendships falter, families begin to fracture. And times of real crisis – a job is lost, finances are uncertain, a relationship unravels. These moments, while deeply challenging, can also be openings – windows into learning, re-evaluation, even transformation. But if those intense periods become our norm – if the pressure never lets up – something begins to break. Without space to decompress, we sleep badly. Our empathy for others wears thin. Our curiosity fades. And in time, our mental health may begin to erode too. That's why I imagine calm as one of the foundational threads that supports everything else. When present, other threads stay strong – when absent, everything else begins to fray.

WHAT CALM MAKES POSSIBLE

Calm Supports Creativity. When you are calm, you are more likely to access the quieter parts of your mind – those that require space and stillness to be heard. I recall a writer once describing her creative brain as a storeroom of ideas she can only unlock when her mind is calm enough to let the unconscious speak.

It Helps You Absorb Shocks. Across a long working life, there will be moments that hit you hard – a parent passes away, a colleague says something that cuts deep, a relationship hits a breaking point. In these moments, it's not discipline or strategy that carries you through but the presence of a wellspring of calm – something internal, cultivated over time – that allows you to remain steady.

It Keeps You Healthy. It is becoming increasingly clear that stress at work is a major cause of physical and mental illness. When you are stressed, your immune system is compromised, your healthy heart is under threat, and you are more likely to resort to unhealthy habits like over-consuming food or alcohol. Intense stress is a barrier to decompression – calm can create that decompression.

It Encourages Empathy. Being empathic will become increasingly core to being human but without periods of decompression, you are less likely to tolerate others or to be empathic. When you are wrapped up in our own issues, you cannot hear the voices of others. Calm helps you hear the voice of others.

HOW TO STRENGTHEN THE THREAD OF CALM

We each have our own form of calm and of being calm. Calm is how we nurture others and how we nurture ourselves. To help you think about this, together we will go through these ideas and exercises:

- → **Find Moments of Calm** – we each have ways to be calm and we begin by reflecting on these moments of calm and the role they have played in your life.
- → **Why Calm Feels Elusive** – many of our working habits push away calm as our working tasks become shorter, more intense and we make more use of technology. Here, we explore how this has happened and the impact it has on your brain and nervous system.
- → **Face the Challenges to Calm** – we take a closer look at the challenges that test us – be they era challenges, life stage challenges or personal challenges. When you are able to name the challenges you face, you are more able to use calm to navigate them.
- → **Gather Your Resources** – when we have these resources, they make an incredible difference to a long life – supporting us to face challenges both now and in the future.
- → **Create Calm in Your Own Way** – we each have our own ways of finding calm and here we explore four ways to ensure that our unique ways of calm, have the space and attention to develop.

FIND MOMENTS OF CALM

We each have moments when calm enters our lives – a pause in the rush, a quiet breath, a place where we feel at ease. These moments may be fleeting, but they remind us that calm is always available, even in the busiest of times. Noticing when and how we experience calm helps us see what restores us and what drains us. By paying attention to these moments, we can begin to weave calm more intentionally into the fabric of our long lives.

Your Story: Of Calm

Tell me a story of a time when you felt calm – grounded, steady, able to cope. Stories of calm show us what restores us and how we build resilience. What was happening? What helped you get there? How did you carry that calm forward? *Notice what this story reveals about the resources you draw on when you need steadiness.*

Calm doesn't appear out of nowhere. It tends to be cultivated, drawn from something you've built over time: a place, a person, a habit, a rhythm. The opening story I shared with you of walking in the French countryside, thinking of my father – captures my place of calm: I am most calm when I am walking. Here are two little stories of feeling calm:

Stories of Walking into Calm – Regent's Park, London, Spring 2023

I'm walking along the path that circles Regent's Park. I start by walking across the playing fields, through the rose garden, along the cherry avenue and back across the open park. It's spring and the cherry blossom is out, the roses have just come into their green leaves, and the borders are ablaze with spring flowers – daffodils, anemones. This is a man-made environment – in spring, the daffodils and crocuses are laid out in intricate patterns, the grass is mown and there are at least 50 varieties of roses planted and tended to. I'm not adverse to the path's man-madeness. It is wonderful now, with the cherry blossom thick on the ground. In autumn, when the lime and horse chestnut trees are shedding their leaves, it's a blaze of colour. This is a path I've walked many, many times – in every weather and in many moods. It's the second year of the COVID lockdown and walking this path has become a daily activity. I am often joined, as I am today, by my dear friend Herminia. With our masks on and socially distanced, we reflect on the day, share our frustrations and congratulate each other on small victories.

The South Downs, January 2024

My sister Heather and I are at the start of our walk to the top of the hills of the South Downs. First we climb up to the top of the downs – feeling our breath shortening and our heart pumping. Then our pathway sweeps down through a thorn coppice. It is late winter. The air is freezing, the mist descends, and we see our breath.

After we scramble down the slope, our path crosses the valley, takes us through a small village, then across a field thick with clay soil that sticks to our walking shoes. Then, passing a bend in the road, we catch a glimpse of the local pub with its welcoming wood fire burning in the hearth. It's a place to stop for lunch and a glass of cider before we set off for the climb to the top of the South Downs and the spot we left the car. As we walk up the steep path, the rain starts but our long weatherproof coats protect us from the rain that is lashing down. We are our father's daughters.

Both these calm stories are about walking. That's my rhythm – my way of slowing down, thinking clearly, returning to myself. Your memories of calm will be different. We are each shaped by our own history, temperament and preferences. There's no single right way to be calm. What matters is finding what works for you – and protecting it.

Everyday Calms

When I walk – up hills, around lakes, across valleys – sometimes talking, sometimes alone, I find my mind settles. I don't wear headphones or listen to podcasts, I just walk, paying attention to the wind, the rhythm of my feet, the sounds of the world around me. It's in these moments that I begin to think more clearly, feel more deeply, imagine more freely.

What is it that happens in our moments of calm? Why do they work so well, how did they evolve? Do they relate to your personality, the role models that inspire?

These calming walks are part of my history. These rituals go back to childhood, walking the fells of the Lake District, learning to be comfortable outdoors and with myself. My walks now echo those early experiences. They create what feels like a holding space: familiar, grounding, safe. They are partly about personality. An introvert, I am happy with my own company or the company of another. These walks are always circular, so I return to where I started. Always repeated and familiar, so I don't have to figure out a new route. Always available, needing no one's permission or co-ordination.

Maybe circular walks aren't on your list. Perhaps it's a run, a book, a yoga class, a swim, a few minutes of quiet with a coffee before the day begins. Whatever it is, these activities have something in common: they give you space to simply be. They allow your nervous system to settle, your thoughts to expand and your sense of self to return.

Mira is beginning to realise that keeping the thread of calm strong is crucial to her. She knows she's introverted and that one of her personality traits is neuroticism – she can feel it in the anger that sometimes wells up inside. She'd learned early to hide her feelings; people don't like to hear anger, and over time to bury her stress levels deep. But the divorce and the trauma around it has surfaced these feelings. She is now acknowledging that calm must – absolutely must – be a constant part of her working life. Everyday habits like walking the dog, listening to music, cooking the meals she loves. Daily habits, repeated into a ritual that keeps her steady.

Your Third Place

Perhaps your calm is a 'third place'.[1] Not home, not work, but somewhere in between. Somewhere expectations fall away and you're not performing a role. These places – cafés, libraries, allotments, workshops, gyms – can become sanctuaries. Places to think, reflect, pause, even dream. And over the course of a long working life, these places may shift. But the feeling they offer, a temporary loosening of the world's demands, remains constant.

For Mira, her 'third place' is a tucked-away corner of her local library. It's quiet, structured and anonymous. She brings a notebook, a flask of tea and loses herself in ideas. Nico finds his at a weekly community gardening project – hands in the soil, surrounded by people who ask nothing of him socially. And Ben has found that his 'third place' isn't a place at all – it's an early-morning cycle along the canal, just before the city wakes up. That's where he feels most free.

Do you have a third place? And if not, could you find – or create – something like it?

Since an adolescent, I've loved Virginia Woolf's book 'A Room of One's Own'.[2] She wrote this with the harassed women of the 1920s in mind, yet it resonates down the century with anyone who feels overwhelmed. One of the promises I made in my thirties was to find a physical 'third place' – and for me that became a small apartment in Sitges, down the Mediterranean coast from Barcelona. It's a place of solace and creativity which, many years ago I promised my future self.

WHY CALM FEELS ELUSIVE

Of course, it is not always possible to find calm and perhaps you struggle to find calm. When I reflect on my own life, I realise there have been times – particularly when my children were young – when I did not take circular walks or find calm. I simply did not have the time. Let's take a closer look at why finding calm in our working life can be so hard.

When Work Fragments Life

Whenever I teach a course for executives at London Business School, I ask my participants what they most want to improve in their life. More calm is often near the top of the list. People long for calm. They talk about wanting time to think, space to breathe, energy to recover. And yet, again and again, I hear the same response: *'I'm just too busy.'* The paradox is real. Even when we recognise how important calm is, we don't feel we have time to make space for it.

Research confirms the same pattern: while leaders understand the benefits of recovery – like mental clarity, better decisions and improved wellbeing – they often don't make time for it. For instance, nearly 70 per cent of senior executives acknowledge that burnout is impairing their decision-making, and 69 per cent are considering quitting as a result.[3]

So, what's stopping you from creating calm and caring for yourself?

My guess is one of the main barriers you are reflecting on is that you simply don't have time to engage in these rituals of calm. You are not alone – many people are feeling the fragmentation of their life, both when they work and when they are at home. I've been watching this fragmentation for decades, charting the ways our use of technology fragments our time, while also predicting how this could play out. In 2011, my book *The Shift: The Future of Work is here*[4] was published. In it, I imagined the day in the life of someone in 2025 – here's how I describe the life of someone – I called her Jill:

A Story of a Day in the Life of Jill – January, 2025

It's 6. a.m., and Jill's awakened to her alarm, her eyes on the 300 messages flashing on her wall screen. Overnight colleagues, friends, current employees and future employees from around the world are keen to share their ideas. As her eyes become accustomed to the dawn light, the first hologram call comes in. Over the next ten minutes, Jill works with her avatar as it is needed for a meeting across the globe that will begin in two hours' time and will require broad directions.

An hour later and Jill's connected to her cognitive assistant, reviewing the day's timetable. Her first conference call is to colleagues in the Beijing office, at the same time she works on another 30 messages – thank goodness for the mute button! By

10 a.m., she is still in her pyjamas. Jill snatches breakfast, holds back on her colleagues' demands for more feedback and logs onto her personal website to view any new work that has come in overnight.

Then it's conference calls to clients, negotiating a couple of deals and agreeing delivery times – a final call with the Mumbai office before they go offline. It's now 10.30 and the team in Boston are awake and keen to ask her opinion about a particular deal they have put together: it involves linking with the Shanghai team so she agrees to brief her Chinese colleagues the following morning.

I'd written this passage in around 2009 – predicting 2025 from the technological trends described at that time. As I wrote in the book: 'Welcome to the fragmented world, where it seems that no activity last more than three minutes, and where those in employment are continuously competing with people across the world to strive to serve the different stakeholders they work for.' Not all the technological predictions happened by 2025 – but the *feel* of Jill's working day? That part landed. The fragmentation, the constant switching, the sheer mental overload. That's become the lived reality for many people in 2025.

If you wrote a day in the life of Jill 25 years hence (let's, say 2050), how would you describe it? Do you think it would be any calmer? Here is the question I asked in 2009: *What can you do to build a life that doesn't leave you depleted – one that protects your energy, not just your output?*

It is a question that matters now as much as it did then. Perhaps even more so. In fact, they are some of the hardest questions I hear when working with senior executives. Not because they don't understand the importance of calm, but because they genuinely can't see where to find it. The exhaustion so many feel at work is real and yet, without calm, it's difficult, perhaps impossible, to think wisely, act with intention or show up with the kind of energy others need from us.

The constant switching and overload of modern work doesn't just eat into our time, it shapes the kind of challenges we face. Fragmentation can turn small pressures into sustained strain, leaving us less able to meet the bigger tests that inevitably arrive. Some of these challenges are shared across generations, others come with a particular life stage and some are intensely personal.

FACE THE CHALLENGES TO CALM

We need calm at every time of our life. But there are times, when our capacity to be calm and care for ourselves comes to the fore. I found it really helpful, as I looked at my own stories, to understand the challenges I've faced – and I think this will be a useful exercise for you.

What are the challenges you are facing now and what have been the challenges you have faced in the past? As you reflect on your own experiences, what comes to mind? What kind of challenges have shaped you? Were they expected, or did they arrive suddenly?

As I looked at my own challenges, I began to realise I've faced three types of challenge: Some are era challenges faced by many people at one time; some are life stage challenges shared by those who are at a similar stage and then there are those personal challenges unique to us. Understanding the nature of these challenges helps you to face them for although they are different, at the foundation is the need to build resilience through calm.

Calm Through Era Challenges

These era challenges are the ones we all face together by virtue of the time we're living in. The 2022 global pandemic is the most obvious example. Overnight, everyone had to change how they worked, cared, socialised and made sense of their days. These collective challenges can feel overwhelming, as the pandemic did, but because so many are navigating them at once, they also generate shared wisdom.

Think about Ben's children – now young and with perhaps 90 years of life ahead of them. They'll face yet another configuration of era challenges, shaped by climate change, AI, shifting models of work and the issues of loneliness and belonging. We can't predict exactly what will come but we can prepare, in part, by building our capacity for calm now.

What era challenges have you already faced and what did they mean to you? What might be ahead? Can you see how strengthening your thread of calm could help you confront these era challenges?

Calm Through Life Stage Challenges

These life stage challenges come at phases of life. For me, one was the challenge of caring for a tiny baby while trying to hold onto my professional identity. Another was the moment in my sixties, walking in a French forest, reflecting on my father's death and questioning how I was living. These challenges are often predictable. They arrive with the decade and because others have faced them too, there is often guidance to draw on – if you know where to look.

Nico describes his way of working to Lucia as 'this stage I'm in'. He works hard – long hours, tight deadlines, high expectations – but he also takes care of himself. Most mornings he runs, keeps a close eye on his step count and drinks the green smoothies his team swears by. He rarely drinks alcohol now. He's even started experimenting with magnesium supplements and guided meditation apps.

But calm? That's harder. He feels engaged by the work, especially when the challenge is real and the team clicks into gear, but at night, his mind doesn't settle. He lies awake replaying meetings, wondering if he misread someone's tone. He mentally reworks how the business is going, tweaking timelines, rehearsing tomorrow's answers. Sometimes he wakes up with jaw tension from grinding his teeth. He keeps his phone just far enough away to claim boundaries, but close enough to check Slack if he needs to. He tells Lucia it's temporary, just a busy stage for the business – but the stage seems to extend.

Nico is beginning to realise that health isn't the same as calm. You can eat well, move often, perform at a high level and still carry a constant hum of mental tension. Calm isn't just the absence of illness, it's the presence of something slower and softer. And that, Nico is still learning how to find.

When do you feel most calm? Not just healthy or productive – but truly at ease. Have you ever realised – like Nico – that wellbeing and calm are not the same? What, for you, brings not just energy, but ease?

Calm Through Personal Challenges

Some challenges feel unpredictable and isolating – a friend dies far too young, a promotion you counted on doesn't come through or a job disappears overnight. These challenges don't come with a guidebook, they require deep internal resource. This is where calm becomes not just helpful, but essential.

All three challenges need calm: to observe others and learn; to take a deep breath and think; to stand back and get perspective. And yet, despite its importance, calm is often the first part of our life that goes. We let it slip beneath the surface of our awareness – pushed aside by deadlines, distractions and the belief that we'll recover later. We rarely schedule time for calm. We don't measure it. And often we don't protect it until we're already running low. But when calm disappears, its absence is felt everywhere. You feel it in your relationships, your focus, your health. That's the real risk. Not that you never had calm, but that you let it erode without realising what you've lost.

However they arrive – sweeping in with the force of a global crisis, creeping in through a life stage shift, or landing suddenly in the middle of an ordinary week – these challenges have one thing in common: they draw on our reserves. In those moments, it's not quick fixes or clever strategies that carry us through, but the depth of what we've built over time.

GATHER YOUR RESOURCES

Calm is not only a state of mind but also something we can prepare for. Just as we keep practical supplies on hand for emergencies, we can collect emotional and psychological resources that steady us when life feels turbulent. These resources may be habits, people or places that restore our perspective and resilience. The more intentionally we gather them, the more readily we can draw on them when calm is most needed.

Your Story: A Challenge Faced

Think of a time when you faced a challenge that really tested your calm – when you had to draw on your resilience. What was the challenge? How did you respond? What did you discover about yourself? *What does this story teach you about your resilience, and the threads that help you endure?*

This is a story of a time that was very tough for me, but from which I learned from my mother about being calm.

A Story of Mum's Bedroom – Lewes, 2018

Mum's health is rapidly deteriorating. I'm teaching and directing a one-week executive program at London Business School. It's a program I've been directing and teaching on for more than 20 years based on my research about human resource strategy in transforming companies. I feel that cancelling the program is out of the question. More than 40 people have travelled from all over the world to be there. I wondered about finding a substitute teacher for the whole week, but at this late stage that's impossible. Yesterday I talked with Mum and my siblings about this. They all say 'teach the program' and Mum said, 'I will be here when you come.'

So, I've taught the program this week. Trying to stay focused on the participants and not be overwhelmed with Mum's deteriorating health. Then this Thursday morning – the fourth day of a five-day program, I've asked two of my colleagues to substitute for me on the program. I jump into the car and race down to Mum's house.

I arrive later that evening. Mum is in her bed, calm but fading. She's slept fitfully that night. By Saturday morning she has begun to fade back and forth into consciousness. Her final wish is to stay at home and we have tried to honour that wish. Her carers have substituted her bed for a medical bed and around her are the various contraptions that monitor her pulse and a driver to administer the morphine which is keeping her pain at bay.

I am here with my sister Heather and brothers Jack and Richard – who has flown over from Australia five weeks prior to be with her. We are seated around her bed in the pale light. Mum's body has shrunk, her bones are visible. Her life is ebbing away from her. We hold her hand and tell her how much we love her and what she has meant to each of us. Looking back, part of Mum's dislike of sentimentality is that she has never said to us 'I love you.' Of course, her actions made this clear. Yet this is not a word she used. We do, and we each tell her how much we love her and what a wonderful mother she had been to us. As she moves into her final hours, I read from her Bible – trying to find psalms that soothe. Mum's last words were, 'I am surrounded by my angels.'

You and I may be distinct in many ways, but we all have mothers or mother figures and there will be a time when these significant others pass away, as my mother Barbara did that week.

What did this story mean to you? Did it evoke feelings about your own life or a future event you know you will be called upon to face?

As I reflect on my memories of Mum's last few days, two conversations come to mind. First, Robert Rowland Smith's advice to 'develop agency of your own, so that when something less advantageous occurs, you can look into your cupboard of personal supplies and find it full, not empty'. And Stew Friedman made a similar point when we spoke about partnership: that it requires meaningful conversations, the permission to have them and the self-care that allows you to show up fully present.

I can see how Mum developed self-care. For her, this focus came in her mid-thirties when she was diagnosed with breast cancer – the prognosis was bad. But she decided to face this head-on and enrolled on a 12-week experimental treatment based on healthy eating, yoga and medication. It was a turning point in her life and became the moment when the habits of calm became a daily practice; she learned how to stay calm and centred.

Mum's final days told a great deal about her life and about how she constantly sought to strengthen her four threads of nurture. The deep friendships she had cherished since at the age of 14, she and Dad had joined Liverpool Youth Club. Even into their eighties, these friends met at least once a year, often in the place they loved most – the Lake District. Her sheer positivity, even as her condition – Sarcoma – caused her skin to constantly peel away, revealing vulnerable and painful skin. And the courage she had to start her treatment of blood transfusions at St George's hospital in London, where every month, over a 12-hour period her blood was passed through a light filter, removing the white blood cells. This gave her another eight months of life – time to see her great-granddaughter born.

There came a time when the treatment no longer worked and it was no surprise that in the final months of her life, Mum's friends were at her side, popping in for coffee, sitting in the conservatory to enjoy her cakes – which to her chagrin had become 'shop-bought'. And it was no surprise that all her children were with her in her last days. Like any family, we had our squabbles and fallings-out yet throughout our adult lives, Mum kept the peace: the intermediary as we fell out with each other, the negotiator when things got tough. She did all of this in such a low-key way that I barely noticed it at the time.

Mum's final challenge was facing her death with generosity and compassion. My challenge was to face the death of my beloved mother. In that moment, I realised how much calm she had woven into our lives – not through grand gestures, but through small, steady acts of care. Her example helped me see that calm is not something we stumble upon, but something we can cultivate, even in the midst of turmoil.

It is in this spirit that I have come to recognise four ways we can create calm in your own way.

CREATE CALM IN YOUR OWN WAY

I believe calm at work, just like calm in life, needs to be built deliberately. It's shaped by our preferences, our context and the constraints we face. Also, by what we decide to protect. There's growing evidence that carving out undisturbed time, even in small amounts, can make a real difference to focus, clarity and wellbeing. Here are some ideas you might like to try out.

Find 'Precious Hours'

For me, one of the most valuable habits I've created is something I call my 'precious hours'. Here's a short story illustrating how they work:

A Story of Three Precious Hours – London, 2019

The door is closed. Notifications on my computer are turned off. My phone is silenced and placed out of reach. In my weekly schedule, there's a three-hour block marked simply: *focus*. No meetings, no calls, no distractions. Just time.

I call them my 'precious hours'. I book them months in advance – protecting them as I would any high-priority appointment. The night before, as I drift off to sleep, my mind often starts preparing, turning over ideas, making space for deeper thinking.

This morning, I sit at my desk and take a long breath, trying to clear the noise. It's not a time for emails or social calls, or to read the *Financial Times* or scroll through messages – that can all wait. This time is for something else. After a break, a coffee, a glimpse into the garden, I return for another hour. I'm not trying to solve everything, I'm thinking. Exploring. When I finally rise from my chair, it's as if time has folded in on itself. Three hours have passed. I've gained clarity – not necessarily in answers, but in the shape of the questions I want to ask next.

I know I'm fortunate to have this kind of autonomy. As a writer and professor, I've built a life where I can protect these windows of time. But I made that choice deliberately – because I need this rhythm of focus to do my best work to stay sane. And even if your working life looks very different, the principle still applies: a protected hour, time without interruption, just to think.

As I reflect on my precious hours, I'm reminded of the work of Mihaly Csikszentmihalyi and his research on *Flow*.[5] He described flow as the mental state where you are fully immersed in a task, with a sense of energy, focus and deep enjoyment. Time seems to stretch or disappear. You feel challenged but not overwhelmed – using your skills at their edge, with just enough difficulty to keep you engaged.

According to Csikszentmihalyi, Flow isn't about relaxation, it's about absorption. It happens most often when you are doing something meaningful, with a clear goal and immediate feedback. For many, this might be writing, coding, designing or solving a tough problem. For others, this might come during a long run, a difficult climb or even a deep conversation. In my precious hours, I can feel that shift. My thoughts deepen, the noise fades. I'm able to connect ideas that normally sit just below the surface. It's not always productive in the traditional sense, but it is generative. Things move. Insights come. I leave that time feeling stretched and restored.

It's as simple as putting time into your schedule. And when I teach executives, by the end of the week most participants have this as a short-term action. They promise that on the following Monday, they will go through their schedule and put in those 'precious hours'.

You may already know what works for you. Maybe you've even made plans to build those precious hours in. But knowing and doing are two different things. I've spoken to so many people who say, 'I know I need time to think, to walk, to rest – but I just can't find it.' Often, it's not because they don't care but that short-term pressures are driving their decisions.

So, how do we push back against this short-termism and protect what really matters? That's where we'll go next. Let's take a look at how you can create more calm in your working life – by shifting your mindset to take a longer view of work, making the investment in your future self and creating slack as a buffer against time scarcity.

Take the Long View

Many of the activities that bring calm – spending time with friends, taking circular walks, carving out precious hours – have one thing in common: they require the deliberate allocation of time. But choosing to invest in calm is hard when life feels full and often, it's the short-term demands that shape our decisions: the meeting that needs preparation, the inbox that won't wait, the people who need answers now. We tell ourselves we'll find time for calm *next week*. Or *next month*. Just as soon as the pressure lets up.

This is what behavioural economists call *present bias*.[6] Our tendency to favour smaller, immediate rewards over larger, delayed ones. It helps explain why saving for retirement, exercising, or even making time for rest can feel so difficult in the moment. Even when we know a longer view would serve us better, we don't act on it. As Robert Waldinger reminded me in our conversation about friendship 'We are generally poor at predicting those activities that generate long-term positive benefits.' That's why I find it so useful to reflect on the image of weaving the fabric of a life: weaving every day, every month, every year. Imagine standing back and looking down at the fabric of your working life from above. Not just seeing this week, but your whole working life: the past, the present and the decades still to come. From that perspective, it makes more sense to value tomorrow as much as today, to invest in your future self.

There will be time to work, to raise children, to learn, to explore. And the longer your life, the more future you have. *The question is: are you making time for what matters most – or deferring it to a future that never quite arrives?*

Looking back, I'm aware that I didn't always take this longer view. I think back to 1990 and the story about trying to work with my baby son Christian strapped to my chest, both of us in tears. I'm trying to write, trying to meet expectations, trying not to fall behind. I'm utterly exhausted. If I'd had a different internal dialogue at the time, it might have sounded like this:

> Lynda, you'll probably work into your seventies. That's another 40 years ahead of you. Your children will be babies for only a tiny fraction of that. Why not move a little leisure from your seventies into now? This is a moment you won't get again but there will be plenty more moments to work.

But I didn't have that conversation. I ask myself why. This was in part because I had no role models to give me an idea of how to be a working mother, but I sense it was more than that. I was also worried what time out with my baby son would do to my career. I was running on a career clock, with pressure to move up, to be able to earn university tenure and a secure job – I didn't feel I could afford to go 'off track'. As it happened, years later when I went up for tenure at London Business School, I didn't get it. But I didn't know that at the time.

So that's how I ended up teaching when Christian was a baby. Standing in front of a class, breastfeeding pads soaked through, jacket buttoned up tightly. So, if you're struggling to protect calm in your life, know this: it's not just about time. It's about role models, policy gaps and the deep, often invisible pressures we absorb from the world around us. It takes courage to step back from the momentum of working life – it turned out I had some of that courage, but not as much as I needed.

Invest in Your Future Self

Here is another way of thinking about time. When you choose to spend time on something calming – something that restores or sustains you – you are making a double investment. You're investing in your present self, giving yourself the benefit of pause or reflection now. But you're also investing in your future self, the version of you who will carry the results of that decision forward. And like any investment, the earlier you start, the greater the return. The sooner you build the habits, routines and relationships that help you feel calm, connected and resilient, the more time your future self has to enjoy the benefits.

This investment in your future self plays out along all of the eight threads. It might be in your skills and mastery. Or in your friendships, your health, your emotional balance. It might be taking those precious hours seriously or reclaiming a long walk that used to be part of your rhythm. The key is to start – and if you've let it go, to start again.

I've felt that in my own life. My circular walks are a calming thread that goes back to childhood. There have been times when I lost touch with them – when work or caregiving or travel crowded everything else out – but like a savings plan, you can come back. You can stop and then start again. The point is to restart before the balance runs too low, before your threads of nurture begin to unravel. And that's what this is really about: seeing calm not as a reward or an indulgence, but as a practice that shapes who you become. It's about making choices now that your future self will be glad you made.

What's one small change you could make this week that your future self would thank you for? It doesn't have to be dramatic. It might be protecting an hour. Reinstating a habit. Saying no to something you'd usually say yes to – so you can say yes to something that matters more to you.

Create Slack

One of the reasons it's so hard to make time for calm is that when time feels scarce, it begins to dominate our thinking. Research shows that scarcity – of any kind – narrows our mental bandwidth.[7] It pushes us into short-term mode, where we focus only on the most immediate problem, often at the cost of longer-term wellbeing.

This is most obvious with money. When you don't have enough cash, you are more likely to make decisions that offer short-term relief but cause long-term harm – like payday loans with punishing interest rates. The same is true of time. When you feel constantly behind, you begin to triage your day. Answering the next email. Rushing to the next meeting. Squeezing in a call. And slowly, you lose the time you need for rest, reflection and restoration. That's why one of the best ways to counteract time scarcity is to create slack – a buffer. A margin. A bit of unclaimed space in your schedule. Not for emergencies, but for breathing room. For me, my circular walks and precious hours have become rituals of slack. They're not just practices of calm, they're safeguards against overload. They help me feel that I have space to think, which in turn allows me to make better decisions about how to use my time.

As we've seen earlier, Lucia has been thinking about this too. She expects to work into her seventies and she's not daunted by that. But she also knows that if she doesn't build slack for rest and space along the way, work could easily become endless and exhausting. So, she's started asking different questions. Could she build in periodic time off – not as recovery, but as rhythm? Could she shift to freelance work for a few years in her forties? Could she take a sabbatical? It's early days, but already, she's realising that calm isn't just something you hope for, it's something you design. And here's the good news: the working world is slowly catching up. Corporate policies are changing. Sabbaticals are more common. Flexible work is no longer fringe. If you're in your twenties, thirties or forties, you may have access to options I couldn't begin to imagine when I was raising my family. This gives you a chance. A chance to pause, to plan and to think across a longer horizon. You can spread your work, your learning, your caregiving and your rest more evenly across time so you don't face the impossible task of doing everything all at once.

CALM: Putting it into Practice

Three Actions to Take Now

1. **Protect a precious hour.**
   Block one hour this week for yourself – no meetings, no emails, no interruptions. Use it to think, walk or simply pause. Notice how your energy shifts afterwards.
2. **Name your third place.**
   Identify one space where you feel at ease – a café, a park, a library, a cycling route – and spend time there. If you don't have one, experiment with creating one.
3. **Choose one small calming ritual.**
   Pick a daily habit that steadies you – a walk, journaling, stretching or cooking – and commit to repeating it for seven days in a row. Treat it as non-negotiable.

Three Promises to My Future Self

1. **I will honour calm as a foundation.**
   I will protect calm not as an indulgence, but as a practice that strengthens all the other threads of my life.
2. **I will build resilience through rhythm.**
   I will create routines and spaces that allow me to restore, so that when challenges come – whether era-defining, life stage or personal – I have reserves to draw on.
3. **I will invest in my future self.**
   I will take the long view, spreading work, rest and care across the decades of a long life, so I can meet the future not depleted, but steady and ready.

As the decades unfold, the moments you create for stillness and reflection will serve you often. Calm restores your energy when work is demanding, steadies your relationships when life feels turbulent, and sharpens your perspective when uncertainty looms. It is one of the threads that holds the fabric of a 100-year life together – unseen at times, but essential for its strength and balance.

To invest in calm is to invest in the capacity to keep weaving your life with intention, resilience and grace.

CHAPTER 13

THE THREAD OF ADVENTURE: Do I Still Feel Alive?

A longer life means more time to try new things – but only if you allow yourself to take those chances. Adventure isn't just for the young, it's a thread you can keep weaving at every stage of life.

Let's talk about energy. Not the steady kind that helps you focus, stay calm or wind down. But the spark. The jolt. The rush that makes you laugh out loud, say yes before you're ready, or walk away with a story you'll be telling for years. If calm is the thread that helps us rest, reset and stay grounded, then adventure is its vibrant counterpoint: it lifts us, surprises us and reminds us what it feels like to be truly alive.

When did you last feel that kind of exhilaration? And here's a question: What would your 70-, 80-, 90- or even 100-year-old self ask of you today?

Yes, perhaps they'd remind you to walk 10,000 steps, sleep well, eat sensibly. But I suspect they'd also say: *'Give me stories. Give me moments I can look back on with joy. Surprise me. Enrich me. Don't just keep me safe – make me feel alive.'*

Your Future Self will ask for adventures and energy. The kind of adventures that make your heart beat faster, when your curiosity kicks in, when the world feels bigger. Those moments that shake you out of routine, soften your fears and reconnect you to courage. They're not just stories to tell, they become markers in your life.

Imagine calm and adventure as points on a spectrum. On one end, calm steadies and on the other, adventure lifts. You need both. And here's the thing: adventure doesn't have to mean leaping off a cliff or changing your life overnight. Sometimes, it's saying yes to something unexpected. Getting lost in a new city. Starting a project that scares you just enough. It's that spark you feel in your body – that edge of risk and wonder that wakes up your sense of possibility.

As you reflect on your life so far, what are the stories that still pulse with energy? The ones that made you feel more awake, more yourself, more human? These are your adventures and in this chapter, we'll follow that thread – through playful work, bold leaps, unexpected turns and the small courageous choices that shape a lifetime.

This feels especially urgent now. In a world shaped increasingly by artificial intelligence, where systems can synthesise information faster than we ever could, what remains uniquely human? The answer, as we explored in the Amplification thread, is our lived experience. Our capacity to take risks, to feel joy, to be changed by a place or a person or an encounter. The memories stories lay down, the empathy we build, the inner world we develop – all of this fuels creativity in a way that no algorithm can replicate. Adventures – big and small – feed that inner life. They sharpen our perception, build our courage, deepen our understanding. They bring us stories and those stories become part of what makes us original.

WHAT ADVENTURE MAKES POSSIBLE

When you are experiencing adventures – at work or out of work – there will be many positive experiences:

Adventure Boosts Energy and Engagement. Adventures wake you up. They pull you out of routine and into flow – banishing lethargy and reminding you what it feels like to be alert, curious, alive. When you say yes to something unknown, you reconnect with a sense of possibility. It's not just about thrill-seeking, it's about feeling part of the rhythm of life again. Even small adventures can shift your emotional state from resignation to readiness. They break the spell of 'learned helplessness' and remind you that you still have agency.

It Creates New Stories and Self-Discovery. Adventure generates narrative. It gives you something to talk about, to remember, to integrate into your sense of who you are. These moments let you test your identity, explore possible selves and see yourself in a different light. A new city, a surprising workshop, a side project that catches fire – these become the raw material of growth. You see what excites you, you learn where you stretch and you carry those insights forward.

It Brings Creativity, Resilience and Connection. Adventure fuels creativity by exposing you to unfamiliar perspectives, environments and challenges. When you move outside your comfort zone, your assumptions are disrupted – and that disruption can lead to fresh insights. These experiences also help build resilience: by facing uncertainty, you practice adaptability. And when you adventure with others – whether in a team, a cohort or even a chance encounter, you build bonds that run deeper than everyday interactions.

HOW TO STRENGTHEN THE THREAD OF ADVENTURE

How are your threads of adventure? Strong, fraying, weak? In this chapter we explore how to strengthen these threads, wherever you are in your life. Here are some exercises and thought pieces we will cover:

- → **Uncover Exhilarating Work** – I will ask you to tell me a story of a time when you felt really alive at work and introduce you to the idea of a Seeking System and how activities can energise and engage our curiosity.
- → **Remember Playful Work** – those projects taking us out of the norm, surprising and engaging. We will explore what it means to have play at work and how this felt to you.
- → **Create More Energising Work** – it often feels as though there are so many barriers to being alive at work. Here, we take a look at concrete, actionable ideas that will boost your energy at work.
- → **Embrace Grand Adventures** – explores how to create a space to let go, be courageous and test yourself. I will show how adventures open up new identities, lay down the markers of your life and connect you deeply.

UNCOVER EXHILARATING WORK

My guess is that as you reflect on your working life, you'll remember moments when your energy lifted – when you were experimenting, stretching yourself, stepping outside the familiar. These are often the experiences we return to, because they show us what we're capable of.

Perhaps your adventures have come through work – taking on a project that was outside your comfort zone or switching to a new field entirely. Maybe you started something on the side: a blog, a podcast, an online store or a short course you built just because you were curious. These experiences often begin with uncertainty, but what they leave behind is energy.

Sometimes adventure shows up in play – a retreat, a workshop or an unexpected collaboration that pushed you into a new way of thinking. I remember a day in Singapore spent with senior executives, exploring the underground system like anthropologists. It sounds mundane, but it wasn't. Times when you were out of your routine, open-eyed, looking closely at something usually invisible. It was playful, surprising and full of discovery.

Ben remembers an unexpected invitation to travel to a South American city. He'd written a piece about digital infrastructure and the city leaders asked him to consult. It wasn't part of his plan but the experience – working in an unfamiliar culture, solving real challenges – left a lasting impression. He still says it was one of the most energising things he's ever done.

For Mira, adventure came in a quieter form. She joined her local choir's tour of the Bavarian churches – an unusual thing for her to do. The travel, the music, the shared meals, the new spaces to perform in – it stirred something in her she hadn't felt in years. She didn't expect to love it as much as she did.

For Lucia, it was Ethiopia. She was just 23, working in a non-profit, surrounded by people whose values matched her own. It was intense, exhausting – and completely formative. Now she sometimes wonders: *Will I ever experience that depth of connection and purpose again?*

Your Story: An Adventure at Work

Tell me a story of when you felt exhilarated at work. Adventure at work demands courage, preparation and presence – and brings that unmistakable jolt of energy. What was the adventure? What did it take from you? What did it give back? *How might this story help you see where you want more adventure in your working life?*

Sometimes adventure doesn't require travel or novelty – it lives inside the work we already do. A presentation. A pitch. A performance. These moments might terrify us in the lead-up, but once we're in them, they can spark something powerful. They show us what it means to stretch and come alive. For me, one such moment lives clearly in the memory. It involved a stage, a suit and a few thousand people. Here's how it felt:

A Story of a Cherry-Red Suit – Radio City Music Hall, New York, 2005

Earlier in that week, I'd picked up my cherry-red silk suit. I'd dashed to the seamstress in east London, who'd just finished the final adjustments to my glorious jacket and a skirt. Yesterday, I'd packed it carefully in my carry-on luggage. Now, clothed in my new red silk suit, I'm waiting at the back of the stage. Glancing around, I see I'm surrounded by the paraphernalia of sound technicians wearing black and speaking in hushed tones.

Five minutes earlier, they've miked me up and I now stand in the wings of the stage for those last few minutes. I can hear the applause for the earlier speaker resonating through the hall. Then, I feel my heart rate increasing and a surge of adrenaline – that tantalising combination of fear and excitement. I'm trying to calm my nerves – reminding myself I've rehearsed my opening paragraph over and over again on the plane journey over. I glimpse the Master of Ceremonies stepping out onto the stage.

On that cue I step out onto the stage, at first dazzled by the footlights. Then as my eyes became accustomed to the light, I look out at the audience. This is the iconic Radio City Music Hall on Avenue of the Americas, home of the Rockettes, today hosting an international business conference. On a Rockette Day, the hall can be packed with almost 6,000 people arrayed across three tiers. Today, it's more like 4,000 people.

I look at the scale of the place, take a deep breath and launch into my rehearsed first paragraph. I've included a story and a joke and I can feel a wave of subdued laughter. I slightly relax, walk to the edge of the stage, open my arms and begin to talk. I can do this...

I can still conjure up the residual excitement of that moment. And I did not, by the way, become a fixture at Radio City Music Hall, but I did have that extraordinary exhilarating moment – that adventure.

How did your story feel to you – can you still feel the excitement it created?

It's rather amusing (to me at least) that even thinking about that memory makes me feel energised and excited. Sometimes these moments of exhilaration are woven into our lives through the thread of mastery. That was the case for me and I can sense the strength of that long thread connecting to the story of teaching at the college of higher education, decades earlier. And I'm not forgetting the connection with the home-sewn prim and proper grey flannel wool suit I'd stitched together for my first real job at British Airways. The red silk suit, no longer made by me, was crafted by a more competent seamstress. This was a garment that in the long history of garments, had marked my changing working identity and visually told 'the story of me'.

As you reflected on your own times of energy and excitement, like me, did you notice how these resonated with you, your sense of self and your sense of uniqueness? And how it connected with earlier parts of your life, perhaps also a link back to your own unique areas of mastery?

Activate Your Seeking System

You may never find yourself on a stage like that, in a cherry-red silk suit, facing thousands. That moment drew on years of my own particular thread of mastery – public speaking, storytelling, performance. But that doesn't mean you haven't had your own version of it.

Maybe it was a big presentation. A conversation you'd been dreading. A moment where you stood up, took the lead or did something you weren't sure you could pull off. Maybe your heart raced, your voice trembled, but when it was over, you felt more alive than before. That's the feeling I want you to look for. Because that's the thread of adventure pulling at you. You don't have to be on a stage, you just have to step forward.

You can feel it in your body – that moment when you're fully engaged, lit up from the inside. Your heart beats faster. Your attention sharpens. You're energised, not by adrenaline alone, but by a deep sense of connection to what you're doing. This isn't stress, it's aliveness.

Neuroscientists call this the activation of the seeking system – our brain's innate drive to explore, to learn, to move towards meaning. Jaak Panksepp, a pioneer in affective neuroscience, studied what happens in the brain when we're curious and filled with anticipation. He found that feelings of interest and engagement activate a neural circuit between the prefrontal cortex and the ventral striatum – areas associated with purpose, reward and drive.[1]

This seeking system isn't just about physical exploration; it's about emotional and cognitive movement – the sense that there's something worth discovering and that you're the one to do it. When the seeking system is alive, we feel open, energised, curious. But when it's switched off, something in us shuts down. As Panksepp puts it, 'When the seeking system is not active, human aspirations remain frozen in an endless winter of discontent.' Strong words, but I imagine you've felt the truth of them. The moments in your life where things flattened out – when your days felt repetitive, your imagination dulled, your forward momentum stalled. That's what it feels like when the seeking system is switched off. And that's why adventure matters – not for its drama, but for its ability to reawaken that inner current.

Yet too often at work we lack this sense of exhilaration. Here's data from a Gallup poll that shows 80 per cent of people say they don't feel they can be their best at work and 70 per cent say they're not engaged at work.[2] Perhaps there are times when you feel the same – not passionate about your work, not looking forward to working, bored and lacking the spark of creativity.

EXPERT VOICES: Dan Cable, Psychologist

Across this book I have sought the counsel of experts. Here, I turn to Dan Cable, Professor of Organisational Behaviour at London Business School, who studies energy, creativity and how people bring their true selves to work.[3] His book *Alive at Work: The Neuroscience of Helping Your People Love What They Do* explores energy at work. In both his research and his everyday behaviour, Dan epitomises energy and excitement – always ready for adventure. His lifelong fascination is how we create work that excites us and opens opportunities for exploration. I asked Dan what he has learned about the connection between energy, creativity and adventure at work.

When we talk about being alive at work, we're not just talking about motivation. We're talking about something deeper – about whether your job gives you a chance to feel curious, to feel useful, to feel that what you do matters. One of the most important systems in the brain is the seeking system. It's what drives us to explore, to experiment, to learn. It's what makes us want to grow – not because we have to, but because it feels good. That system evolved for a reason. And when it's activated, we experience positive emotions like excitement, interest and enthusiasm. We're more creative, we're more resilient. We take more initiative.

But in too many workplaces, the seeking system gets shut down. Not deliberately – but through control, measurement, standardisation. The focus is on compliance, not curiosity, so people begin to disengage. They do what's required, but they don't feel alive.

And when people feel physiological arousal – heart racing, mind active – they often interpret that as anxiety rather than anticipation. And that interpretation matters. If you assume you are under threat, you become more rigid, less open, less creative. But if you frame it as excitement – as a signal that you are doing something meaningful – you lean in.

What happens to your energy at work? When do you feel most alive and when do you start to shut down?

Dan's insight about the seeking system is clear: we are built to explore, to try, to stretch. But many of us end up in roles where our curiosity gets parked. Over time, that can dull more than just our performance – it can dull our sense of self.

You don't need to change jobs to reignite the seeking system but you do need to notice what's dimming it – and take one small step to turn the light back on.

Lucia and Nico: Paths to Feeling Alive

Lucia's adventure was visceral – the heat, the noise, the unfamiliarity. When she boarded the plane to Ethiopia with a single backpack, Nico stood back and watched, feeling a flicker of envy. Lucia was heading into the unknown, he was heading back to the office to finish a slide deck.

He visited her once that year. What struck him wasn't just the tin-roofed hut or the lack of running water, but how fully she had settled into the life. The bed was thin, the food unfamiliar, the mornings loud with unfamiliar sounds, but Lucia seemed lit up from the inside, alive in a way he hadn't seen before.

Nico craves rhythm, control, comfort. He packs the same running shoes for every business trip, stays in familiar hotels, orders what he can pronounce. His adventure is at work. He finds it in the rush of a high-stakes client meeting, the adrenaline of turning around a failing project, the late-night clarity when a complex solution finally clicks. It's not the destination that excites him, it's the pressure, the urgency, the edge of not quite knowing if he'll pull it off.

Lucia's adventures pull her far from home. Nico's keep him grounded, but alert. One seeks out the unknown in the world, the other finds it in challenge and intensity. Both are forms of courage, both are ways of stepping beyond comfort.

And you? Where do you find that feeling of being vividly alive – outwardly in place and people, or inwardly in stretch and risk?

REMEMBER PLAYFUL WORK

Not all adventure is bold or public. Sometimes, it is moments that surprise you: when you laugh out loud in a meeting, when you try something completely new, when you feel that brief, unmistakable sensation of being a child again – curious, engaged, free.

Your Story: Playful at Work

Tell me a story about when you felt really playful at work – maybe it was a workshop, a team challenge, or a trip somewhere new. What happened? How did it feel? What did you learn from it? *As you reflect, notice how play shows up in your work – and how you might welcome more of it.*

These are the moments when work becomes playful. When energy rises not from pressure, but from possibility. They may not happen often, but when they do, they stay with us. Here's one that stayed with me. It took place not in a classroom or an office, but deep underground – in the Mass Rapid Transit system of Singapore.

A Story of a Subway – Singapore, 2001

I'm in Singapore with a group of senior leaders from around the world – banking, aviation, energy, consumer goods. Today is a day of adventure. We are exploring the city's Mass Rapid Transit (MRT) system like anthropologists: no agenda, no guide, just notebooks, questions and open eyes. With 140 stations, 200 kilometres of line and moving more than three million people a day, the subway is key to the city's efficiency. We are here to explore why it's so efficient, clean and timely. We only have one day. By 6 p.m., we're expected back to present our findings to the MRT's senior leadership.

We fan out in teams and head straight to the nearest station. For most of us, it's our first time on the MRT and we're struck by the clarity of the signage, the spotless platforms, the ease of navigation. On board the trains, we talk to commuters, observing carefully, asking about their experience. At one station, we chat with the staff about daily routines and what makes the system run smoothly. We hop from stop to stop, comparing notes, laughing at ourselves as we scribble in notebooks and get politely stared at by bemused locals.

By early evening, we return to headquarters with a cascade of questions: how do they sustain this level of order? What's the culture like? Is it profitable? One of our group, a New Yorker, is particularly fascinated – he's used to a far messier commute. Over dinner, the conversations deepen. We talk about what we noticed, what surprised us, what this way of working reveals about Singapore – and ourselves. It's playful, unexpected, rich with discovery.

What did you feel when you read my story of being playful at work? It wasn't a grand adventure – just an afternoon spent on a subway. And frankly, spending a day in a subway hardly feels like an 'adventure'. I take the London Tube often and it doesn't feel like an adventure but I have included this story precisely for that reason. Yes, adventures can be bold and amazing and exhilarating, but they can also be commonplace. The difference between my normal journey on the London Tube and the adventure on the Singapore MRT is that this was a day of playfulness, no real outcome in mind (except the promise to observe like an anthropologist), no plan of action. And for these senior teams, coming from jobs where every minute would be scheduled, a blessed relief to simply go with the flow, to hang out, to open their eyes wide and to be excited by the company of each other.

I guess the point is this: you don't have to climb Everest or row across the Atlantic or walk through an African state to have an adventure and feel energised (though these are all enormous adventures). All you need is some space, a playful mindset and people who are prepared to play with you.

We are most energised and alive when we have a safe zone to play and connect with each other. Here, I'm making the link to the *Knowing* thread, the idea that when you're relaxed and yet attentive, you're not simply comparing ideas with what you've heard. You are embarking on a more active process, challenging your long-held assumptions, bringing your curiosity and excitement to the fore. In the days that followed the MRT adventure, we reflected with the group about how you learn from these adventures and brought in the model of appreciative inquiry[4] as a way of thinking about how to understand and converse.

Create More Energising Work

What's stopping you having more exhilarating and playful work? I asked Dan Cable to tell me what he had seen:

> I've seen that how we work and the context of our work can really sap our energy. A real barrier to feeling alive at work is that we experienced being overly controlled by measurement and monitoring. We work in a job where the tasks are so narrowly defined that there is no space for us to experiment or play. When our jobs become so specialised, we feel constrained. Corporate policies can also stifle our desire to explore and try new things. That's very much the case in companies with deeply entrenched assumptions and policies about control and standardised performance metrics, incentives and punishments, promotion tournaments and so on. Without perhaps realising it, these organisations are deactivating their employees' 'seeking' systems and activating their 'fear' systems. And if you are working in one of these organisations, then over time this narrows your perceptions and encourages your submission.

> We noticed that when people work in these types of corporate environments, over time they develop *learned helplessness*. They give up and passively accept what happens, they feel there is nothing they can do. If you find yourself in such a situation, this alters your emotional stage (you grow resigned), it lowers your motivation (you no longer even try) and it changes your cognitive reasoning (you generalise your experience to other environments). So, you find yourself in a crossfire between your biological seeking systems and the realities of your organisation. Your built-in biology urges you to explore your environments, experiment and learn – but you feel it's not possible to do any of these things so you begin to ignore the urges of your seeking system – you shut off and your anxieties dominate.

How did you feel about Dan's explanation? Have there been workplaces where you have felt helpless and frustrated, when there is simply no space for playfulness and energy?

If any part of you recognises that feeling – of stagnation, of routine, of a sense that your work is no longer sparking something inside you – here are four practical, energising steps to help reignite your curiosity and reawaken your sense of possibility.

Start Small

You don't need to upend everything or embark on a radical reinvention. Begin with a manageable project, something new or adjacent to your existing responsibilities. Even if it's informal – something you volunteer for or something you simply take the initiative to shape – it can offer a fresh context for thinking and acting. Look for chances to step into a different space. Can you ask to solve a different kind of problem, something slightly outside your usual domain? Even a minor stretch in your scope can reintroduce a sense of challenge and novelty, which are often precursors to renewed engagement.

Ask Deeper Questions

Instead of defaulting to the familiar 'What do I need to do?', try reframing your internal dialogue. Ask yourself: 'What would make this more interesting for me?' or 'Is there a way I could approach this task in a way I haven't tried before?' These questions can shift you from a passive mindset – of completing tasks – to an active one of exploration. They invite you to imagine what's possible, not just what's required. They also help you uncover elements of a task that might align more closely with your strengths, values or learning goals.

Find Micro-Moments of Ownership

These are small but potent opportunities to make a task or process more your own. Could you tweak how something is done – just a little? Is there space to add your insight, your design, your way of thinking? Perhaps it's how you run a meeting, prepare a report or present an idea. When you inject something personal – your style, your thoughtfulness – it transforms even mundane tasks into expressions of your agency. These modest experiments can reawaken a sense of control and contribution that often fades when work feels repetitive.

Talk to Energising People

The people around us matter more than we often realise. If you're feeling flat, seek out colleagues, collaborators or mentors who exude energy, optimism or curiosity. Their enthusiasm can be contagious. Even a brief conversation with someone who sees things differently or who is excited about what they're working on can jolt you into a new perspective. Sometimes, we don't need more time or more resources, we just need a fresh spark. The right person can help you remember why you started doing this work in the first place or show you new directions you hadn't considered.

These steps won't fix everything overnight but taken together – starting small, asking different questions, owning your work in micro-ways and finding energisers around you – they can form a quiet but powerful path back to engagement. And in that journey, you might rediscover not only your curiosity, but also your sense of meaning and momentum.

EMBRACE GRAND ADVENTURES

Some adventures are light and playful. Others are deeper, more stretching – what I think of as *grand adventures*. These are the ones that take you far from home, far from routine and often far from who you thought you were. They take time, courage and a little bit of letting go.

For some, these big adventures involve travel – across cultures, across landscapes, across different ways of living. For others, it might be a sabbatical, a solo retreat, a volunteering trip or a career break that gives them a new perspective on what matters. These adventures don't require money so much as intent. They're not about luxury, they're about stepping into the world with open eyes and an open heart.

In a long life, we have the chance to build in experiences like this – not just once, but many times. They don't happen by accident. We have to make space for them, notice the moment when the opportunity appears and be brave enough to say yes. What follows is one such story from my own life – an adventure that began on a roundabout in the Lake District and took me all the way to a kibbutz on the edge of Israel.

A Story of Hitchhiking to Israel – Keswick, 1976

Mum dropped me off at Keswick roundabout. In the Lake District there are few roundabouts. The town of Keswick has a roundabout that connects Penrith in the north of England on the newly built motorway – the M6 and the M1 that snakes down to London.

My plan is to hitchhike to Israel to complete my final-year undergraduate dissertation on a study of the child rearing practices in a kibbutz. I've chosen a community located on the east side of Israel, near the Lebanese border. My aim is to contrast these child rearing practices in the kibbutz with another child practice – children in an orphanage in Liverpool.

I begin by hitchhiking down to London and meet my travel companion. Extraordinarily, at another roundabout in Paris we are picked up by a Lebanese businessman. He is driving a Mercedes he's bought in France and is planning to go to Beirut to sell the car (it turns out that second-hand Mercedes cars are a highly prized accessory in the Lebanon).

My next memory is our glorious entry to the city of Istanbul over the straits of Bosphorus, a long, elegant bridge connecting Europe and the Asian continent. We've heard from other travellers about the famous 'Pudding Shop'. It turns out to be basically a rundown place, but for a few lira we can roll our sleeping bags on the roof of the shop and wake up to the calls of the nearby mosques.

Then my memory is filled with the scent of jasmine. We are now in Syria, at the ancient town of Aleppo. Walking through the tight, dark passageways of the city, I come across vast round trays of freshly cooked honey cakes – the air pungent with their fragrance. A scent memory that remains with me. Later, we travel to the ancient city of Palmyra, a ruin since its destruction in 273BC. Sleeping that night under the stars, I extract a small scorpion from my sleeping bag before gingerly putting my feet into it.

Jumping on a local bus, I cross the border from Syria to the neighbouring country of Jordan and into the Sinai desert that surrounds the ancient city of Petra. There is no accommodation in the city and I'm invited by a Bedouin family to sit with them in their tent and share their simple evening meal of bread and goat. My teeth grind on the sand as I eat the unleavened bread cooked in an open oven in the desert floor. I am sitting with an old Bedouin woman with her long flowing black thawab. I feel incredibly peaceful, looking out from the tent into the vast desert sky.

How does this story feel to you? How did you respond to the idea of that kind of adventure – leaving home, stepping into something unknown, going further than you've gone before? Does it sound exciting? A little terrifying? Out of reach? Or exactly what you've been longing for?

Your Story: A Grand Adventure

Tell me a story about an adventure you have had – at any time in your life. It doesn't have to be dramatic; it may be something small but bold. What did you do? Who was with you? What did it awaken in you? *What does this story remind you about your courage, and the adventures you still want to take?*

The thread of adventure has run strongly through my own life – and it's something I've encouraged in my children as well. I wanted them to know the world not just through books or screens, but by being in it – curious, open and sometimes just a little bit lost.

Christian, my eldest son, took that invitation seriously. At 18, between school and university, he set out on a year of discovery – working as a (very amateur) journalist in India, China and Singapore. One story from that time has stayed with me. It's vivid, slightly terrifying – and a powerful reminder of what it means to step into the unknown.

A Story of Arriving in Mumbai, 2008

Christian told me this story soon after it happened. For those unfamiliar with Mumbai transport circa 2008, a 'tuk-tuk' is a (very noisy) three-wheeled vehicle powered by a (polluting) motorbike engine. This was how he described that first arrival:

He landed in Mumbai, stepping into the dense heat and clamour that hits you the moment you leave the airport. Determined to save money, he waved away the taxis and found a tuk-tuk driver outside, pointing to his destination on a crumpled piece of paper. They agreed on a price and off they went – Christian squeezed into the back as the rickety vehicle bumped and rattled through the chaos of the city.

Over the noise of traffic, the driver struck up a conversation, telling Christian he lived in Dharavi, one of the largest slums that circles Mumbai. Then, quite casually, he asked, 'Would you like to come meet my family?'

And Christian – jetlagged, aged 18, freshly arrived from London – said yes.

They veered off the main road into a warren of tiny, potholed alleys, descending into the shadows of overhanging tin and timber. Christian began to realise he was carrying his passport, all his clothes and every rupee he had for the first part of his travels. He had no idea where he was.

Eventually they stopped outside a dark set of rooms and the driver jumped out, taking Christian's bag. He spoke softly to an older man – his father, Christian assumed – and then to a young boy standing nearby. The boy disappeared inside and moments later, sprinted off down the street.

Christian was invited in, given a low stool to sit on. The adrenaline of the journey began to wear off. Jet lag hit. Sweat soaked his T-shirt. His mind began to spiral: what if the boy had gone to fetch a gang? What if this was a trap?

Ten long minutes passed. Then the boy reappeared, grinning, holding a single cold bottle of Coca-Cola. He handed it over proudly. Christian learned that the driver's father had scraped together enough rupees to buy this one bottle and had sent the boy to the local café to fetch it.

There was only one bottle – and in proud silence, the entire family watched as Christian drank it.

When Christian first told me this, I felt a wave of emotion – gratitude that he was safe, awe at his courage (and yes, perhaps his youthful recklessness) and a deep appreciation for the generosity of a family who, with so little, gave so much.

And for Christian? I think that moment marked the beginning of a thread that would run through his working life. Years later, I asked him what that year of travelling and working had taught him. He said it helped him realise that while journalism intrigued him, it wasn't his vocation. More profoundly, it gave him an early and unforgettable lesson in humility – and in the generosity of others.

I've been thinking about that. About how early work experiences – especially those that push us outside our comfort zone – can stay with us for decades. They don't just teach us skills, they teach us how to pay attention. They give us glimpses into lives unlike our own. They expand what we notice – and what we care about.

What about you? Have you ever had a moment – early or late in your working life – that cracked something open? That made you more curious, more grateful, more awake to the world around you?

Sometimes it's the work itself, sometimes it's what happens on the margins. Either way, these moments can be seeds – threads of experience that, with time, shape who we become.

Next is my final story of an adventure – tinged with insights and sorrow. Chad is a landlocked country in north-central Africa. Our plan was to visit Zakouma National Park and the incredible positive impact the charity African Parks has had on this country:

A Story of a Marketplace, Chad, 2017

It's market day in Kach Kacha and there is much excitement. Hundreds of people from the neighbouring villages have travelled from the break of dawn to be sure to get a place. Many have ridden miles on donkeys and by the time Nigel and I arrive at 10 in the morning, the donkey park is already filling up with these beasts of burden – glad to be resting as the midday sun brings the temperature up and protected from the dust swirls around them.

I'm so happy to be here – for the truth is I love markets and this is a market with many wonders. In this region of Chad, many people are nomadic, following their animals and the seasonal shifting of the lush grass. So, this market has a temporary feel – hastily erected tents, rickety restaurant chairs and tables set into the dust, goods laid out on the ground with their owners squatting next to them.

Two days ago, we had flown over the countryside of Chad in a light aircraft to arrive at the desert camp where we are staying. As I gazed from the aircraft portholes, I saw the land of Chad laid out below. Many circular villages, each with huts radiating out from one central hut to make a daisy motif. The explanation is that when a daughter of the family has a family of her own, she is given the land adjacent to her parents' house on which to construct her own house. Each house made of local mud and thatched – no electricity and no paved roads connecting the villages.

Now, as I look around the marketplace, there is a working practice I have never seen before. In the street in front of me are two men sitting on the ground in front of their simple forges. Each has made a hole in the ground and in that hole is a small pile of charcoal which, with the help of a bellows, now glows bright. The heat from these little charcoal pits is sufficient to melt the tin that makes up many of the utensils. Around them are arrayed the utensils they will work on over the course of the morning: bent spoons, teapots with holes in them, misshapen bowls. One by one, the metal worker picks up the object and with the simplest of tools, straightens the spoons, fixes the holes in the teapots, hammers the bowls back to shape. For these semi-nomadic people who carry everything they own on the back of a donkey, each utensil is precious and fixing them is part of its long history.

How very unlike the working lives with which I am familiar. The lives of these nomadic tribesmen have been repeated for hundreds of years: the donkeys, the charcoal pits, the prized utensils. Theirs is a pre-industrial working life based often on barter and exchange. A life which is fragile with little resilience. A drought, a local war lord, refugees from another state – all disrupt this life.

I watched the news with tears in my eyes in early 2023 as some regions of Sudan erupted into violence. Pictures of exhausted parents piling their babies and all their worldly goods onto donkeys to begin the trek into Eastern Chad, away from violence. A path that would take them through arid desert and finally to makeshift refugee camps. As this part of the Sahel becomes warmer and more arid, disputes over water and natural resources are flaring up with increasing frequency and once families are on the move, they become incredibly vulnerable. The people I saw in the market had very little – but they had a place to return to and family around them. At the end of the day, they would saddle their donkeys and make the journey back to their home villages. Now they are joined by families who have crossed the border from Sudan, carrying what they can after fleeing violence in Darfur. They join millions of others across Africa uprooted by the twin forces of drought and conflict, forced to move in search of safety and survival.

What I witnessed in Chad – and what later unfolded there – has stayed with me. These kinds of adventures aren't always uplifting. Sometimes they stir sorrow, humility, even helplessness. But they also deepen our capacity to care, to notice, to be present in the world as it is.

As I think about my own Grand Adventures, I realise they are a chance to explore who I am – to create a sense of my multiple selves. They mark a passage in time, giving me a sense of what has been and what could be, helping me to connect more deeply to myself and be more empathic to others.

Glimpse Your Multiple Selves

It seems to me these times of excitement, exhilaration, playfulness together define who we are. I've thought a great deal about these adventures from the vantage point of my seventh decade of life. I realise these adventures (of which the Israel expedition was only one) began to define who I was, and who I became. I am a professor in a business school – yet I'm also partly the girl with the Peruvian skirt and partly the girl who hitch-hiked across Europe, then Turkey, Syria, Jordan and then Israel. In the fragments that make up my identity, the three months I spent on that adventure have a disproportionate weight.

These periods of adventure and excitement are also times of self-knowledge. As I reflect on the Keswick roundabout and the memories of Aleppo and Petra, I'm struck by my younger self. By my risk taking, courage – and foolishness. This adventure gave me an opportunity to think about myself and my world: that the world is an extraordinary place, that there are generous and kind people, and that to embark on an adventure is one of the great joys of life.

Mark Life's Passage

Before we move on, let's take a moment to think about the adventures that have shaped you. They might not have involved distant cities or desert tents, but you'll know them by the way they live in your memory – bright, visceral, often defining. These are the moments that mark a passage in your life. They're more than stories, they're part of how you became who you are. That passage of time is very much at the heart of the story my son Christian told me. For while we can recall adventures and their exciting memories, we can rarely recreate them. Here, I am reminded of the conversation with Robert Rowland Smith about the nature of our past. This is what he told me:

> We stand in the flow of time. Once you step out of the river and step back in, it's never the same river. You cannot go back. Our mind is able to move across time – we can remember episodes from the past or look forward to the future. The body inhabits space – it has no such licence. From birth onwards we cling to time, forever streaming one way. Not only can we never go back: we cannot outpace time and get ahead of ourselves.

I'm thinking again about Robert's phrase: 'Once you step out of the river and step back in, it's never the same river.' I can return to Aleppo in my memory, but not in body. The city I walked through in the 1970s – alive with scents and sounds – no longer exists. The Syrian civil war that began in 2011 devastated much of the historic Old Town. I've never gone back – possibly never will.

But I did return to Jordan and the magnificent ancient city of Petra. In 2021, I found myself there again – not as a young hitchhiker, but as a guest on a curated trip with fellow patrons of the British Museum. This time, I slept not in a desert tent, but in crisp linen sheets in a hotel now built just outside the city gates.

These are snapshots caught in a moment in time. Creating memories that can be more vivid than much of everyday life. In the weaving of our working life, we can pull the thread from one time to another – as I did when I returned to Petra – viscerally, vividly connecting what I was, to who I am now.

And as I pulled the thread of time, these two events, though separated by time, become closer. And though some of the context can be the same (Aleppo might no longer exist as it did, but Petra is similar), I am not the same person. The second visit to Petra, I slept in a comfortable bed with linen: how would I have felt about sleeping on the ground in a Bedouin tent? The first time I was alive to the scents of the town and wandered around. Certainly, I missed much and knew little. The second time I came to Petra prepared – I'd read in advance about the city, was accompanied by a knowledgeable group, knew more. But that does not negate the intense feelings of that first time – or the visceral memories I still have.

It feels like in the weaving of our life, these times of adventure and excitement are times when the thread changes. These are the stories and narratives that help you connect more deeply with who you were. They are also an invitation to think about your future. For me, the question for my future self is: 'do I have what it takes to wander around the world as I did in my twenties? Have I become so used to linen sheets that Bedouin tents are an impossibility? Will I ever be able to feel again the innocence of simply wandering without the burden of knowledge?'

Think back to a time when you did something bold, unfamiliar or new. How old were you? What did you learn – not just about the world, but about yourself?

Now ask: if you returned to that place, that experience, that version of you, what would feel the same? What would feel completely different? You don't need to recreate the past, but you can honour the adventurer you were – and ask how they might guide you now.

You don't need to be 20 to have an adventure but there's something about the first adventures that stays with us. They carry a kind of rawness, a clarity of emotion, a sense that the world is opening up. Before we go on, take a moment to reflect. What adventures – big or small – have opened your eyes in a way you didn't expect? Where have you been that changed how you see your own life? And how do those moments sit with you now?

We all have an intrinsic urge to explore and curiosity is a potent emotion. I see how it helps us move away from our comfort zone and old habits, and in doing so reduces our natural resistance to change. Exploring nourishes our imagination, gives us stories to tell.

Shift Your Mindset

Reflection: what's stopping you and how could you overcome these barriers and be more excited and alive?

Given how essentially human and joyful it is to have work that makes us feel excited and adventures that nourish our sense of self, why is it so hard to have these experiences in our working life? Why do we let lethargy or even anxiety become our dominant emotional state? As I talk to people about what is stopping them being playful, having adventures, they talked about the work itself and the time squeeze – they simply don't have enough time.

My advice, as you think about your long working life, is to consider how you are going to make time for adventures. I was able to fit in my adventure hitchhiking to Israel as part of my final year at university – a period designed to give stretches of time to think and explore. My son Christian used the potential year between school and college to see the world. Once working, these unencumbered times become less frequent and more precious. I did not take a sabbatical or a substantial break between jobs, yet I can see others who have and how much they gained from these experiences.

To make time for adventure requires a shift in mindset about what the fabric of a long working life looks like and to imagine multiple stages of life. This could mean taking time out following a sequence – perhaps six months break every five years. Or it could mean developing a portfolio where within any timeframe you are able to switch to various jobs. I am doing this now as I switch from an academic teaching role to the founder of a consulting practice, to a writer and a speaker, to someone who goes on adventures.

Later, in the final chapter of this book, I will invite you to look again at how you are imaging the weave of the fabric of your working life – and whether indeed there are more opportunities for these Grand Adventures than you imagine. For now, let's take a closer look at actions you can take now – and promises to your future self.

ADVENTURE: Putting it into Practice

Three Actions to Take Now

1. **Say yes to one small adventure this week.**
   It doesn't have to be dramatic – a new route home, a bold idea in a meeting, a different recipe. The point is unfamiliarity – something that stirs curiosity or delight.
2. **Revisit a time when you felt most alive.**
   Where were you? What were you doing? What made it feel vivid? Use this memory as a compass to guide new choices.
3. **Schedule something unfamiliar into your calendar.**
   A new class, a new person, a new place. Don't wait for the perfect opportunity, give adventure a time and place to begin.

Three Promises to My Future Self

1. **I will keep choosing aliveness over comfort – at least sometimes.**
   Even when it's easier to stay where I am, I will stretch towards what makes me feel awake and engaged.
2. **I will resist the trap of routine in a long life.**
   Stability is valuable – but I will make room for wonder, disruption and renewal. I will keep making memories, not just managing time.
3. **I will pursue adventures that reflect who I'm becoming.**
   What thrills me may shift, but I'll keep seeking experiences that nourish growth, joy and imagination.

Don't let routines close in. A 100-Year Life gives you not just more years, but more chances to explore. Over time, adventure becomes one of the threads that keeps your life vibrant and open, reminding you that possibility doesn't fade with age. Whether it's a bold leap or a small spark, each act of adventure helps you weave a story of renewal, discovery and curiosity across the decades of a long life.

PART THREE:

Short-Term Choices, Long-Term Promises

LIVING FORWARD

The long lives ahead of us give us space to evolve – but they also ask us to take responsibility for how we live them. Part Three helps you balance action today with the needs of your future self.

You've already travelled far in this book. We've explored eight threads – mastery, cooperation, knowing, amplifying, intimacy, friendship, calm and adventure – discovering which is strong, which threads are frayed, and how each can be strengthened, or rewoven across a lifetime. Now comes the pivot: what do you do with this knowledge?

Here lies a central tension: the present demands action, yet the future calls for imagination. Focus only on today and life risks becoming fragmented; focus only on the future you may lose energy and joy. To live forward is to do both – acting with intention now while recognising that your future self is not fixed but continually shaped by the choices you make.

Living Forward is about this work of agency. It asks how you balance urgency and uncertainty, how you prepare without predicting, and how you move into the future with courage rather than paralysis.

Chapter 14 takes up these questions directly. It explores the images we hold of our future selves, the patterns that are shaping working life, and the shift in responsibility between worker and organisation. It shows that while you cannot fully know your future self, you can prepare – by strengthening your threads, by making promises, and by acting with intention now.

This is the invitation of *Living Forward*: not to follow a perfect blueprint, but to embrace a lifelong practice of weaving – reflecting, reimagining, renewing – so that when you look back, the fabric of your life is strong, resilient and uniquely your own.

CHAPTER 14

Your Future Self

IMAGINE YOUR FUTURE SELF

Imagine standing back at the age of 80 and surveying your working life – if you are in your early thirties, like my two sons, you will be looking back 50 years.

What do you see and how would you describe your working life? What did your life look like – what were the highlights, the crises?

Now let's reverse the observation. Think back to when you were young, perhaps in your teens. What were the images you had of your future?

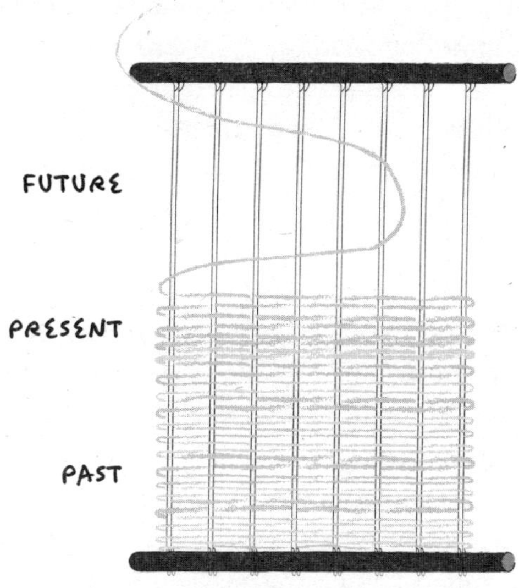

In weaving a life, we draw on stories of the past, an understanding of who we are now, and images of who we might yet become. Psychologists Hazel Markus and Paula Nurius offer a helpful way to think about these imagined futures.[1] They suggest that each of us carries several 'possible selves': the self we *hope* for, the self we *expect*, and the self we *fear*. These imagined versions of ourselves act like forces – some pulling us forward, others pushing us away from paths we do not want to follow.

Your *Hoped-for Self* is the future in which you flourish. You may picture this self as confident, creative, purposeful or deeply connected to others. The details will differ for each of us, but the function is the same: this image helps orient your aspirations. It invites you to stretch.

Your *Expected Self* is subtle but equally powerful. It is the future you can realistically imagine – shaped by your environment, your past choices, and the assumptions you hold about what is possible for you. This self often guides the decisions we make day to day, sometimes more than we realise.

Your *Feared Self* represents the future you wish to avoid: perhaps a version of you that is stuck, lonely, irrelevant or overwhelmed. This self is not a sign of dysfunction. It can be a healthy part of self-regulation, alerting you to risks and motivating you to take preventative steps. But when the feared self becomes too dominant, it can narrow your vision of the future and create anxiety or paralysis.

For many people – myself included – the *Hoped-for Self* is the hardest to picture clearly. The future contains so many possibilities that the outline remains sketchy. And as the psychologist Randall Peterson reminds us, our future self will not be a radical departure from who we already are. Personality tends to remain stable. Our future self is a variation on our current themes. Some parts of our world will change, but others will stay recognisable. Understanding this can make the idea of the future self feel less abstract, more grounded in the rhythms of our own lives.

Your Story: Your Future Self

Was there a time in your life when you had a concrete image of your future self? What was the self you imagined? How clear was the picture? How did it guide your choices? And how might this story of your future self shape the next chapter of your 100-year life?

When I look back at my pile of stories, I find only a few moments where I imagined my future self. Here's one from adolescence, when dreaming about the future is almost a full-time occupation for most 16-year-olds.

A Story of Hot Pants (spring 1970) and a Velvet Cape (summer 1972)

I'm walking up Helvellyn mountain with Dad, lost in daydreams of my future self. An image is taking shape.

The future 'me' is an image. I am wearing a pair of cream hot pants, pale tights, boots that lace to above my knee and a cream polo-neck sweater. I've seen something similar in the pages of *Petticoat* magazine and know this is definitely the future me.

Armed with the trusted Singer sewing machine, a *Vogue* pattern capable of adaptation and off-cuts of silk from the local curtain fabric shop, Mum and I begin to cut, pin and sew the hot pants. Then money from my waitressing job at Pillar House buys the boots. Not exactly the glamorous (and dare I say sexy?) thigh-length boots I had in mind, but a perfectly serviceable pair that finish just below my knee and have the requisite laces up the front. The cream striped polo neck is then an easy purchase. I survey the new me – I feel like a million dollars.

Fast forward now 17 and again marching in rain behind Dad, daydreaming. I'm going to university that September and I sense this is an opportunity to explore a completely new identity. I will no longer be the girl from a small town in the valley of Cumberland – I can be anything. I explore the possibilities and over a number of walks, an image of my future self emerges. I imagine entering the university city and striding down the main street. Clasped around my shoulders is a flowing full-length bottle green velvet cape with a peacock blue silk lining. The cape has a large hood capable of drooping over my eyes. Very mysterious.

It's back to the sewing machine, *Vogue* pattern and the remnants box of the local fabric shop. Once complete, I bundle the cape into my case for university. And I do indeed walk down the street wearing this glorious full-length cape with a hood, though I cannot recollect whether it had the impact I had hoped.

Did you ever have a complete vision of your future self – and do you have one now? Many people don't. When I look back, my clearest images were not of what I would *do*, but of what I would *wear*: hot pants with knee-high boots, a velvet cape sweeping through a university town. I couldn't picture my studies or future career – only my future outfit.

That's often how we imagine the future: in fragments, vivid but incomplete. An outfit, a job title, a place. These sketches are shaped as much by fantasy as by intention. The fuller picture only emerges as we live – making choices, encountering surprises, and revising the image until we discover what truly matters.

Act Into Your Future

Here, I return to Herminia Ibarra's insight: 'When we imagine our future self, we are inevitably constrained by what we have already experienced and what we see others doing.' As a teenager, I could picture my outfits, but not my life as a writer. I read voraciously – Dostoevsky, Flaubert, Camus, Woolf, de Beauvoir – but knew no one who wrote for a living. The gap between my own clumsy writing and their brilliance felt unbridgeable. That version of me lay outside my field of reference.

At 16 and 17 my vision of the future was less about what I'd *do* – and more about what I'd *wear*. Only later through action – side projects, late-night data analysis and anxious presentations, did a different self begin to emerge. The patterns we weave rarely start as fixed designs, they take shape through experience – we act our way into the future.

My teenage visions were vivid but incomplete – fragments rather than a map. It was only through doing, experimenting, failing and learning that a more grounded self took shape. And with that emerging self came something else: the beginnings of a pattern, a sense of how my working life might unfold over time. We rarely see these patterns early on, but they reveal themselves gradually as we act our way into the future.

SEE WORK LIFE PATTERNS EMERGE

As you think about your future self, you also begin to imagine the shape your working life might take. In the early years, this shape is rarely clear. It forms gradually, as experiences accumulate and a version of yourself becomes more recognisable. Over time, what once felt like disconnected choices starts to reveal a pattern.

Across generations, these patterns of working life appear again and again – sometimes crafted deliberately, sometimes formed by circumstance or habit. They are not prescriptions or paths you must follow. Rather, they offer a way to understand the landscape you are moving through. And in a longer life, being able to recognise these patterns matters. Each carries its own rhythm, its own opportunities, and its own constraints. Seeing them helps you navigate more intentionally, choosing the path that best fits who you are becoming.

The Three-Stage Pattern

For many of our parents and grandparents, life unfolded in three distinct stages: first full-time education, then full-time work and finally full-time retirement. This three-stage pattern was neat, linear and for some, reassuring. Institutions – schools, companies, pensions – were built to support it. Here's how it looks:

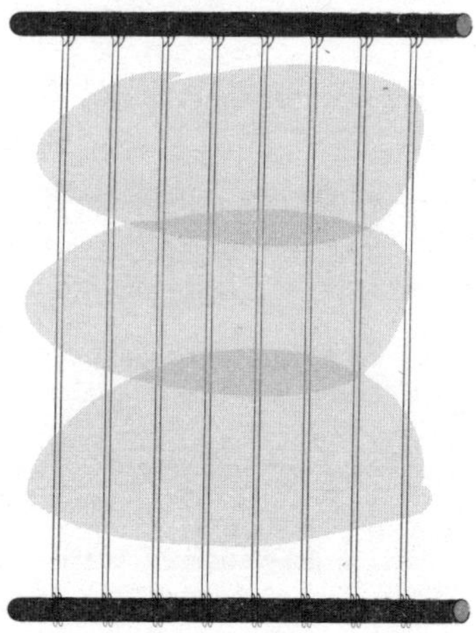

The Three-Stage Pattern

There is an elegance to this model. It offered stability and clarity: few transitions to navigate, clear age-based cohorts moving through each stage, and an easy way to describe one's place in the world – 'I'm in education', 'I'm working', 'I'm retired'.

Yet when stretched across a 100-year life, this pattern begins to show its cracks. A single front-loaded period of education leaves you vulnerable to becoming obsolete. Fifty years of continuous full-time work, from your twenties to your seventies, is unrealistic for most people – emotionally, physically and practically. And retiring at 65 when you may live into your nineties risks decades on a fixed income, decades in which contribution, growth and renewal can be prematurely set aside.

What once felt elegant can now feel confining. The simplicity that served earlier generations does not always serve a longer, more varied working life.

The Multi-Stage Pattern

As lives lengthened, the tidy three-stage model began to loosen and stretch. Education, work and retirement no longer fit neatly into single blocks, and so a new pattern emerged: the multi-stage life. It looks something like this:

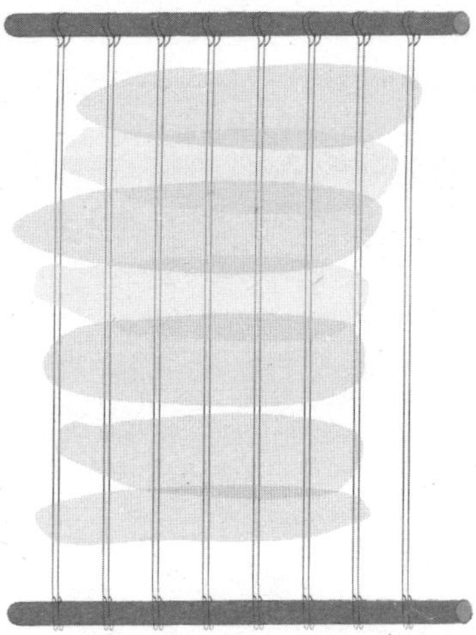

The Multi-Stage Pattern

In the multi-stage pattern, there are more steps along the way – a gap year here, a midlife sabbatical there, periods of parental leave, retraining or phased retirement. Life is still broadly structured and still roughly sequenced by age, but now there are pauses built in, moments to step out, step back or step sideways.

This pattern brings welcome flexibility. It allows for more switching, more transitions and more opportunities to assemble a working life that fits your needs and circumstances. Yet it also introduces new complexity: each transition requires navigation, and each choice carries implications for skills, identity, finances and wellbeing.

The multi-stage pattern is an improvement on the simplicity of the three-stage life, but it rests on a familiar assumption – that life unfolds in a predictable order. And in a long life shaped by uncertainty, reinvention and changing aspirations, that assumption may no longer hold.

The Portfolio Pattern

Then there is a pattern that doesn't climb at all but spreads wide: the portfolio pattern. Instead of completing one stage before beginning the next, you hold several roles at the same time. Teacher and parent. Volunteer and writer. Consultant and learner. Caregiver and adventurer. Some roles fuel each other; others compete for attention. But together they create a fabric that feels dynamic and alive.

The portfolio pattern reflects a world in which work, learning, caring and contribution no longer sit in tidy chronological boxes. It offers variety, autonomy and renewal – but also demands coordination, boundaries and constant rebalancing.

This is the pattern I live now, and perhaps you do too:

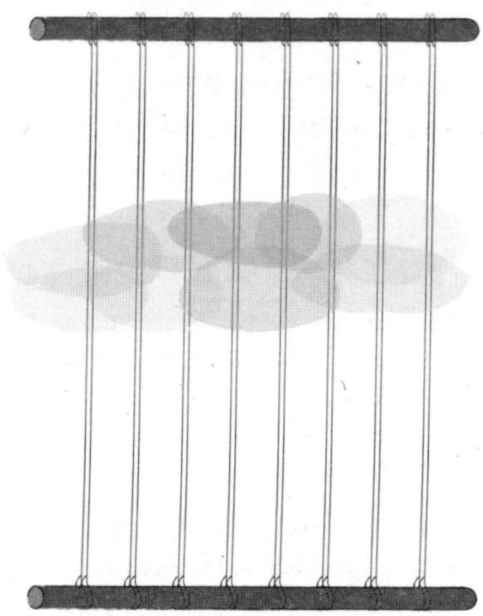

The Portfolio Pattern

When the Portfolio Pattern first emerged in the 1980s and 1990s, it was often viewed as a late-career strategy – a way for semi-retired consultants or seasoned professionals to ease into flexibility. But that has changed. Today, people in their twenties, thirties, sixties – and every decade in between – are actively shaping portfolio lives.

Of course, this pattern has its challenges. The biggest is identity stretch. When you move between roles – teacher, founder, parent, volunteer, learner – it's easy to feel fragmented. Who are you when you do so many things? What deserves your attention? What inevitably falls away?

A portfolio life demands resilience and self-trust. Identity can stretch thin when you are pulled in multiple directions. Yet the rewards are real: energy, creativity and the freedom to live more fully now, not only later. In the past, many people waited until retirement to explore passions or experiment with new ways of living. Today, that exploration can begin in midlife – or even earlier.

The Portfolio Pattern reflects what a 100-Year Life makes possible: a way of working that's fluid, adaptable and uniquely your own.

Discover Your Unique Pattern

These patterns – the Three-Stage Life, the Multi-Stage and the Portfolio – aren't rules. They're tools. Ways of seeing. For some, one pattern might feel like a natural fit; for others the real power lies in blending them: choosing what fits now, shifting as life changes, combining structure with freedom.

That's the gift of a long life. You don't have to follow a fixed model. You can create a pattern that's uniquely your own – woven from your circumstances, your choices, your values and the threads you want to strengthen next.

The truth is you don't have to choose between these patterns. In a 100-Year Life, you can move between them as your needs, ambitions and circumstances evolve. You might begin with a multi-stage pattern, moving sequentially through education, work, a sabbatical, parental leave. This can build foundational threads: Mastery, Cooperation, Intimacy – supported by rhythm, structure and institutional structure. Later you might shift into a portfolio pattern: blending roles, experimenting with side projects, balancing caregiving with creative work. This horizontal phase can reawaken threads like Adventure, Knowing and Calm.

Or the sequence might reverse: you may start with a diverse portfolio in your twenties, then choose to anchor into a more linear path for stability and return to a portfolio life later, on your own terms.

The point is this: your pattern doesn't have to be fixed. It can evolve, recombine and stretch across time. That's the freedom – and also the responsibility – of a longer life. Recognising your pattern is the first step; shaping it is the next.

TAKE AGENCY AND RESPONSIBILITY

Once you recognise the patterns a working life can take, the question becomes: *what is your role in shaping these patterns?* Here I return to Robert Rowland Smith's observation we explored earlier:

> Develop agency of your own. So that when something less advantageous occurs, you can look into your cupboard of personal supplies for dealing with it – and find that it is full and not empty. Having fate, as we all do, means being vulnerable. It calls us away from others and into a future that we can never completely predict.

That idea - preparing ourselves inwardly to meet what the future brings – reaches beyond the individual resilience. It signals a wider shift in how responsibility is held and invites us to rethink the role of the organisations we work for and with.

From 'Parent–Child'

Over the decades I've seen a deep change in the social contract between workers and companies. It's an idea I explored in *The Democratic Enterprise.*[2] In this book I described the traditional 'deal' between employer and employees as a kind of *parent–child* relationship. The company, like a parent, took responsibility for the worker: fostering, guiding and at times controlling. And the worker, like a child, accepted limited autonomy in exchange for the promise of care and direction. It was this arrangement that made the Three-Stage Pattern possible – a stable, linear path built on loyalty and predictability.

At its best, this relationship and deal could feel secure. Companies benefited from loyal employees who knew the culture and were willing to go the extra mile. Workers felt looked after, confident that someone had their long-term interests at heart. There was comfort in that stability, even if it came at the cost of flexibility. But the parent–child deal was never quite as cosy or dependable as it appeared. Looking back, it often seemed more like a veneer.

I remember, as a child, hearing my parents in a fraught conversation behind closed doors: my father's voice low and distressed, my mother's tearful words. Later they told me that Dad had been 'let go'. His company had faced a difficult year and made cuts. As a young engineer, he was part of the 'last in, first out' group. He'd worked hard, taken his responsibilities seriously, supported a young family – yet the promises of that traditional deal did not hold. The parent–child relationship, at least for him, was only a mirage.

And it's even less true now. In a longer, more unpredictable working life, that world – if it ever truly existed – has faded.

To... 'Adult–Adult'

As I reflected in *The Democratic Enterprise*, if the old parent–child model was defined by protection and dependence, the emerging adult–adult relationship is grounded in accountability, responsibility and mutual obligation. In this framing, the organisation is no longer a benevolent parent handing down direction, and the employee is no longer a dependent child awaiting guidance. Instead, each recognises the other as capable, autonomous and answerable.

The organisation has an obligation to create an environment where people can learn, contribute and thrive. The employee has a responsibility to bring energy, skill and commitment. The organisation is accountable for the fairness of its practices, the clarity of its purpose and the integrity of its leadership; the employee is accountable for their choices, their impact and their ongoing growth.

I see this not as a one-way contract but rather a mutual one. Obligations flow both directions. When this adult–adult deal works well, it generates respect rather than control, dialogue rather than compliance, and partnership rather than dependency. It reflects a more mature way of thinking about work – one that recognises the longer arc of a 100-Year Life, and the need for both sides to take responsibility for sustaining it. You are not a child in your working life, and the company is no longer a parent. The freedom – and the responsibility – now rest with you.

This may feel daunting at times, but it opens space for something more intentional. It invites you to approach your working life not as something handed down, but as something you actively shape – through the choices you make, the threads you strengthen and the patterns you begin to weave. You may not control every outcome, but you can decide where to place your energy next.

Even if your image of your future self is hazy, you can still stock that 'cupboard of personal supplies'. And in a 100-Year Life, those supplies are your threads – the inner resources that hold the fabric of your life together. Taking adult–adult responsibility means tending to them, strengthening what supports you and renewing what has grown thin.

Reflect and Act on the Threads

A long life is sure to test the strength of every thread. Some threads will remain strong for decades: anchored by personality, upbringing or a deep sense of purpose. Others may fray – worn down by pressure, distraction or neglect.

As you've moved through each chapter, you've likely seen certain threads that feel naturally strong – perhaps woven early in your life, sustained through your character or reinforced through the work you've chosen. You may also have noticed threads built through effort – deliberate weaves of study, practice and care. And there may be threads that feel elusive: harder to tend, easier to postpone. For me, this was friendship. For years, I focused on the thread of mastery, often at the expense of friendship and intimacy. Only recently have I seen how much these threads need strengthening and reweaving.

As you pause here, revisit your notes. Consider your profile at www.livingthe100yearlife.com. What's strong? What's fraying? And which thread might you begin to strengthen next?

You strengthen your threads through intentional action. Throughout this book we've explored what these actions could be – from short-term steps to longer-term promises. You've seen how different choices can strengthen different threads: side projects that build mastery, learning that renews knowing, to activities that reconnect you with calm.

As you've been reflecting on your own threads, we've also travelled alongside Lucia, Nico, Ben and Mira. These fictional characters – drawn from research, teaching and countless conversations – were never meant as templates. They are companions on the journey, each showing one way a long life can unfold, each reminding us that the questions we wrestle with are shared by many.

Lucia is still searching for how to align her values with her work, experimenting with ways to bring more purpose into her career. Nico is building his second venture carefully and deliberately, recognising that in a long life there is room to play the long game. Ben continues to juggle responsibility at work and home, but he and Yuki are asking new questions about presence, legacy and meaning. Mira is reweaving her working life after divorce, discovering that reinvention is slow but possible – each application, each conversation adding strength to her threads.

Their stories are unfinished, just as yours is. They show that a long life is not something to solve in one move, but something we shape gradually: strengthening and renewing the threads that carry us all forward.

And that brings us back to you – and to the present moment, which always begins with a choice.

CHOOSE YOUR NEXT STEPS

So the question turns to you – not in theory, but in this moment of your life. What do you need next? Before rushing to decide, pause. Notice where you are, what is shifting and which thread is calling for attention – energy, meaning, relationships, risk or renewal.

There are times when simply staying put feels right. Times when you feel a change is beginning. Moments when you crave more autonomy. And those rare, pivotal times when a bigger shift becomes not just possible, but necessary. You've likely encountered all of these before – and you will again. Now is a chance to ask: *what do I need next*?

Perhaps your next step is modest. You may *stay in your current job but sense it's time to grow*. You could stretch into a new task, pivot towards something adjacent, start a side project that reawakens curiosity, enrol in a programme that builds mastery, or volunteer for something that reconnects you to purpose. Sometimes, staying still is the most powerful place to grow.

Or your next step may be bolder – a *job change, a new environment, a new identity*. This might be a moment to shift domains, or to hop – with intention – towards a role better suited to a changing world. In work shaped by fast-changing technology, this can be a chance to stay ahead of the curve. A job change isn't only about finding something new; it's also about creating space for who you're becoming.

Perhaps what you long for now is *more autonomy*. You've built strong productivity threads and now you want more freedom in how, when and for whom you work. You might move towards freelance work, rebalancing your energy and time. Or you may choose to build something of your own – a business, a practice, a platform.

Or maybe this is a *turning point*. You're ready for something more radical: a real change of direction. That could mean a return to full-time education, a sabbatical to reset, stepping away to support family with clarity and care, or saying yes to a grand adventure – not to escape, but to reimagine. A longer life brings more freedom and with it, more responsibility. In the past, institutions set the pattern. Now that scaffolding has loosened and the weave is in your hands.

Throughout this book you've explored eight threads – sometimes strong, sometimes frayed, always evolving. You've imagined new ways of working and made promises to your future self. That self isn't a stranger, they are you – shaped by experience, moved by new priorities, woven from new patterns. So picture them for a moment. What age are they – 40, 60, 85? What thread are they hoping you'll pick up now? Perhaps friendship, so the middle years feel less lonely. Perhaps mastery, so later decades are rich with capability. Or adventure, so your stories stay vivid and your eyes wide.

And as you strengthen these threads, you will change in ways you never imagined. I never imagined myself as a writer. I spent my teenage years devouring books, but there were no models for the kind of writing life I now live – the path wasn't visible, so I didn't walk it.

Sometimes we miss our future self because the image feels too far away or doesn't fit what we've seen before. But here's the truth: we don't become someone after we've figured it all out. More often, we become someone because we take a step, especially when the path is uncertain.

So, choose a thread. Make a promise, take one step.

And remember, your story doesn't end here. It unfolds – thread by thread, choice by choice – in the years ahead. You are not just living a longer life, you are designing it.

WHAT I'M LEARNING FROM LIVING THE 100-YEAR LIFE

It began with a walk. Back in August 2022, my story was of walking with Dad – long since dead, but present in that everyday moment. This period became a turning point. I found myself circling around a question that felt urgent and expansive all at once: *Who Am I?* It was a question that touched not only my past and present, but also the many years I hoped still lay ahead. That question set everything else in motion, leading me to another: *What are the actions I can take now, and the promises I want to make to my future self?*

Over the three years that followed, I immersed myself in the lives of others – real and imagined. I listened to experts, challenged my assumptions and revisited long-held ideas. Gradually, a central insight became clear: living a 100-Year Life is not a solitary concern. It is a shared experience – one that will define this generation and those to come.

I realised that the question I had asked – *Who am I?* – is one we are all asking in some way. How do we make sense of our working lives when those lives are longer, more fluid and more uncertain? And once we do make sense of them, how do we choose where to focus our energy, attention and time?

Thread by thread, the ideas came into focus. I explored how cooperation shapes our communities; how mastery sustains us; how friendship and intimacy bring meaning to our days; how calm helps us regain balance; how adventure opens new possibilities; how knowing and amplifying expand our potential. These eight threads gave me language and structure – but more than that, they gave me hope. They also gave me something more personal: a new way to imagine my own future.

Through them, I came to understand that the 100-Year Life is not just a demographic fact or a policy challenge. It is a possibility. It asks us not only to extend our lives, but to enrich them. It calls for wise decisions, courageous reimagining and a deeper commitment to becoming the person we want to be. That is why this project became more than just a book: it became a passion, a commitment to support others in navigating the long arc of their working lives.

That's why I'm creating the website www.livingthe100yearlife.com and building tools to support reflection and action – the Assessment, the Workbook, the Journal. And it's why I'm exploring how we might come together in coaching circles, reading groups and organisations to bring these ideas to life in practical and inspiring ways.

When *The 100-Year Life* was first published, I could see clearly that longevity was reshaping our world, but didn't yet know how I personally might respond. Now I do. Living the 100-Year Life requires imagination, courage and reflection. It asks us to return again and again, to the question: *Who am I becoming?*

Writing this book has reminded me that none of us live our 100-year lives alone. We learn from those who came before us. We walk alongside friends, family and colleagues. And we imagine futures that will be shaped by those who follow.

My hope is that the eight threads have given you both insight and inspiration – ways of seeing your own life as a fabric you can weave with care, strength and creativity. Your fabric will be unique – sometimes loose, sometimes tightly woven – but always evolving.

Thank you for allowing me to accompany you for a while on this journey. May you keep asking questions, keep making promises to your future self, and keep weaving a life that is wise, joyful and deeply your own.

STEP INTO THE WEAVE

Join the Living the 100-Year Life Community

I've long believed that reflection matters but I believe something more now: reflection is more powerful when it's shared – when our stories spark conversations, when our insights echo across communities. The journey of living and working wisely is not one we must take alone.

So, this isn't just a book to be read, it's a practice to be lived.

And it doesn't end here. I've created a space where your exploration can continue. A digital home where your insights, your intentions and your questions can live and grow alongside others. Visit: www.livingthe100yearlife.com

WHAT YOU'LL FIND THERE

The Living the 100-Year Life Assessment: Thread Strength Test
A free, online tool to assess the strength of your eight threads. You'll receive a personalised assessment showing which threads are strong, which ones may be fraying and areas you can focus on.

The Living the 100-Year Life Workbook: Life Design Guide
A free downloadable workbook to help you revisit our three Guiding Questions: *Who am I? How am I working now? What actions will I take – and*

what promises will I make to my future self? Use it in your own time, or return to it at every turning point.

The Living the 100-Year Life Journal: Reflect, Reimagine, Renew
Inspired by my own desk with drawings, ideas, reflections – this journal is a space to pause. It includes exercises, prompts and room to reflect on each of your eight threads. I've designed it to be a journey that will take you through your own insights, stories and resources. Beautiful and practical, it's designed to sit beside you as you weave forward. Begin now and over the coming months the Journal will be your companion for your commitments and actions. You can purchase it from the website or your normal on-line provider.

The Life Threads Podcast
Alongside this book, I've created an eight-episode podcast, *Life Threads*, with each episode exploring one of the threads through a conversation with the experts you've encountered here, together with a guest whose life brings the thread into focus. It's a way of hearing these ideas unfold in dialogue and in practice. If you'd like to continue the journey, you can find *Life Threads* wherever you listen to podcasts, or at livingthe100yearlife.com, as a companion to your own evolving weave.

The Living the 100-Year Life Circles: Living Forward
In Japan, *The 100-Year Life* was embraced not just individually, but collectively – read and discussed in many groups. My readers told me how transformational these book groups became for them so I've created resources to help you host your own conversations, wherever you are. You can download these resources from the website.

A FINAL INVITATION

You don't have to weave this life alone. Whether you're in your thirties or your seventies, switching careers or searching for meaning, there's room here for your story.

Come visit.
Come reflect.
Come weave with us.
www.livingthe100yearlife.com

Acknowledgements

This book began with a walk in France and a year of writing my stories. At the time, I did not know quite what they would become, but I did know that I wanted to write a book that was different – one that brought together the issues we all face in our working lives, and illustrated them with our stories, beginning with my own.

A small group of friends read those early drafts and urged me to continue. I owe special thanks to my dearest friends Herminia Ibarra, Shirley Cramer, Tobsha Learner and Diane Gherson, and to my sister Heather Gratton, for their encouragement at that moment of uncertainty; without their belief, this book might never have taken the form it did.

My literary agent at PFD, Caroline Michel, and the writer Tim Binding then encouraged me to keep the stories in – and, indeed, to begin the book with that walk in France. I had never brought my stories into a book in this way before. It felt unusual, exposing even, and required a measure of courage. Their reassurance helped me see that weaving the personal with the analytical could create something distinctive – that the stories were not just embellishments but part of the fabric of the book itself.

Alongside personal encouragement, I also drew deeply from the wisdom of expert voices. Robert Rowland Smith, Randall Peterson, Herminia Ibarra, Selin Kesebir, Tomas Chamorro-Premuzic, Jennifer Petriglieri, Robert Waldinger, Dan Cable and Stew Friedman all gave generously of their time and wisdom. Their reflections enriched the threads of mastery, cooperation, knowing, amplifying, intimacy, friendship and calm. I thank them not only for their expertise but also for the spirit of curiosity and generosity with which they entered these conversations. I remain grateful to my co-author Andrew J. Scott for our collaboration on *The 100-Year Life*, which laid the foundations for this new work.

I am also grateful to my colleagues and community at London Business School. The support of the Dean and the School has sustained me through the years of research and writing that underpin this book. A special thanks to Savio Kwan, whose encouragement convinced me that living a 100-year life was not only possible but something to embrace with optimism.

My thanks also go to the senior team at my advisory company, HSM – Harriet Molyneaux, Sarosh Khan and Oliver Ferriman – who gave me the space to think and write, and to my assistant, Cara Birkett, who managed my schedule with patience and care. Their support created the time and clarity I needed to bring this book to life.

As the manuscript evolved, a number of people read drafts and offered invaluable feedback. I am especially grateful to Harriet Molyneaux, Kate Dinon and Christy Johnson for their thoughtful comments, which helped me to see the manuscript more clearly and sharpen its message. My thanks also go to Max Mockett and Joseph Wright, whose insights were particularly valuable in shaping the chapter on Amplification.

I am indebted to Nigel Newton at Bloomsbury, who published *The 100-Year Life* and encouraged me to see this book as a worthy follow-up. His personal belief in me and in the project gave me courage at the outset. I also want to thank my Bloomsbury editor, Tomasz Hoskins, who was excited about the project from the very beginning and ushered it through the publication process with patience, insight and good grace. As a visual person, I loved working on the illustrations for this book. My thanks go to Mary Moysis, who worked with my sketches to create the wonderful illustrations you now see on these pages.

Alongside the book itself, I've developed a wider set of resources to support you in putting these ideas into practice, including the website, diagnostic, and accompanying journal. I am deeply grateful to my creative partner, Kate Dinon, whose instinct for craft, structure, and user experience has shaped how this work lives beyond the printed page. I also want to thank George Saad, who designed the glorious cover of this book and created the visual language for all the supporting materials, bringing coherence, clarity, and beauty to the entire body of work.

My heartfelt thanks go to my two sons, Dominic Seiersen and Christian Seiersen, who not only allowed me to tell some of their stories but who, of course, have been central to my own. Our stories thread through this book, and I am profoundly grateful for their generosity in letting me share them.

I also want to thank my husband, Nigel Boardman, who has generously allowed some of his own stories to be told here. We have travelled the world together, and the stories of Chad and Petra are as much his as mine. Thank you, Nigel, for your intimacy, for sharing our story, and for walking alongside me through the three years of bringing this book to life. You have seen it through countless edits, offering wise comments and steady encouragement throughout.

Finally, I want to acknowledge you, the reader. A book is never complete until it is read. My hope is that the ideas here help you weave a life of curiosity, adventure, calm, intimacy and meaning. Just as the love and support of those I thank here are woven into these pages, may you weave your own unique tapestry of a 100-year life.

References

Preface

1 Lynda Gratton and Andrew Scott, *The 100-Year Life: Living and Working in an Age of Longevity* (London: Bloomsbury, 2016).

Chapter 1: MY HERITAGE: The Family, Culture and History That Brought Me Here

1 **On Robert Rowland Smith:** If you'd like to read more from Robert – here are some interesting books: Robert Rowland Smith, *Breakfast with Socrates: An Extraordinary (Philosophical) Journey Through Your Ordinary Day* (London: Profile Books, 2010). Robert Rowland Smith, *Driving with Plato: The Meaning of Life's Milestones* (London: Profile Books, 2011). Robert Rowland Smith, *Autobiophilosophy: An Intimate Story of What It Means to Be Human* (London: 4th Estate, 2018).

Chapter 2: MY PERSONALITY: My Natural Preferences, Habits and Patterns

1 Claudia Roden, *A Book of Middle Eastern Food* (London: Penguin Books, 1968).

2 **On Randall Peterson:** If you'd like to read more of Randall's work consider: Randall S. Peterson, *Leading and Managing People in Dynamic Organizations* (London: Routledge, 2009); Randall S. Peterson, *Disaster in the Boardroom: Six Dysfunctions Everyone Should Understand* (with Nigel Nicholson, Basingstoke: Palgrave Macmillan, 2022).

Chapter 3: MY WORKING IDENTITY: How Work Has Shaped Me – and How It Could Evolve

1 Margaret Mead, *Growing Up in New Guinea: A Comparative Study of Primitive Education* (New York: William Morrow, 1930).

2 **On Multiple Selves:** If the theme of 'multiple selves' interests you – here are two books: Roy F. Baumeister, *The Self in Social Psychology* (Philadelphia: Psychology Press, 1999). Kenneth J. Gergen, *The Saturated Self: Dilemmas of Identity in Contemporary Life* (New York: Basic Books, 1991).

3 **The side project with Ivan Robertson:** Ivan T. Robertson and Lynda Gratton, 'The Impact of Personnel Selection and Assessment Methods on Candidates', *Human Relations* 44, no. 9 (1991): 963–83. Ivan T. Robertson and Lynda Gratton, 'The Psychometric Properties and Design of Managerial Assessment Centres: "Dimensions into Exercises Won't Go"', *Journal of Occupational Psychology* 60, no. 3 (1987): 187–96. Robertson, Ivan T., Lynda Gratton, Paul A. Iles and David Sharpley, 'The Impact of Personnel Selection and Assessment Methods on Candidates', *Human Relations* 44, no. 9 (1991): 963–83.

4 **On Herminia Ibarra:** Here are three important pieces from Herminia – her book length argument, her seminal article on provisional selves, and her later work on narrative identity. Herminia Ibarra, *Working Identity: Unconventional Strategies for Reinventing Your Career* (Boston: Harvard Business School Press, Updated 2023). Herminia Ibarra, 'Provisional Selves: Experimenting with Image and Identity in Professional Adaptation', *Administrative Science Quarterly* 44, no. 4 (1999): 764–91. Herminia Ibarra and Roxana Barbulescu, 'Identity as Narrative: Prevalence, Effectiveness, and Consequences of Narrative Identity Work in Macro Work Role Transitions', *Academy of Management Review* 35, no. 1 (2010): 135–54.

PART TWO: HOW AM I WORKING NOW?

1 Paul Evans Fernando Bartolomé, *Must Success Cost So Much?* (New York: Basic Books, 1980).

Chapter 5: THE THREAD OF MASTERY: Am I Creating What I Love?

1 **On the 10,000- hours:** If this is a topic that interests you – here is the original study: K. Anders Ericsson, Ralf T. Krampe and Clemens Tesch-Römer, 'The Role of Deliberate Practice in the Acquisition of Expert Performance', *Psychological Review* 100, no. 3 (1993): 363–406. It was this book that captured the popular imagination: Malcolm Gladwell, *Outliers: The Story of Success* (New York: Little, Brown and Company, 2008).

2 **Debate about the 10,000-hour rule:** The so-called '10,000-hour rule' has been widely debated. Anders Ericsson, whose research inspired it, emphasised that 10,000 hours was an average among elite violinists, not a universal benchmark, and that what mattered was *deliberate practice* – structured, effortful and feedback-driven. Later meta-analyses showed that practice explains only a modest share of performance differences (around 12 per cent), with wide variation across domains: in some fields, mastery may take far fewer hours, while in others, far more. Critics argue that talent, opportunity and context play significant roles, making the rule a useful metaphor for effort, but a misleading formula for success.

3 **On Systems Thinking:** Richard T. Pascale, Mark Millemann and Linda Gioja, *Surfing the Edge of Chaos: The Laws of Nature and the New Laws of Business* (New York: Crown Business, 2000). Peter M. Senge, *The Fifth Discipline: The Art and Practice of the Learning Organization*, Revised and Updated Edition (New York: Doubleday/Currency, 2006). Chris Argyris and Donald A. Schön, *Organizational Learning: A Theory of Action Perspective* (Reading, MA: Addison-Wesley, 1978). Russell L. Ackoff, *Creating the Corporate Future: Plan or Be Planned For* (New York: Wiley, 1981).

4 **On the Craftsman:** Richard Sennett, *The Craftsman* (New Haven: Yale University Press, 2008). This book explores craftsmanship not only as a set of technical skills but as an enduring human value – how taking pride in good work shapes identity, community and meaning.

5 **On the evolution of skill clusters:** See, for example, James Manyika et al., *Jobs Lost, Jobs Gained: Workforce Transitions in a Time of Automation* (New York: McKinsey Global Institute, 2017); Burning Glass Technologies, *The Hybrid Job Economy: How New Skills Are Rewriting the DNA of the Job Market* (Boston: Burning Glass Technologies, 2019); LinkedIn, *The Skills Genome: Mapping the Skills That Drive Talent and Business* (LinkedIn Economic Graph, 2017).

6 Liu Lu, Wang Yang, Sinatra Roberta, Lee Giles, Song Chaoming & Wang Dashun (2021). 'Hot Streaks in Artistic, Cultural, and Scientific Careers', *Nature Communications* 12, no. 1 (2021): 1–9.

Chapter 6: THE THREAD OF COOPERATION: Do I Work Deeply With Others?

1 Andrew and I wrote two books together: Gratton, Lynda and Andrew Scott, *The 100-Year Life: Living and Working in an Age of Longevity* (London: Bloomsbury, 2016), and Gratton, Lynda and Andrew Scott, *The New Long Life: A Framework for Flourishing in a Changing World* (London: Bloomsbury, 2020). Andrew followed the theme and wrote: Scott, Andrew J, *The Longevity Imperative: Building a Better Society for Healthier, Longer Lives* (New York: Basic Books, 2024).

2 Boris Groysberg, *Chasing Stars: The Myth of Talent and the Portability of Performance* (Princeton, NJ: Princeton University Press, 2010).

3 Our two articles are: Diane Gherson and Lynda Gratton, 'Managers Can't Do It All: It's Time to Reinvent Their Role for the New World of Work', *Harvard Business Review*, March–April 2022; and 'Highly-Skilled Professionals Want Your Work but Not Your Job', *Harvard Business Review*, May–June 2024.

4 See Sumantra Ghoshal and Lynda Gratton, 'Integrating the Enterprise', *MIT Sloan Management Review* 44, no. 1 (Fall 2002): 31–8; and Lynda Gratton and Sumantra Ghoshal, 'Beyond Best Practice', *MIT Sloan Management Review* 46, no. 3 (Spring 2005): 49–57.

5 See Lynda Gratton, *Hot Spots: Why Some Teams, Workplaces, and Organizations Buzz with Energy – and Others Don't* (San Francisco: Berrett-Koehler, 2007); and *Glow: How You Can Radiate Energy, Innovation and Success* (London: Financial Times/Prentice Hall, 2009).

6 Lynda Gratton and Sumantra Ghoshal, 'Improving the Quality of Conversations', *Organizational Dynamics* 31, no. 3 (Winter 2002): 209–23.

7 **On Connections and Networks:** If networks fascinate you – here are two references: Granovetter gives you the theoretical grounding, and Cross & Parker make it practical for modern organisations. See Mark S. Granovetter, 'The Strength of Weak Ties', *American Journal of Sociology* 78, no. 6 (1973): 1360–1380; and Rob Cross and Andrew Parker, *The Hidden Power of Social Networks: Understanding How Work Really Gets Done in Organizations* (Boston: Harvard Business School Press, 2004).

8 **On the Flaneur:** Here is the piece in the original French Charles Baudelaire, *Le Peintre de la vie moderne* (Paris: Michel Lévy Frères, 1863). The English translation: Charles Baudelaire, *The Painter of Modern Life and Other Essays*, trans. Jonathan Mayne (London: Phaidon Press, 1964).

9 **On Heuristics:** If you'd like to go deeper on heuristics and explore how we make quick judgments and the role of mental shortcuts, here are some classics and modern guides: Kahneman, Daniel, *Thinking, Fast and Slow* (New York: Farrar,

Straus and Giroux, 2011); Tversky, Amos, and Daniel Kahneman, 'Judgment under Uncertainty: Heuristics and Biases', *Science* 185, no. 4157 (1974): 1124–31; Gilovich, Thomas, Dale Griffin, and Daniel Kahneman, eds *Heuristics and Biases: The Psychology of Intuitive Judgment* (Cambridge: Cambridge University Press, 2002) and Gigerenzer, Gerd, Peter M. Todd, and the ABC Research Group, *Simple Heuristics That Make Us Smart* (New York: Oxford University Press, 1999).

Chapter 7: THE THREAD OF KNOWING: Am I Expanding What I Know?

1 **On Selin Kesebir:** Here are two interesting articles from Selin Kesebir which look at identity and meaning: Kesebir, Selin. 2012, 'The Superorganism Account of Human Sociality: How and When Human Groups Are Like Beehives', *Personality and Social Psychology Review* 16 (3): 233–61, and Kesebir, Selin, and Shigehiro Oishi. 2015, 'Income Inequality Explains Why Economic Growth Does Not Always Translate to an Increase in Happiness', *Psychological Science* 25 (1): 190–6.

2 **On John Bowlby:** This is the classic text on Bowlby's theory of attachment, Bowlby, John, *A Secure Base: Parent–Child Attachment and Healthy Human Development* (New York: Basic Books, 1988).

3 **On John Rawls:** This is John Rawls' classic work on the veil of ignorance: Rawls, John, *A Theory of Justice* (Cambridge, MA: Harvard University Press, 1971). Here is Rawls' own attempt to summarise and clarify his arguments: Rawls, John. *Justice as Fairness: A Restatement*. Edited by Erin Kelly (Cambridge, MA: Harvard University Press, 2001). This is a short introduction to Rawls' thoughts: Freeman, Samuel, *Rawls* (London: Routledge, 2007).

4 **On James Hollis:** I have been drawn to James Hollis's writing for decades. The reference here is: Hollis, James, *The Swamplands of the Soul: New Life in Dismal Places* (Toronto: Inner City Books, 1996). I have also found these books very thought provoking – here are others that can help during tough times: Hollis, James, *Finding Meaning in the Second Half of Life: How to Finally, Really Grow Up* (New York: Gotham Books, 2005). Hollis, James, *Living an Examined Life: Wisdom for the Second Half of the Journey* (Boulder, CO: Sounds True, 2018).

5 **On Warren Bennis:** Warren G. Bennis and Robert J. Thomas, 'Crucibles of Leadership', *Harvard Business Review* 80, no. 9 (September 2002): 39–45 and Bennis, Warren G., and Robert J. Thomas, *Geeks and Geezers: How Era, Values, and Defining Moments Shape Leaders* (Boston: Harvard Business School Press, 2002).

6 This was the Consortium for Advancing Adult Learning & Development (CAALD), convened by McKinsey & Company starting in **2016.** We wrote a couple of articles – including: McKinsey & Company, 'Competitive Advantage

with a Human Dimension: From Lifelong Learning to Lifelong Employability', *McKinsey Quarterly*, December 2019.

7 Gherson, Diane, and Lynda Gratton, 'Managers Can't Do It All', *Harvard Business Review*, March–April 2022.

Chapter 8: THE THREAD OF AMPLIFYING: Can AI Extend My Reach?

1 Lynda Gratton, *The Shift: The Future of Work Is Already Here* (London: HarperCollins Business, 2011).

2 **On Generative AI and Job Tasks:** This is an interesting analysis of the impact of Generative AI on tasks – Acemoglu, Daron, David Autor, Jonathon Hazell and Pascual Restrepo, 'Artificial Intelligence and Jobs: Evidence from Online Vacancies', *NBER Working Paper* no. 28257 (October 2021). In this article Daron Acemoglu models AI's taskbased effects on automation and productivity, projecting modest increases in GDP and total factor productivity – no more than 0.53 per cent–0.66 per cent over the next decade. He also suggests AI may widen the gap between capital and labor income, unless new 'good tasks' are created: 'The Simple Macroeconomics of AI' (Economic Policy, January 2025). Acemoglu is a voice worth following – see for example – MIT Policy Memo: 'Can We Have ProWorker AI?' (September 2023). Co-authored with Autor and Johnson, this memo argues that generative AI need not displace workers – it can be designed to complement and elevate their capabilities, particularly those without college degrees – but this requires intentional institutional design and policy support. David Autor also continues to play an important role in this conversation – see for example: Autor, David, and Neil Thompson, *Expertise Ex.* Cambridge, MA: MIT Department of Economics, Working Paper, June 18, 2025.

3 **On AI and Medical Diagnostics:** The essay I am drawing on here is: David Autor and James Manyika, 'A Better Way to Think About AI', *The Atlantic*, August 24, 2025. They cite the study with radiologists – Liu, Yuan, Albert W. Wu and Matthew P. Lungren, 'How Clinical AI Deployment Impacts Physician Performance: Evidence from CheXpert', *Nature Medicine* 29, no. 3 (2023): 574–82. In this analysis of case studies, doctors plus AI achieved about 85 per cent better diagnostic accuracy than doctors alone, and 15–20 per cent better than AI alone: Singhal, Karishma, Pranav Rajpurkar and Eyal Oren, 'Large Language Models Improve Medical Reasoning', *Proceedings of the National Academy of Sciences* 121, no. 5 (30 January 2024).

4 **On Tomas Chamorro-Premuzic:** Tomas is a voice worth following – see for example: Chamorro-Premuzic, Tomas. *I, Human: AI, Automation, and the Quest to Reclaim What Makes Us Unique* (Boston: Harvard Business Review Press, 2023); Chamorro-Premuzic, Tomas, *The Talent Delusion: Why Data, Not Intuition, Is the*

Key to Unlocking Human Potential (London: Piatkus, 2017); Chamorro-Premuzic, Tomas, *Confidence: The Surprising Truth About How Much You Need and How to Get It* (New York: Portfolio, 2013).

5 Li, FeiFei, 'If We Want Humane AI, It Has to Understand All Humans', *WIRED*, October 30, 2015.

Chapter 9: THE THREADS OF NURTURING

1 H.-J. Wolfram and Lynda Gratton, 'Spillover Between Work and Home, Role Importance and Life Satisfaction', *British Journal of Management* 25, no. 1 (January 2014): 77–90.

Chapter 10: THE THREAD OF FRIENDSHIPS: Am I Forging Deep, Sustaining Connections?

1 **On Robert Waldinger:** This book distils decades of insights from the Harvard Study: Waldinger, Robert, and Marc Schulz, *The Good Life: Lessons from the World's Longest Scientific Study of Happiness* (New York: Simon & Schuster, 2023). His TEDx talk has over 40 million views, Waldinger, Robert, 'What Makes a Good Life? Lessons from the Longest Study on Happiness'. Filmed November 2015 at TEDx Beacon Street, Boston, MA. Video, 12:47. Published January 2016. https://www.ted.com/talks/robert_waldinger_what_makes_a_good_life_lessons_from_the_longest_study_on_happiness. His personal website explores topics such as mindfulness, relationships and applying Zen philosophy to everyday life. For example: Waldinger, Robert, 'Mindfulness and Relationships', *Robert Waldinger Blog*, March 15, 2022. https://www.robertwaldinger.com/blog/mindfulness-and-relationships

2 Neugarten, Bernice L. 1996. *The Meanings of Age: Selected Papers* (Chicago: University of Chicago Press).

3 Cicero, *Laelius: On Friendship.* Translated by Michael Grant. (London: Penguin Classics, 1971.)

4 **On Rob Goffee and Gareth Jones**: Goffee, Rob, and Gareth Jones, *Why Should Anyone Be Led by You? What It Takes to Be an Authentic Leader* (Boston: Harvard Business School Press, 2006). Goffee, Rob, and Gareth Jones, *Clever: Leading Your Smartest, Most Creative People* (Boston: Harvard Business Press, 2009).

5 I describe this data in: Gratton, Lynda. 2022, 'Why You Should Make Friends at Work', *MIT Sloan Management Review*, October Gallup data.

6 Hadley, Constance N., & Mortensen, Mark, 'Are Your Team Members Lonely?' *MIT Sloan Management Review*, (8 December 2020).
7 Lynda Gratton, 'Cut the Meetings, Make More Friends', *Financial Times*, 27 July 2022.
8 Cicero. *Laelius: On Friendship.* Translated by Michael Grant. (London: Penguin Classics, 1971.)

Chapter 11: THE THREAD OF INTIMACY: Am I Giving and Finding Love?

1 **On Anthony Giddens:** One of the clearest thinkers on relationships – see for example: Giddens, Anthony, *The Transformation of Intimacy: Sexuality, Love, and Eroticism in Modern Societies* (Stanford, CA: Stanford University Press, 1992); and Giddens, Anthony, *The Politics of Sexuality* (Cambridge: Polity Press, 1993).
2 Milkie, Melissa A., Marybeth J. Mattingly, Kei M. Nomaguchi, Suzanne M. Bianchi and John P. Robinson, 'The Time Squeeze: Parental Statuses and Feelings About Time With Children', *Journal of Marriage and Family* 66, no. 3 (August 2004): 739–61.
3 Winnicott, Donald W, *The Child, the Family, and the Outside World* (London: Penguin, 1964).
4 **On Stew Friedman:** This pioneering study – co-authored with Jeffrey H. Greenhaus – is based on surveys of over 800 business professionals. It investigates how work and family roles interact, Friedman, Stewart D., and Jeffrey H. Greenhaus, *Work and Family – Allies or Enemies?: What Happens When Business Professionals Confront Life Choices* (New York: Oxford University Press, 2000). See also, Friedman, Stewart D, *Leading the Life You Want: Skills for Integrating Work and Life* (Boston: Harvard Business Press, 2014); and, Friedman, Stewart D., and Alyssa F. Westring, 'How Working Parents Can Regain Control Over Their Lives', *Harvard Business Review*, 5 March 2020 and Friedman, Stewart D., and Alyssa F. Westring, 'Navigating Pandemic Fatigue as a Working Parent', *Harvard Business Review*, 27 January 2021.
5 Stew wrote about the zero sum in Friedman, Stewart D., Perry Christensen, and Jessica DeGroot, 'Work and Life: The End of the ZeroSum Game', *Harvard Business Review*, November–December 1998, 119–29.
6 **On Jennifer Petriglieri:** Petriglieri, Jennifer, *Couples That Work: How Dual-Career Couples Can Thrive in Love and Work* (Boston: Harvard Business Review Press, 2019) and Petriglieri, Jennifer, 'Couples That Work', *Harvard Business Review*, September–October 2018, 118–25 and here is a TED talk: Petriglieri, Jennifer, 'How Working Couples Can Best Support Each Other (The Way We Work)'. *TED Talks*, November 2020.

CHAPTER 12: THE THREAD OF CALM: Can I Slow Down?

1 **The 'third place'** – Oldenburg, Ray, *The Great Good Place: Cafés, Coffee Shops, Bookstores, Bars, Hair Salons, and Other Hangouts at the Heart of a Community* (New York: Paragon House, 1989).

2 Woolf, Virginia, *A Room of One's Own* (London: Hogarth Press, 1929).

3 Brower, Tracy, 'Senior Leaders Are Stressed and Quitting – 5 Things to Look for in Leadership', *Forbes*, 21 July 2022.

4 **Reference to The Shift** – You will find the passage on page 55 of *The Shift: The Future of Work Is Already Here* (London: HarperCollins, 2011).

5 **On Flow:** Csikszentmihalyi, Mihaly, *Flow: The Psychology of Optimal Experience* (New York: Harper & Row, 1990).

6 **On Present Bias**: the foundational work is: Laibson, David, 'Golden Eggs and Hyperbolic Discounting', *Quarterly Journal of Economics* 112, no. 2 (1997): 443–77. Made more accessible as a concept in: Thaler, Richard H., and Cass R. Sunstein, *Nudge: Improving Decisions About Health, Wealth, and Happiness.* (New Haven, CT: Yale University Press, 2008).

7 Mullainathan, Sendhil, and Eldar Shafir, *Scarcity: Why Having Too Little Means So Much* (New York: Times Books, 2013).

Chapter 13: THE THREAD OF ADVENTURE: Do I Still Feel Alive?

1 **About the Seeking System:** Panksepp, Jaak, and Lucy Biven, *The Archaeology of Mind: Neuroevolutionary Origins of Human Emotions* (New York: W. W. Norton & Company, 2012). The quote comes from *Affective Neuroscience: The Foundations of Human and Animal Emotions* (New York: Oxford University Press, 1998).

2 Gallup, *State of the Global Workplace 2025 Report*, 23 April 2025.

3 **On Dan Cable**: In this important book Dan describes his basic thesis: Cable, Daniel M, *Alive at Work: The Neuroscience of Helping Your People Love What They Do* (Boston: Harvard Business Review Press, 2018). This book describes his perspective on unlocking potential: Cable, Daniel M, *Exceptional: Build Your Personal Highlight Reel and Unlock Your Potential* (San Francisco: Chronicle Books, 2020). This is a fascinating read, Cable, Dan, 'Turn Your Boring Job into a Job You'll Love', *Harvard Business Review*, 16 February 2021.

4 **On Appreciative Inquiry:** Whitney, Diana, D.D. & Amanda Trosten-Bloom, *The Power of Appreciative Inquiry: A Practical Guide to Positive Change.* 2nd ed. (San Francisco: Berrett-Koehler Publishers, 2010).

Chapter 14: YOUR FUTURE SELF

1 **On Possible Selves:** Markus, Hazel R., and Paula Nurius, *'Possible Selves'*, American Psychologist 41, no. 9 (September 1986): 954–69.

2 Gratton, Lynda, *The Democratic Enterprise: Liberating Your Business with Freedom, Flexibility and Commitment* (London: Pearson Education, 2004).

Index

Index

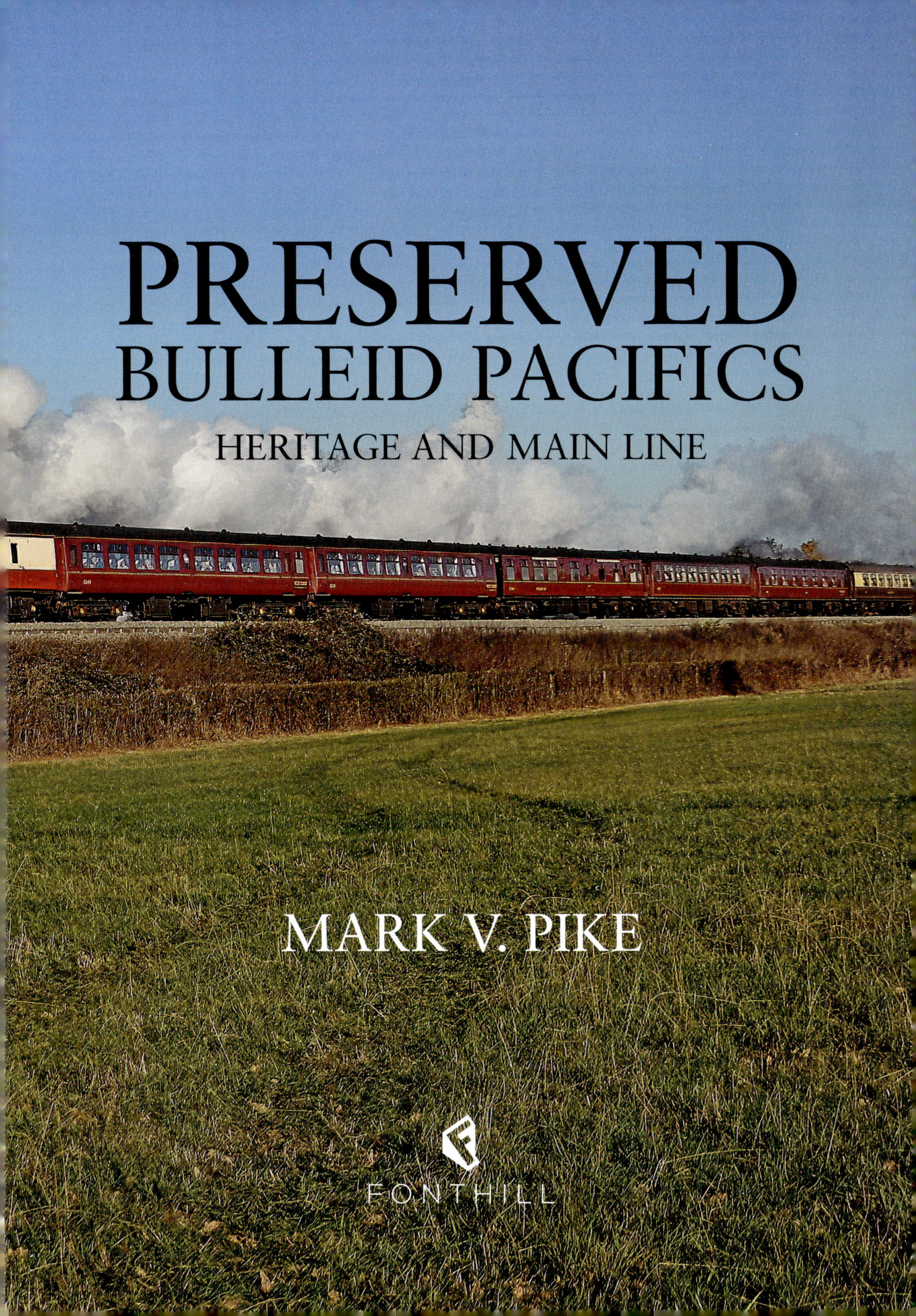
PRESERVED
BULLEID PACIFICS
HERITAGE AND MAIN LINE
MARK V. PIKE
FONTHILL

First published in Great Britain in 2026 by
Fonthill
An imprint of
Pen & Sword Books Ltd
Yorkshire – Philadelphia
www.fonthill.media

ISBN 978-1-03619-370-6

A CIP catalogue record for this book
is available from the British Library.

Typeset in SabonLTStd 10/13 by
SJmagic DESIGN SERVICES, India.
Printed and bound in India by Replika Press Pvt Ltd

MIX
Paper | Supporting responsible forestry
FSC™ C016779

The Publisher's authorised representative in the EU for product
safety is Authorised Rep Compliance Ltd., Ground Floor,
71 Lower Baggot Street, Dublin D02 P593, Ireland.
www.arccompliance.com

For a complete list of Pen & Sword titles please contact
PEN & SWORD BOOKS LIMITED
George House, Units 12 & 13, Beevor Street, Off Pontefract Road,
Barnsley, South Yorkshire, S71 1HN, England
E-mail: enquiries@pen-and-sword.co.uk
Website: www.pen-and-sword.co.uk

or

PEN AND SWORD BOOKS
1950 Lawrence Rd, Havertown, PA 19083, USA
E-mail: uspen-and-sword@casematepublishers.com
Website: www.penandswordbooks.com

Contents

1

Main Line: Merchant Navy Class

35005 *Canadian Pacific*
35018 *British India Line*
35028 *Clan Line*

To begin this pictorial album dedicated to preserved Bulleid Pacifics, we look at the three mighty Merchant Navies currently to have worked on the main lines of the UK. Readers will become aware that most of the images in this book have been taken

This is undoubtedly the most famous loco of all three, and as such features most frequently in this chapter. 35028 *Clan Line* looks magnificent as it approaches Sherborne (Dorset) with a Yeovil Junction to Salisbury charter. After a few days working test runs in the area, this was the first public run. It is hard to believe this was almost forty years ago now, twice as long as the locomotive was in BR service! 5 October 1986.

in the South of England, which is appropriate for these former Southern Railway locomotives. The first sixteen shots in this chapter depict a few of the earlier days of main line operation in the south upon the lifting of the nineteen-year steam ban in place from 1967–1986.

Above: The following weekend saw the running of 'The Blackmore Vale Express' from Salisbury to Yeovil Junction and return. This is 35028 during a photo run-past at Templecombe station. There were once substantial goods yards either side of the line here that were all swept away in the late 1960s with the closure of the station. That was not the end of the story though. Just three years prior to my visit here the station reopened in 1983 due to public demand and since that time has justified this decision over and over again. In the intervening forty years it is just about impossible to do a shot such as this as huge trees line the tracks here. 11 October 1986.

Opposite above: Later that same day I went up to Yeovil Junction for more views of the train. The low autumn sunshine glints across the superb lines of 35028 as it backs on to its train at was originally the former 'down' platform used by stopping trains to Exeter and beyond, for the return journey to Salisbury. This is another station that is just a shadow of its former self after the decimation of the Salisbury to Exeter route in the late 1960s. The only part still in public use today is an island platform from which this shot was taken. 11 October 1986.

Opposite below: A brief visit further north this time as we see 35028 powering through the station on the 'up' through line at Oxford with 'The White Rose' operated by Flying Scotsman Services. This charter started out diesel hauled from London Paddington to Didcot Parkway, from where the Pacific took over the train working it up to Derby. 7 July 1990.

35028
BLACKMORE
VALE EXPRESS
35028

35028
THE
WHITE ROSE

Above: Back to the south now and we are at Salisbury to see 35028 arriving with 'The Woking Centenarian' charter organised by the Woking Borough Council. Details for this are a bit vague but I think this train originated at either Woking or London Waterloo. 24 March 1995.

Opposite above: Upon arrival at Salisbury the locomotive was turned on the nearby Laverstock Triangle. Upon return to the station, it is seen here basking in the spring sunshine while being serviced in the down bay platform at Salisbury station. 24 March 1995.

Opposite below: Here is a real nostalgic view of 35028 just arrived at platform one at Southampton Central with a near perfect re-creation of the famous 'Bournemouth Belle' pullman train, that was a regular on the Waterloo to Bournemouth route for many years up until 1967. This particular working was an unidentified private charter. The loco has stood in this very spot literally hundreds of times in its BR career. The only drawback on this day was the miserable weather! 4 February 2001.

35028
THE WOKING
CENTENARIAN
35028

35028
BOURNEMOUTH
BELLE

Above: At the time of writing, 35028 has been in preservation for an incredible fifty-eight years and in that time has visited many places around the UK that it would never have ventured to in BR days. Here we see the loco awaiting departure westbound from Taunton with 'The Mayflower' charter that ran from Finsbury Park with Class 67 diesel No. 67019 as far as Bristol Temple Meads, from where 35028 took over to Plymouth. 21 October 2000.

Opposite above: Moving on from 35028 for now, the second example to grace the main lines of the UK was 35005 *Canadian Pacific* during the late 1990s/early 2000s. Rather controversially around that time it was also painted in blue livery for a while, a colour scheme that the rebuilt locos never carried while in BR service. I personally think it looked rather good! Anyway, here is the loco arriving at Salisbury with 'The Bournemouth Belle' charter that had started out from London Victoria. From here Class 37 diesel No. 37042 reversed direction of the train and worked it to Poole, from where the Merchant Navy later worked the train back to London Victoria (see the next image) in the evening. 12 February 2000.

Opposite below: With a nice glint from the rapidly setting winter sunshine, this is 35005 getting to grips with the commencement of the demanding 1-50 incline of Parkstone Bank. It is working hard from a standing start from Poole station, about a mile or so distant from this point as it heads back to London Victoria. The water (background right) is part of Poole Park Lake. Until the early 1970s the view to the left of this image would have been very different as the waters of Poole Harbour originally came right up against the bottom of what was then a concrete covered embankment that carried the line on a causeway. This fine viewpoint has long since become overgrown. 12 February 2000.

35005

Above: 35005 is another well-travelled loco, although it has not operated on the mainline in preservation as long as 35028. Here it is in Woodborough Loop on the Great Western 'Berks & Hants' line about to take on water. I have no details for this charter but I believe it started from Bristol Temple Meads and was heading for London. This is another location where it is hard to believe a station ever used to exist until closure in 1966. All trace of it has vanished. 29 January 2000.

Opposite above: While in the loop here at Woodborough I used the opportunity to grab a broadside shot of 35005 that really shows off its unique blue livery as it was being watered. I will leave the reader to make up their mind regarding how good or bad it looks! 19 January 2000.

Opposite below: A couple of years later and a now green-liveried 35005 is again seen in a broadside view, but this time on the turntable at Yeovil Junction. It had worked here with 1Z91, the 0910 Eastleigh to Yeovil Junction charter train. This service operated as part of a week that the main freight operator at the time, EWS, undertook training for some of their staff on steam locos. Tickets were also made available to the public and they turned out to be very popular. It used what at the time was the Mid-Hants based 'green train' stock. The turntable here is an amazing survivor from steam days and now forms part of the Yeovil Steam Centre which is well worth a visit if you are in the area, it is still used occasionally when main line steam pays a visit (see also later in this chapter). 16 April 2002.

35028
THE ROYAL WESSEX

35028
NINE ELMS ENGINEMEN 1838–1967

Above: Of course, for about the last twenty years or so 35028 has been associated with the Belmond British Pullman (formerly VSOE) luxury train that utilises the fabulous and historic Pullman coaches that were used in famous trains of the past such as the Bournemouth Belle and Devon Belle. Back in those days a Merchant Navy Pacific would be the regular and preferred motive power for these prestigious services. This is 35028 soon after arrival at Bristol Temple Meads with 1Z28, the 0846 London Victoria to Bristol Temple Meads 'Historic Bath/Brunel's SS Great Britain by Steam' charter operated by Belmond. Despite being deep in former GWR territory the loco by no means looks out of place here. 6 October 2021.

Opposite above: The next few images also show 35028 on former GWR territory. Here we see the loco passing through Cholsey on the GWR main line with 1Z97, the 0845 London Victoria to Oxford charter operated by VSOE. This fine open view has now been lost to the overhead electrification that was installed here during the late 2010s. 28 October 2009.

Opposite below: An even more rural setting as we see 35028 rounding the curve at Cole, between Castle Cary and Bruton with 1Z65, the 1631 Exeter St Davids to London Victoria 'Atlantic Coast Express' operated by UK Railtours. At this point the train was running some twenty minutes early and I literally just made it here for this shot. I was standing on the old embankment of the former Somerset & Dorset line that crossed the GWR at this spot until closure in 1966. The loco was starting to work hard here as it was commencing the climb up the gradient to Bruton and then up to the summit at Brewham, a distance of around 5–7 miles. 23 September 2017.

35028

35028
ATLANTIC
COAST EXPRESS

Above: A rather menacing sky can be seen above part of the City of Bath as 35028 departs and gets to grips with 1Z63, the 0844 Southend Central to Bristol Temple Meads 'The Cathedrals Express' operated by Steam Dreams. This charter was originally advertised to be hauled by A4 Pacific 4464 *Bittern*, but that was unavailable so it was initially substituted for A1 60163 *Tornado*, but unfortunately that failed its Fitness to Run exam so 35028 stepped in at the last minute! 16 March 2013.

Opposite above: For some years now there have been regular summer weekend charters to the ever-popular South Devon coast and 35028 has been involved in a few of these. Here we see the loco south of Trowbridge and coming around the curve at Hawkeridge Junction on the approach to Westbury with 1Z27, the 0800 Bristol Temple Meads to Kingswear 'Torbay Express' operated by Torbay Express LTD. 20 August 2017.

Opposite below: Inevitably, 35028 has undergone quite a few overhauls since being purchased from BR in the late 1960s and has been privately owned for far longer than it was by BR. It returned to the main line way back in 1974 with a trip from Basingstoke to Westbury. On the exact 50th anniversary of that tour we see the loco about to pass beneath the Dundas Aqueduct, in the Avon Valley between Bradford-on-Avon and Bath Spa with 1Z21, the 0914 London Victoria to Bath Spa 'The Clan Line 50th Anniversary Pullman', operated by UK Railtours. It was good to see that this train covered part of the route from that original outing from 1974. 27 April 2024.

35028
TORBAY
EXPRESS

Above: We will come back to 35028 again later, but now we have some views of the latest Merchant Navy to return to the main line, No. 35018 *British India Line*. This was the first of the Class to be rebuilt by BR in 1956 and unlike 35028 it was withdrawn in 1964 before the end of Southern Steam. It was then taken to the famous Barry scrapyard for disposal. However, the loco was saved in 1979 and has since moved to/from various preservation sites until it was eventually returned to steam (and the main line) in 2017. It is currently based at Carnforth from where it operates charter trains with West Coast Railways (WCRC) mostly in the North of England. One of the regular trains it worked for some time was the 'Scarborough Spa Express' between York and Scarborough. It is seen here beneath that fabulous roof of York station soon after coupling up to 1Z21, the 0741 Carnforth to Scarborough. Once again, the loco does not look out of place even though it is well away from its original stamping grounds! 23 August 2018.

Opposite above: 35018 is seen departing York on to the Scarborough line with 1Z21 seen in the previous shot. 23 August 2018.

Opposite below: During the last few years, the loco has (perhaps inevitably) worked a handful of charters in the South of England, most of which I have managed to catch up with. It is seen here arriving into Basingstoke with 1Z50, the 0822 London Victoria to Weymouth 'Bournemouth Express' charter operated by The Railway Touring Company. 3 July 2021.

THE SCARBOROUGH SPA EXPRESS
35018
35018

RAILWAY TOURING COMPANY
35018

Above: An extended stop at Basingstoke enabled another view as the train prepares to depart south. I believe there was a broken rail in the Micheldever area on this morning that caused the train to work wrong line from Micheldever to Winchester, providing an extra bonus for passengers! The superb loco makes an interesting comparison to the modern Class 450 unit in the adjacent platform. 3 July 2021.

Opposite above: Just six days later and 35018 was back in action on the South Western Main Line. Here it is again arriving at Basingstoke, but this time at platform 1 with 1Z50, the 0820 London Victoria to Yeovil Pen Mill 'The End of Southern Steam' charter, operated by The Railway Touring Company. This was running exactly fifty-four years to the day that steam ended on the Southern Region. 9 July 2021.

Opposite below: With many of these charter trains having to stop for water or await service trains in passing loops etc, it is often quite easy to get in front of them, as I have shown earlier in this book. This was possible again here as I jumped on a service train from Basingstoke back to my local station at Gillingham (Dorset) from where I was able to get this shot of 35018 with 1Z50 as it slowly passes through the station and draws up to a red signal (just out of picture to the right) to await the passage of an Exeter to London Waterloo service train. The signal box just visible above the loco tender was closed in 2012 but is retained as a ground frame to work the sole remaining siding here. 9 July 2021.

35018

35018

Above: Now we see 35018 passing through Southampton Central with 1Z82, the 0846 London Victoria to Weymouth 'The Bournemouth Belle' charter operated by the Railway Touring Company. This was another of the annual charters that commemorated the end of Southern Steam and ran as close to the anniversary (9 July) as possible. Another long closed signal box can be glimpsed to the left of shot. 6 July 2019.

Opposite above: We now start a sequence of shots taken on the same day showing 35018 with 1Z92, the London Victoria to Yeovil Pen Mill/Weymouth 'End of Southern Steam' charter operated by the Railway Touring Company. This is the first leg of the tour arriving at platform 4 at Salisbury. 9 July 2019.

Opposite below: The next view shows 35018 with 1Z92 arriving into the former down platform line at Yeovil Junction. The rusty rails tell their own story here as this line is rarely used these days and then usually only by the odd track machine. Although the station is still open to main line services using an island platform to the left, it was decimated at the end of the 1960s when the whole line from Salisbury to Exeter was rationalised. 9 July 2019.

35018
RAILWAY TOURING COMPANY

35018
RAILWAY TOURING COMPANY

Above: On arrival at Yeovil Junction the Merchant Navy was detached and the charter train continued on to Weymouth hauled by WCRC operated Class 47 diesel No. 47245 *VE Day 75th Anniversary*. Meanwhile 35018 was serviced at the Yeovil Railway Centre that is situated adjacent to the station. The first job was to reload the tender with coal, seen here being undertaken next to the former down loop platform. 9 July 2019.

Opposite above: Once coaling was completed the loco proceeded towards the turntable, taking a brief stop here by an old water crane for a rather authentic-looking steam-age shot! 9 July 2019.

Opposite below: Around 150 tons of locomotive is gingerly eased onto the surviving ex-BR turntable here at Yeovil Junction. Witnessed by part of the large public gathering to the right of shot, this process makes for very popular viewing. In fact, the Yeovil Railway Centre has constructed a special viewing grandstand overlooking the table here for just that purpose. The table itself is an amazing survivor, being retained after the ravages of the line's destruction for the use by the civil engineer's department for turning track machines etc. 9 July 2019.

35018
RAILWAY
TOURING
COMPANY

35018

Above: Finally, the loco has now been turned and serviced and is coming through the former down platform in readiness to take the spur to Yeovil Pen Mill and run light engine down to Weymouth to be reunited with its charter train. It then worked 1Z94, the 1739 Weymouth to London Victoria via Poole & Southampton. 9 July 2019.

Opposite above: Moving forward another four years and this is 35018 again, this time heading through the lovely countryside on the Somerset/Dorset border at Milborne Port between Templecombe and Sherborne. Although this section is still double track, closer inspection will show that the train is actually travelling over the up main line. The signalling in this section allows for trains to travel on either track in either direction (obviously not at the same time though!). The white building to the far right of this view is the former station building at Milborne Port, which was closed in the 1960s. It has long since been converted into a private dwelling. 9 July 2023.

Opposite below: For the last view of 35018 on the main line, we are back on the London Waterloo to Weymouth line at Redbridge, west of Southampton. The loco is coming off the line from Romsey with 5Z95, the 1013 Southall to Swanage ECS working. This working was running in conjunction with the upcoming Bulleid Pacific Gala to be held at the Swanage Railway where the loco and coaches were to take part in 'Strictly Bulleid II', a fine gathering of Bulleid's finest! 5 June 2024.

30
35018
35018

Above: As far as I know, this is the only time the Merchant Navy Locomotive Preservation Society (MNLPS) have allowed their loco to be temporarily renamed/renumbered. This is 35028 *Clan Line* (masquerading as 35017 *Belgian Marine*) glinting in the winter sunshine awaiting departure from London Victoria with 1Z84 1226 circular Christmas luncheon service via Shalford. I am not 100 per cent sure of the reason for the renaming. The real 35017 was withdrawn from service in July 1966 and scrapped not long after. 9 December 2011.

Opposite above: On the same date here is a broadside image of '35017' at London Victoria. 9 December 2011.

Opposite below: You can appreciate from this image that the transformation of the loco into '35017' was done very professionally. Often, when a loco number is temporarily changed you can see that the new number is simply overlaid resulting in the original still being visible, but not so here. The MNLPS certainly do things properly! 9 December 2011.

35017

8P
35017

Above: A little later in the day '35017' is captured coming up the gradient and joining the main London Waterloo to Weymouth line at Byfleet & New Haw with 1Z84, after being routed via Staines. 9 July 2011.

Opposite above: We are now returning to 35028 in its normal guise for a whistlestop (excuse the pun!) trip from Worting Junction, near Basingstoke, down to Exeter. The loco is seen here approaching Worting Junction with 1Z82, the 0752 London Waterloo to Exeter St Davids 'Atlantic Coast Express' operated by UK Railtours. The loco would have passed here many times in its BR career, and undoubtedly with this famous train in tow. 10 August 2019.

Opposite below: On a later date 35028 is arriving at Salisbury with 1Z82, the 0752 London Waterloo to Exeter St Davids 'Atlantic Coast Express', which was almost an identical run to the one seen in the previous view, but this time operated by the Railway Touring Company. This spot was the scene of a horrific train crash almost exactly 116 years earlier, on 1 July 1906, when an up express train from Plymouth was trying to go far too fast around this very tight curve and derailed, hitting another train and causing total carnage, with the loss of some twenty-eight lives. 2 July 2022.

35028
ATLANTIC
COAST EXPRESS
6

35028
ATLANTIC
COAST EXPRESS

Above: Here is a view that was once an everyday part of the railway scene in steam days. 35028 is coming to a halt at the western end of platform 4 at Salisbury with 1Z90, the 0844 London Victoria to Salisbury 'The Great Britain XVII' (Day 1 of 9) charter operated by the Railway Touring Company. In the steam era this was the scene of many an engine change and in later years, when engine changes ceased, a race to change crews and get the loco watered before setting off west once again. 26 April 2025.

Opposite above: The loco and support coach was taken off the train here at Salisbury and moved to the down bay to be serviced before continuing later in the day on to Bristol Temple Meads. These days, water cranes are mostly just a distant memory so watering usually has to be done using a road tanker. 26 April 2025.

Opposite below: Moving down the line we reach Tisbury where we see 35028 in full cry passing the loop provided here in 1986 and approaching the station with 1Z63, the 0713 London Victoria to Exeter St Davids 'Atlantic Coast Express' operated by UK Railtours. This train returned to London via Westbury and Melksham and a view of it at Cole (near Bruton) appeared earlier in this book. 23 September 2017.

Salisbury
THE
GREAT BRITAIN XVII
35028

Above: On a different occasion we see the loco soon after passing Tisbury station and getting to grips with the climb to Semley as it heads west with 1Z67, the 0955 London Waterloo to Weymouth 'Cathedrals Express' operated by Steam Dreams. On arrival at Yeovil Junction the loco was removed for servicing while the train proceeded to Weymouth hauled by a diesel loco. 35028 later travelled down to Weymouth light engine and returned the train to London via Poole. 9 July 2012.

Opposite above: Taken from a public foot-crossing between Tisbury and the closed station at Semley, this is the stirring sight of 35028 tackling the gradient and reverse curves as it heads west with 1Z67, the 1041 London Waterloo to Yeovil Junction 'Waterloo Sunset' charter operated by UK Railtours. It is hard to imagine now that this was once a busy double track main line. 9 July 2017.

Opposite below: I mentioned the closed Semley station in the previous shot and in this view, it was, and the remains are still, behind the camera as 35028, carrying its black-backed nameplates, is breasting the summit of the climb from Tisbury with 1Z82, the 0846 London Victoria to Sherborne 'John Farrow Salute' charter, operated by UK Railtours. This train ran to commemorate John Farrow, the founder of UK Railtours who passed away during 2020. The area to the left of this shot was originally part of Semley station goods yard. 18 August 2021.

35028
THE WATERLOO SUNSET

35028
THE JOHN FARROW SALUTE

Above: This is Gillingham (Dorset) during a sharp summer shower as 35028 arrives with 1Z94, the 0846 London Waterloo to Weymouth (via Yeovil Junction) 'End of Southern Steam' charter operated by the Railway Touring Company. 9 July 2024.

Opposite above: Just west of Gillingham is the well-known location of Buckhorn Weston Tunnel, largely hidden in this view, where we see 35028 exiting in a cloud of smoke and steam with 1Z68, the 1740 Yeovil Junction to London Waterloo which is the return of the 'Waterloo Sunset' charter seen in an earlier shot. Note the 'banana' effect of the train as it passes over the summit of the climb up from Templecombe. 9 July 2017.

Opposite below: We saw 35018 here earlier in this book, and this time it is the turn of 35028 to be serviced at Yeovil Junction; first, it is seen on the turntable at the commencement of the turning process. The loco had earlier worked 1Z92, the 0846 London Victoria to Sherborne 'Carols at Sherborne Abbey' charter, then ECS to Yeovil Junction. It also marked the 70th birthday of the loco, hence the subtle '70' on one of the headcode discs on the front. 20 December 2018.

35028
THE WATERLOO
SUNSET

35028
70
35028

Above: Unusually, rather than it being carried out in the Yeovil Railway Centre, the coaling of the loco was done opposite the site in one of the remaining sidings. In lovely winter sunshine, it is being topped up for the return journey back to London. 20 December 2018.

Opposite above: A few miles west of Yeovil Junction lies Sutton Bingham reservoir which supplies an area of Somerset with drinking water. On an overcast morning 35028 is seen passing this substantial body of water with 1Z28, the 0714 London Waterloo to Exeter St Davids 'Atlantic Coast Express' charter operated by the Railway Touring Company. 12 October 2024.

Opposite below: To conclude this chapter on main line Merchant Navies we see 35028 approaching Exeter Central with 1Z91, the 0844 London Victoria to Exeter St Davids 'Cathedrals Express' charter, operated by Steam Dreams. This section of line, about a mile or so, was exceptionally busy in the steam era, especially with light locomotives moving between Exeter Central and the former Exmouth Junction steam shed. It is much quieter nowadays though! 3 May 2012.

SY
50
SY
48
34028
15

34027
EDDYSTONE
34028

Above: The loco is now seen departing from platform 1 (presently no longer in use) with another shuttle heading for Eastleigh. 28 June 1992.

Below: The following year 34027 was in action again on the Salisbury to Exeter line. It is seen here pulling away from the Sherborne stop with a London Waterloo to Yeovil Junction charter. I am not sure where the loco had worked from, but possibly Salisbury. 10 April 1993.

Above: Just east of Sherborne and this is the return charter seen in the previous shot. 34027 is producing some serious 'clag' as it heads up the rising incline towards Templecombe. Despite appearances, the young lady standing on the drain cover and waving is not related, just a lucky coincidence! 10 April 1993.

Below: We are now at Yeovil Junction again where 34027 is seen arriving from the west with 'The Sarum' charter from Exeter St Davids. 19 September 1993.

Above: Now at the eastern end of Yeovil Junction station, 34027 has been watered and is raring to depart with the charter seen in the previous shot. 19 September 1993.

Opposite above: On a thoroughly wet and miserable afternoon, this is 34027 passing Wool (Dorset) with the 'Dorset Phoenix' which was the first through train from Weymouth to London Waterloo to be worked by steam since 1967. On the rear, electro-diesel 73003 can just be made out, having worked the train from London Waterloo to Weymouth that morning. 13 November 1993.

Opposite below: As we noted earlier in this volume, some locos have carried non-authentic liveries during the time they have been in preservation, usually rather frowned-upon by the steam purists. Showing this off to good effect is 34027 (temporarily re-named *Hogwarts Express*) standing 'on the blocks' at the unlikely location of London Kings Cross in its striking maroon livery, applied as part of the filming for the 'Hogwarts Express' in a Harry Potter film entitled *Harry Potter and the Goblet of Fire*. Personally, as I said for 35005 *Canadian Pacific*, I quite like it. This train toured the country visiting many locations over the course of a few days with the author J. K. Rowling on board. 8 July 2000.

34027
THE DORSET PHOENIX
WO
3

10:02:54
34027
THE HOGWARTS EXPRESS

Above: On a hot summer's day, 34016 is seen powering up the gradient at Upton Scudamore, between Westbury and Warminster with a Bath to London Victoria 'Cathedrals Express' charter run by Steam Dreams. This steep climb, be it either steam or diesel hauled, very often required banking assistance in the rear, but I cannot recall any on this occasion. 26 July 2001.

Opposite above: A cold day this time, and 34016 is viewed arriving at its destination with 1Z96, the 1100 London Waterloo to Salisbury 'Cathedrals Express' operated by Steam Dreams. After spending a large amount of its preserved life based at the Mid-Hants Railway it eventually left for pastures new based at Carnforth with the West Coast Railway Co (WCRC) who eventually intend to get it back on the main line. 9 December 2003.

Opposite below: We now move on to a more recent addition to grace the national network in the form of 34046 *Braunton*. After a long restoration this loco eventually returned to service on the West Somerset Railway during 2008. Ten years later however it was purchased by Locomotive Services LTD (LSL) and is now very active across the UK, and is often out based at Southall, West London. This first shot shows the loco powering away from Hawkeridge Junction, just north of Westbury with 1Z40, the 0620 Rugby to Bristol Temple Meads 'Great Western Envoy' operated by Saphos Trains. It was routed via Hanwell Bridge Loop from where 34046 had worked through to destination. 15 April 2023.

34016
THE CATHEDRALS
EXPRESS
30

34046

Above: Passing the delightfully named hamlet of Wyke Champflower, near Castle Cary 34046 heads west with 1Z27, the 0800 Bristol Temple Meads to Kingswear (via Westbury) 'English Riviera Express' operated by Saphos Trains. Interestingly, when in BR service this loco was allocated to Bournemouth shed for a good part of its working life and as such was regularly seen working over the former Somerset & Dorset Railway. A short distance to the rear of train was the point that the S&D crossed the line along which this train is travelling. See earlier in the Merchant Navy section a view of 35028 *Clan Line* travelling in the opposite direction taken from the remains of this embankment. 16 June 2019.

Opposite above: The Light Pacifics were a regular sight at Exeter St Davids in BR days on services to Plymouth (via Tavistock) and also services to North Devon/Cornwall via Barnstaple. 34046 makes a fine sight as it passes through non-stop with 1Z60, the 0748 Slough to Kingswear 'English Riviera Express' operated by Saphos Trains. The loco worked the train from Norton Fitzwarren (Taunton) as it was temporarily based on the West Somerset Railway at the time. 18 June 2022.

Opposite below: Immaculate as always, 34046 curves around past Dawlish Warren with 1Z36, the 0424 Nantwich to Kingswear 'English Riviera Express' operated by Saphos Trains. The loco once again had worked this train from Norton Fitzwarren. It is worth noting that the shield above the nameplate on this loco was added in preservation, it never wore one in BR service. 4 May 2024.

34046
When an abuser controls your finances, they control you.

34046
BRAUNTON
34046

Above: During 2016/17 34046 was renamed as Battle of Britain 34052 *Lord Dowding* by its owner, the original loco being one of the few examples that worked right up until steam on the Southern Region ceased in July 1967. One of its first workings in this guise was 1Z46, the 1008 Clapham Junction to Southampton Central 'The Eagles Express', organised by Crystal Palace Football Club. This is the first 'Footex' that had been hauled by steam since it was abolished by BR. The train is seen here just after arriving at Southampton Central. 15 May 2016.

Opposite above: This interesting view shows the disguised 34046 with 1Z43, the 0647 Three Bridges to Weymouth crossing the River Hamble on the approach to Bursledon, Hants, which the loco worked throughout. The marina here looks to be almost at breaking point with boats! 8 April 2017.

Opposite below: Such were the timings of this charter that it was booked to stop for some time at Mount Pleasant, near Southampton, so I was easily able to get a service train back to the city to obtain a couple more shots. Here the train has just exited Southampton Tunnel and is approaching platform 3 at Central station. 8 April 2017.

34052

Above: The last shot of this charter shows the loco in platform 3 at Southampton Central with a good head of steam as it prepares to depart south. 8 April 2017.

Opposite above: Another well-known stamping ground for these Pacifics was of course the West of England Line from Salisbury to Exeter. Here is 34046 arriving with 1Z92, the 0834 London Victoria to Bath Spa 'London to Bath' charter, operated by Steam Dreams. 24 May 2023.

Opposite below: Passing a wonderful stand of Rosebay Willowherb the loco (running as 34052) is getting into its stride as it thunders up the gradient at Hatch, just after passing through Tisbury with 1Z67, the 0900 London Waterloo to Yeovil Junction 'The End of Southern Steam' charter, operated by the Railway Touring Company. Upon arrival at Yeovil Junction the train then proceeded to Yeovil Pen Mill and was then hauled to Weymouth by Class 33 diesel No. 33207 *Jim Martin*. The Pacific later went light engine to Weymouth to return the train to London via Poole and Southampton. 8 July 2017.

THE STEAM DREAMS RAIL CO · EST 1999
34046
BRAUNTON
6

34052

Above: Two or three miles further south we are at an overbridge at Motcombe, near to Gillingham (Dorset) to see the loco pounding up towards Semley on the western side of the gradient seen in the previous shot with 1Z69, the 1650 Weymouth to London Victoria 'Cathedrals Express' operated by Steam Dreams. This charter worked the exact opposite route from the one in the previous image. 26 June 2014.

Opposite above: Slowly passing the closed signal box at Gillingham (Dorset) is 1Z70, the 0830 London Victoria to Yeovil Junction charter operated by Steam Dreams. This train once again went on to Weymouth via the same route as described a couple of shots ago. The signal box closed in early 2012 but has been retained as a ground frame for the siding seen in the foreground. 27 June 2023.

Opposite below: Our short trip down the West of England line concludes here at Exeter Central as 34046 arrives with 1Z82 London Victoria to Exeter St Davids, the first leg of the 'Great Britain VII' around Britain charter. In its heyday this location was a hive of activity, as can be witnessed by the wide area between the platforms that used to accommodate two more tracks. 26 April 2014.

STEAM DREAMS
34046

34046

Above: Far removed from the South West of England, this is 34046 passing through Wandsworth Road with 1Z82, the 0720 Alresford (Mid-Hants Railway) to Kingscote (Bluebell Railway) operated by Steam Dreams. This was the first charter train to operate between these two heritage lines. Note the famous long-closed Battersea Power Station in the background, which has now been restored as a trendy shopping village of all things! 2 October 2014.

Opposite above: Of all the routes used by steam in the South of England, the section from Reading to Basingstoke rarely features. Our last look at 34046 (running as 34052 again), sees it going well with 1Z82, the 0740 West Brompton to Salisbury 'Cathedrals Express' charter operated by Steam Dreams just south of Mortimer as it heads for Basingstoke. 29 November 2016.

Opposite below: In the course of composing this volume, the latest Pacific to gain a main line certificate is 34028 *Eddystone*, owned by Southern Locomotives and based on the Swanage Railway in Dorset for almost thirty years. After much work to fit all the necessary equipment during the last six months or so, this is its very first main line outing speeding through Basingstoke, with whistle blowing in the company of the Swanage Railway's Class 33 diesel D6515 'just in case' running as 0Z28, the 1026 Swanage to Southall WCRC. 3 September 2025.

34028

Above: Making a fine sight, 34067 thunders past the disused sidings just east of Aldermaston on the Berks & Hants route from Reading to Westbury. The train is 1Z27, the 0920 London Paddington to Yeovil Junction 'The Somerset Explorer', operated by the Railway Touring Company. I am not sure if these sidings still exist but the main lines are now cluttered with overhead electrification equipment. 14 February 2009.

Opposite above: The next selection of images show the loco working on various parts of its former stamping grounds. Going at a good speed through Farnborough (Main) we see it heading east with 1Z82, the 0800 Swanage to London Waterloo 'The Capital Christmas Express' operated by the Railway Touring Company. The loco again worked the train throughout as well as the return. 28 November 2009.

Opposite below: Here is an unusual, almost aerial view as the loco passes beneath the horrible concrete structure that carries the M3 motorway across the line just south of Winchfield. It is hauling 1Z67, the 0844 London Victoria to Weymouth 'Dorset Coast Express', operated by the Railway Touring Company. During the days of Southern Steam this area was a favourite location for photographers of the day, but that was prior to this carbuncle of a bridge appearing of course! 3 September 2014.

34067
THE
ROYAL WESSEX

Above: A few miles further south we are at Basingstoke station to see 34067 arriving with the same train as we saw a couple of shots ago at Farnborough (Main). These steam charters are often given slack timings so it was easy to get a service train from here to get ahead of it. 28 November 2009.

Opposite above: Making our way further south along the South Western Main Line, this is the loco in full cry once again approaching Winchester with 1Z67, the 0844 London Victoria to Weymouth 'Dorset Coast Express', operated by the Railway Touring Company. 2 September 2015.

Opposite below: A week later and 34067 was busy again, here approaching Eastleigh with 1Z67, the 0844 London Victoria to Weymouth 'Dorset Coast Express', operated by the Railway Touring Company once again. This was the last run of this train for the season. 9 September 2015.

34067

34067

Above: Beneath a very dramatic sky, 34067 heads south near Woodfiddley, in the heart of the New Forest National Park with 1Z92, the 0810 Clapham Junction to Weymouth 'Sunny South Express' operated by Steam Dreams, on the 42nd anniversary of the end of Southern Steam operations on BR. As one can imagine, in the ensuing sixteen years or so since I took this shot the tree growth here has earned it the 'Forest' part of the name, quite literally! This charter was later marred by an almost two-hour late departure from Weymouth, through no fault of the loco! 9 July 2009.

Opposite above: Looking magnificent as it leaves a trail of smoke across the New Forest, 34067 is just south of Beaulieu Road station with 1Z67, the 0755 London Waterloo to Weymouth 'Cathedrals Express'. This was another of the annual trains run to coincide with the last day of Southern Steam in 1967. The later Weymouth to Yeovil section traversed by this charter unusually involved ex-LMS 2-8-0 48151, which is not very often seen on the main line in the South. 9 July 2011.

Opposite below: This time 34067 has just stormed through the small New Forest station at Sway as it heads east towards Brockenhurst with 1Z87, the 1015 Poole to Bristol Temple Meads 'Bath & Bristol Xmas Express' operated by the Railway Touring Company. 24 November 2011.

34067
464
34067

Above: West from Salisbury and this is the loco working hard on the gradient on the approach to the long-closed station at Semley with 1Z82, the 0745 London Victoria to Exeter St Davids 'The Great Britain VI' (Day 1 of 9) round Britain charter operated by the Railway Touring Company. Despite all the huge trees lining most of the West of England line, this spot was surprisingly clear at the time. It has, however, now been lost. 20 April 2013.

Opposite above: Just about a quarter of a mile east of the previous shot and this is 34067 racing down the grade from Semley in the opposite direction with 1Z67, the 1437 Exeter St Davids to London Victoria 'The Atlantic Coast Express' (Day 2 of 2) operated by Steam Dreams. This charter ran to commemorate the final run of the train of the same name back on 5 September 1964. 8 September 2014.

Opposite below: Here the loco is about to make a very smoky departure from Exeter St Davids with 1Z85, the 1301 Bristol Temple Meads to Wareham 'Somerset & Dorset Remembered' charter, operated by Kingfisher Railtours. The loco was just about to tackle the notorious 1-37 incline up to Exeter Central station. The Light Pacific's were an everyday sight here in steam days. 2 September 2006.

34067
ATLANTIC
COAST EXPRESS

34067

Above: To conclude our main line survey, we have a couple of images of 34067 a bit more off the beaten track. In near perfect conditions we see it crossing the River Arun at Ford, West Sussex, with the returning 1Z83 1518 Bognor to London Victoria 'Sussex Belle' operated by the Railway Touring Company. 23 September 2006.

Below: Finally, to bring the main line preservation story of 34067 up to date, the loco is crossing the famous Ribblehead Viaduct on the Settle–Carlisle line with 1Z64, the 1422 Carlisle to Newcastle 'Northern Belle' Pullman charter. Since the late 2010s the loco has been used almost exclusively in the North of England. 28 May 2022.

3

Heritage Lines & Non-operational Merchant Navy Class

35005 *Canadian Pacific*
35006 *Peninsular & Oriental SN Company*
35011 *General Steam Navigation*
35018 *British India Line*
35028 *Clan Line*
35029 *Ellerman Lines*

The list above are locos I have photographed in the preservation era, but are not all operational at the time of writing. Other examples of the Class exist but I have not

We start this section with 35005 *Canadian Pacific*, which has been based on the Mid-Hants (Watercress Line) for many years and in early 2025 it was returned to service after a long overhaul. In the main line section, it was seen at work on various charters, but when not required it was regularly used on internal services. Here we see it at Medstead & Four Marks with an Alresford to Alton train during the 20th anniversary of the line in 1993. 3 July 1993.

managed to catch up with those—yet! Because of their weight these big Pacifics are not ideally suited to heritage lines, but nevertheless it is an important part of their continued work and maintenance requirements, and for the enthusiast it is great to see and enjoy them close up working at lower speeds etc.

Above: The loco is seen here waiting impatiently at Alresford for its next turn of duty. Often these large powerful locos (not just Bulleid Pacifics) are referred to as 'caged beasts' on heritage lines! 23 September 2005.

Opposite above: Complete with a 'Royal Wessex' headboard, the loco sets off from Ropley with an Alresford to Alton service. 21 September 2007.

Opposite below: The signal is off and 35005 is ready to depart tender first from Medstead & Four Marks with an Alton to Alresford service. 2 February 2008.

35005
THE
ROYAL WESSEX
35005

Above: It is not very often these days that one can get to compare the rebuilt forms of Merchant Navy and West Country Pacifics side by side. This, however, is the view at Alton with 35005 next to its smaller cousin, 34016 *Bodmin*. 23 September 2005.

Opposite above: 35005 has also made visits to other heritage lines in the preservation era. In a powerful view, it is ready to depart from Bishops Lydeard with a service for Minehead on the West Somerset Railway. 30 September 2005.

Opposite below: Later the same day, the Pacific departs from Crowcombe Heathfield with another Bishops Lydeard to Minehead service. 30 September 2005.

35005

35005

Above: Moving to the Swanage Railway and this is 35027 *Port Line*, which operated on the line for a while in the early 2000s, and prior to this did a stint on the Bluebell Line soon after restoration from a Barry scrapyard wreck. However, it has never worked on the main line in preservation. The loco is seen here at Swanage station before commencing its day's duties at the annual steam gala. 8 September 2001.

Opposite above: Here is the loco a bit later in the day arriving at Harman's Cross station bound for Norden. Although it would never have worked this branch line, it was based at the nearby Bournemouth MPD for a good deal of its working life. 8 September 2001.

Opposite below: With Harman's Cross signal box (built 1996) to the right, 35027 awaits departure north to Corfe Castle and Norden. 8 September 2001.

35027
281

BP
35027
PORT
LINE

Above: The highlight of the day's proceedings was the pairing of 35027 with Battle of Britain 34072 257 *Squadron*. The pair are seen here coming across Corfe Castle Viaduct and approach their destination with a Swanage to Norden train. 8 September 2001.

Opposite above: Another popular event held annually on the Swanage Railway is the 'Winter Warm-Up', usually between Christmas and new year. 35027 is again seen at Harman's Cross awaiting departure for Corfe Castle & Norden. 28 December 2002.

Opposite below: Also taken during this gala day, the loco presents a powerful sight as it approaches Corfe Castle with a service from Swanage to Norden. 28 December 2002.

35027
381
HARMANS CROSS

35027
381

Above: With part of Corfe Castle glimpsed to the right of shot, 35027 is not far from its final stop at Norden with a train from Swanage. This weekend steam gala was one of the last times it worked on the line as it was later found to have serious cracks in its firebox that would prove to be very expensive. It was, therefore, sold to millionaire Jeremy Hosking in 2005. I am not sure of its current status but I believe the plan is for it to eventually go main line. 13 September 2003.

Opposite above: Our last view of 35027 sees it at Afflington, soon after departing from Harman's Cross with a Norden-bound train. 14 September 2003.

Opposite below: This is our friend 35028 *Clan Line* again, but this time at the unlikely location of Swanage shed! At the time the heritage line had not long been reconnected to the national network and 35028 had worked in with 1Z97, the 0845 London Victoria to Swanage 'The Royal Wessex', operated by UK Railtours. I think this was one of the first visits the loco made to a heritage line. 27 April 2012.

35027

35028
35028
THE
ROYAL WESSEX

Above: Moving on again and we are at Cheltenham Racecourse to see 35006 *Peninsular & Oriental SN Company*, having just run round its train and awaiting to depart with a train for Broadway. 4 August 2016.

Opposite above: My visit here was made not long after the loco returned to service. The loco being rescued from Barry scrapyard, the long road to restoration took just over thirty years of hard work. Amazing to think that 2025 marks the end of its current boiler certificate. Here, the loco awaits the signal to depart from Cheltenham Racecourse. 4 August 2016.

Opposite below: 35006 was unusual among the thirty Merchant Navies, in that it was the only example to remain allocated to one shed for all of its working life of about twenty-six years; that shed being Salisbury. With a nice patch of Rosebay Willowherb to the left, this loco is seen shortly after departing from Cheltenham Racecourse with a train for Broadway. 4 August 2016.

35006

35006

Above: During its time in service since restoration 35006 has visited a couple of other heritage lines, one of these being the Swanage Railway. It is seen here at Corfe Castle station during the line's 'Strictly Bulleid II' gala. 7 June 2024.

Opposite above: This 'Strictly Bulleid II' gala was an incredible spectacle involving no less than EIGHT Pacifics, including two West Country's, four Battle of Britain's and two Merchant Navies! For many though, the highlight was the daily diagram of a pair of Merchants. This was the first time this had happened since 2 July 1967, when 35007 *Aberdeen Commonwealth* and 35008 *Orient Line* worked a Weymouth to Waterloo charter right at the dying days of Southern Steam. The superb sight of 35006+35018 are seen here departing Harman's Cross with a service for Norden. 9 June 2024.

Opposite below: The crew on board 35018 look rightly proud as the locos await departure from Corfe Castle for Norden. That unmistakeable landmark looms above the scene. 7 June 2024.

35006
CANBERRA
P & O-ORIENT LINES

35018

Above: Believe it or not, this is 35018 *British India Line* that the crew are looking out from in the previous shot! Eighteen years earlier it is stored in the yard of South Coast Steam Ltd at Portland, Dorset, of all places. The loco was here for eight years until it was moved north to Carnforth, the base of West Coast Railways (WCR), and at the end of 2016 finally returned to steam for the first time since 1964. It has been a regular performer on the main line, mostly in northern England since then. 29 August 2006.

Opposite above: This one is not in the best of health! The remains of 35011 *General Steam Navigation* are seen outside the depot at Williton on the West Somerset Railway. There has been much movement between various sites over the time this example was rescued from Barry scrapyard in 1983 but it has most recently been at the Swindon and Cricklade Railway, where some degree of restoration has taken place over the last few years. In mid-2025, however, the loco owners asked them to vacate the site and a new home has thankfully been found at the Yeovil Railway Centre, adjacent to Yeovil Junction station. The intention is to eventually 'de-rebuild' the loco back to its original form with the 'air-smoothed' casing etc. A very ambitious project indeed. 15 March 2008.

Opposite below: I am pretty sure that many readers of this volume are familiar with 35029 *Ellerman Lines*, displayed as a sectioned exhibit at the National Railway Museum for many years now. We close this series with a couple of shots of it in the great Hall. At the time the loco was chosen there was some talk about why such a prestige loco was chosen over many 'lesser' locos to choose from at the time, but I don't think any real answer was forthcoming. Here is the loco showing its 'good side'. 23 August 2018.

TFL BTN 566151

35029
ATLANTIC
COAST EXPRESS
35029

Above: A couple of years later the loco is facing the opposite direction in the Ropley shed yard. 14 May 2005.

Opposite above: This time we see the loco running into Ropley with a service from Alton to Alresford. The 'Cunarder' headboard was one of many that were carried on various boat trains that used to run to/from Southampton Docks. 21 September 2007.

Opposite below: A few years earlier 34016 was to be found double heading with Merchant Navy 35005 Canadian Pacific, providing an interesting sight of the two Pacific locos together. I am sure this was not unheard of in steam days but it would certainly have been rare. 29 July 2001.

SPL
21
34016
THE
CUNARDER

34016

Above: Another early restoration was 34105 *Swanage*, the youngest preserved example. The immaculate loco is seen departing Ropley with an Alton-bound service. The loco worked until the late 1990s but has now been out of service for many years. However, at the time of writing I believe this loco is now in an advanced state of restoration. 3 July 1993.

Opposite above: During its time awaiting overhaul, 34105 briefly changed identities with class mate 34102 *Lapford*, which was one of the final un-rebuilt examples to remain in service. It is seen here in a rather sorry looking state in the yard at Ropley. 13 March 2009. frogpupp

Opposite below: From one of the youngest, to the oldest preserved example. This is 34007 *Wadebridge* approaching Ropley with an Alton to Alresford service. Originally restored to working order in the mid-2000s, it is now reaching the end of another overhaul with an expected date of completion sometime during 2026. 13 March 2009.

34007

Above: 34007 is seen at Ropley station with another service bound for Alresford on the same day as the previous shot. 13 March 2009.

Opposite above: With 34102 (105) in the yard, 34007 heads north from Ropley with a train for Alton. Since this view was taken there is now a footbridge crossing the line at this point. 13 March 2009.

Opposite below: If you thought 34105 looked a bit sad, look at this poor example! 34073 249 *Squadron* is viewed in the head shunt at Ropley in an un-restored state and exposed to the elements. What remains of this loco has since been moved to West Coast Railway Company at Carnforth and mainly used as a source of spares for 34067 *Tangmere*. It is very doubtful that 34073 will ever steam again in its own right. 18 May 2003.

34102
34007

34073

Above: This is more like it! Carrying its original malachite green Southern Railway livery, visiting 34081 92 *Squadron* is pulling away from Ropley with an Alresford to Alton service. 26 September 2003.

Below: Here is 34081 awaiting to depart south from Ropley with a train for Alresford. 26 September 2003.

Above: At the same spot but from the platform side, the loco fits in very well with its surroundings. 26 September 2003.

Below: This time we see 34081 pulling away from Alresford with an Alton bound train. 26 September 2003.

Above: One of the most elusive (for me at least!) of the preserved Bulleid's has been 34039 *Boscastle* and I have only managed to catch up with it once when I had a ride behind it on the Great Central Railway. The loco is seen here at Loughborough Central prior to my ride. 29 May 2000.

Opposite above: This is 34039 on the completion of my ride at Leicester North station with the driver removing the destination disc for the return tender first trip. Unfortunately, just a few days after my visit the loco was withdrawn with a troublesome firebox and has yet to return to service at the time of writing. 29 May 2000.

Opposite below: Seen earlier in this book during its exploits on the main line, this is 34046 *Braunton* looking absolutely immaculate at Bishops Lydeard on the West Somerset Railway, where it was based for a short while. This image was taken just one month or so after it had undergone the massive task to restore it from a scrapyard wreck. Further information on its second main line career was given earlier in the book. 25 October 2008.

34039

34046
BRAUNTON

Above: Later the same day, the loco is seen on the approach to Blue Anchor with a Minehead to Bishops Lydeard service. Note the suitably clad person in the front coach wearing goggles to keep the coal dust from getting in his eyes, a common practice 'back in the day'. 25 October 2008.

Opposite above: Here is a final view of 34046 for the time being soon after departing from Bishops Lydeard, as it returns tender first with a Minehead service. 25 October 2008.

Opposite below: Still on the West Somerset Railway, this is the rare sight in preservation of rebuilt and un-rebuilt Battle of Britain's double heading. 34053 *Sir Keith Park* + 34070 *Manston* make a wonderful sight as they slowly approach Blue Anchor with a Minehead to Bishops Lydeard train. 6 March 2016.

Above: Here is another view of the pair at Blue Anchor station. Both locos were visiting the line for the 50th anniversary gala of the closure of the Somerset & Dorset Railway. 6 March 2016.

Opposite above: With the addition of a turning triangle formed at Norton Fitzwarren during the 2010s, it has become possible to turn locos at the southern end of the line. The same pair are seen here at Cottiford, between Stogumber and Williton with a Minehead bound train. 6 March 2016.

Opposite below: Still on the West Somerset Railway, and keeping to the Somerset & Dorset theme, this is visiting 34067 *Tangmere* piloted by BR Standard Class 4 2.6.0 76079 that was running as long-lost class mate 76009 that often worked on the S&D. The pair are running tender first just east of Crowcombe Heathfield with a Bishops Lydeard bound service. Part of the Quantock Hills can be seen in the background. 19 March 2006.

Above: Seen on the Mid-Hants earlier in this section, this is 34007 *Wadebridge* creating a pretty good recreation of an inter-regional train from the late 50s/early 60s with its complete rake of maroon stock. It is at Bishops Lydeard having just arrived from Minehead. 17 March 2007.

Opposite above: Here the loco is about to take on water after coming off the train in the previous shot. 17 March 2007.

Opposite below: Our last look at 34007 sees it coaled and watered and awaiting its next duty at Bishops Lydeard. 17 March 2007.

34007
WADEBRIDGE

34007
WADEBRIDGE

Above: Moving on again and this is the first of a few shots taken on the Bluebell Railway in Sussex. Unfortunately, I have not been able to visit again since the time these shots were taken in the early 2000s. This view sees long-time resident on the line 21C123 *Blackmore Vale* approaching Kingscote with a train from Sheffield Park. Back at this time this station was the eastern terminus of the line. 28 July 2001.

Opposite above: Later in the day at the same location we see 21C123 piloting visiting 34081 *92 Squadron* approaching with a train from Sheffield Park. I believe this was the first time since Southern Railway Days that two Bulleid's carrying malachite green livery had been paired up. 28 July 2001.

Opposite below: The immaculate 21C123 stands at Kingscote station awaiting its next move. Interestingly, the version of the name carried here was the one it carried for a couple of years when new in 1946, but this was changed to the correct spelling Blackmore Vale during 1948. 28 July 2001.

SOUTHERN
21C123

SOUTHERN
21C123
21C123
SOUTHERN

Above: With loco and train looking very smart indeed, 21C123 departs from Horsted Keynes with a train from Sheffield Park to Kingscote. Surprisingly, to date this loco has never visited any other heritage line in the UK as far as I am aware? 28 July 2001.

Opposite above: Visiting loco 34081 *92 Squadron* stands at Sheffield Park awaiting its next service. This loco never received a '21C' number as that practice was discontinued from 34071 onwards when British Railways came into being. 28 July 2001.

Opposite below: Our last look at the Bluebell line sees 21C123 awaiting departure from Sheffield Park with a Kingscote bound service. 20 July 2002.

BRITISH RAILWAYS
34081
34081

SOUTHERN
21C123
21C123
SOUTHERN

Above: The rest of this section is dedicated to the various light Pacific's either based at, or visiting the Swanage Railway over the years at various locations along the route. Starting with some early shots, the first example to grace the line was 34072 257 *Squadron*, seen at Harmans Cross on Remembrance Day, very soon after its transformation from a Barry scrapyard wreck had been completed. At this time trains were only running to here from Swanage. The headboard is a nod to the massive involvement by Tarmac contributing to the rapid restoration of this loco. 11 November 1990.

Opposite above: On the same day as the previous shot, 34072 is captured passing Herston with a Swanage to Harmans Cross train. 11 November 1990.

Opposite below: A few years later on another early visit to Swanage, this is the great sight of two un-rebuilt Pacific's together at the station. 34072 257 *Squadron* and visiting 34105 *Swanage*, both carrying headboards of famous Southern Region named express's briefly pose for photographs, before 34105 set off with a train for Harmans Cross. 21 March 1993.

34072
TARMAC
SWINDON

34072
ATLANTIC
COAST EXPRESS
34105
BOURNEMOUTH
BELLE

Above: After 12 years of service on the line, 34072 was withdrawn in early 2003 with firebox problems. On its last day in service, it is waiting to depart from Swanage with a train for Norden. 5 January 2003.

Opposite above: After withdrawal, the loco was put into open storage at various locations on the line until a place could be found in Herston Works for an overhaul to commence. It is seen here soon after being admitted and in the process of being stripped down and assessed. 13 March 2010.

Opposite below: It is always nice to see a bit of humour along with the serious work that lay ahead, especially when restoring a huge steam loco! 13 March 2010.

34072

257 SQUADRON
BATTLE OF BRITAIN CLASS
(BURMA) SQUADRON
ROYAL AIR FORCE
GOERING
BATTLE OF BRITAIN (RUNNER UP) CLASS

Above: 34072 eventually returned to service in late 2018 and is seen here crossing Corfe Castle Viaduct with a Swanage to Norden service. 28 July 2019.

Opposite above: Here the loco is arriving at Harmans Cross five months later with a Swanage to Norden train during the line's annual 'Winter Warm Up' mini gala. 28 December 2019.

Opposite below: Looking very clean as usual, the loco is approaching Afflington, soon after departing Harmans Cross with a Swanage to Norden service. 30 April 2022.

34072

34072

Above: After coming up the incline more or less all the way from Swanage, the loco is just starting to slow on the approach to Harmans Cross station with a Norden bound train. 28 July 2019.

Opposite above: Since the mid-2010s the Swanage Railway have often used the Norden to Frome River Bridge section (where there is no station) during galas, usually with locos in 'top & tail' mode. 34072 is seen here about to cross Stoborough Heath, near Furzebrook with a Frome River Bridge to Swanage train. This section extends the normal operating distance from Swanage to Norden by an extra three to four miles. 13 October 2018.

Opposite below: A low level view of 34072 this time as the loco crosses Corfe Viaduct and approaches its destination of Norden with a train from Swanage. 29 March 2025.

34072
34072

34072

Above: Later in the same day as the previous shot, the loco is seen working tender first at Afflington with a goods train, as it catches a glint from the weak sunshine. Note all the people in that guard's van that are no doubt getting a good view in close-up of the working Pacific! 29 March 2025.

Opposite above: This time we catch the loco arriving at Corfe Castle with a Swanage to Norden train. 22 August 2025.

Opposite below: With that one and only backdrop, 34072 awaits departure for the last quarter of a mile or so to Norden. 22 August 2025.

34072

34072

Above: Arguably one of the best views to had on any heritage line in the UK, seen from the top of West Hill 34028 pulls away from Corfe Castle the short distance to the end of its journey at Norden. 13 September 2008.

Opposite above: A powerful image of 34028 as it slows for the stop at Corfe Castle station with a Norden bound service. 13 April 2008.

Opposite below: Another shot taken in the low, early winter sunshine as the loco comes across Corfe Viaduct and approaches Norden station with a train from Swanage. 19 November 2011.

34028

34028

Above: An alternative view of the attractive Corfe Viaduct as 34028 crosses tender first with a Norden to Swanage service. 19 February 2008.

Opposite above: It was certainly not unusual to see the light Pacific's working freight trains in BR service, but it was the exception rather than the rule. Here is a demonstration freight coming across Corfe Viaduct with the loco looking equally at home with a rake of trucks. 1 April 2005.

Opposite below: Framed by the branch of a Yew tree, 34028 awaits departure from Corfe Castle with a train for Norden. 25 September 2005.

34028
16

34028
L. & S.W.R.
TRESPASSERS
WILL BE
PROSECUTED

Above: More framing here as we see the loco through a gap in the hedgerow heading away from Harmans Cross with a Swanage to Norden train. Shame about that maroon coach on the rear! 1 April 2005.

Opposite above: Corfe Common provides a great place to watch the trains, with quite a few vantage points. Here 34028 is about to pass beneath the small Townsend occupation bridge with a Swanage to Norden train. 13 September 2009.

Opposite below: Services are often timed to cross at Harmans Cross station and in this view, we see 34028 awaiting to depart for Norden, while running in from Corfe Castle is 34070 *Manston* (more on this loco presently). Hard to believe that signalbox only dates from 1996! 3 April 2010.

34028

NOT
EDDYSTONE
7P 5FA
34028

Above: Almost at its destination, 34028 slows for the stop at Norden. East Hill looms in the background. 3 October 2008.

Opposite above: A real sight for sore eyes for Bulleid Pacific followers! 34028 is piloting 34053 *Sir Keith Park* across Corfe Castle Viaduct with a train from Swanage to Norden. On the rear is 34072 257 *Squadron*. 7 June 2024.

Opposite below: 34028 was withdrawn from service during 2014 for an overhaul which took seven years, delayed by various factors including the covid 19 pandemic. Here we see the loco at Corfe Castle station. 7 June 2024.

34028

34028
EDDYSTONE

Above: A few months later and the loco has now been fully lined out, including the tender. It makes a great sight in the early winter sunshine as it departs Corfe Castle for Norden. 6 December 2008.

Opposite above: For various reasons the rededication of 34070 was delayed for a year but in 2009, soon after Battle of Britain day it was formerly launched in a ceremony at Swanage station. This is actor Edward Fox who lives nearby, and was one of the stars in the 1969 film 'The Battle of Britain' revealing the nameplate. 19 September 2009.

Opposite below: Not a bad view from an upstairs window! 34070 is passing the cottages on the approach to Corfe Castle station with a Norden to Swanage service. 9 September 2011.

MANSTON
BATTLE OF BRITAIN CLASS
34070

34070

Above: We saw 34028 hauling a demonstration goods train earlier and this is 34070 hauling a similar one in the opposite direction. Here it is at Afflington and on the approach to Harmans Cross station bound for Swanage. 19 April 2015.

Opposite above: One might be advised to heed the warning here as 34070 is captured on the lesser photographed extension between Norden and the Frome River Bridge at Stoborough Heath, working a Swanage to Frome River Bridge service. This part of the line is usually only used when there is a gala of some sort in operation. 31 March 2017.

Opposite below: That ever present historical landmark is seen in the background as the loco draws near to Harmans Cross with a Swanage bound train. 17 February 2010.

Stop
Look
Listen
Beware
of trains
34070

Above: Powering beneath Townsend Bridge, the Pacific looks magnificent as it makes for Harmans Cross and Swanage with a train from Norden. Yes, that is a lone cow on top of the hill! 17 February 2010.

Opposite above: We have seen a few pictures of Corfe Castle Viaduct in this volume but not from this side of the line which is only good for photography in early morning, as the sun soon moves away quite soon. 34070 crosses with a train for Norden. 9 September 2012.

Opposite below: Next we see the loco at Woodyhyde, just north of Harmans Cross as it passes with a Norden to Swanage train. A recent visit here found it very overgrown and impossible to replicate this shot. 17 February 2010.

34070
Swanage
A351
Wareham
A351
Norden
Park & Ride

BRIDLEWAY
BRIDLEWAY

Above: Here the Pacific has just crossed Corfe Common and is approaching Afflington Bridge with a Norden to Swanage train. 11 February 2023.

Opposite above: Norden station is just to the top left of this shot as 34070 departs with a train for Swanage. In the far top right, you can just make out the edge of Poole Harbour. 11 February 2023.

Opposite below: For our last view of 34070, this is the same spot as the previous shot but taken at ground level as the loco makes a smoky departure from Norden bound for Swanage. 11 February 2023.

34070

Above: The third Pacific to make this its home line (for a short while) is 34053 *Sir Keith Park*. The loco returned to service during 2012 and initially worked on the Severn Valley Railway before moving to Swanage for a while. After mechanical problems the loco went to the Spa Valley Railway as Swanage already had both 34028/34070 in service. It has also visited the Swanage line on various occasions for galas etc. In heavy rain, it is seen approaching Corfe Castle with a demonstration goods train bound for Swanage. 12 October 2019.

Opposite above: On the less used northern section from Norden again, 34053 comes past Creech Bottom crossing with a train from Swanage to Frome River Bridge. 31 March 2017.

Opposite below: An imposing view of 34053 as it arrives at Corfe Castle with a Swanage to Norden train. 2 June 2018.

34053
S. R.
TRESPASSERS
WILL BE
PROSECUTED

Above: After arrival of the charter into Swanage the loco is seen being serviced at Swanage Depot. It later worked a couple of internal services on the line before working back to London later in the day. 2 May 2009.

Opposite above: With 34067 visiting on a different occasion later the same year, the opportunity was taken to pair the loco up with resident 34070. The pair are seen coming across Corfe Castle viaduct both tender first with a train from Swanage. 29 November 2009.

Opposite below: I think this was the first time a pair of un-rebuilt Battle of Britain Pacifics worked together in preservation. With the autumnal colours showing well, the pair have just departed from Norden as they make their way back to Swanage. It is interesting to note the two shades of green worn by the locos. 29 November 2009.

Above: We also saw 34046 *Braunton* in the main line section of this book, and this is another example that has visited the Swanage line. At the time of this visit, it was carrying the identity of Battle of Britain 34052 *Lord Dowding*. It is seen just about to cross Stoborough Heath with a Frome River Bridge to Swanage train. 31 March 2017.

Opposite above: In this fabulous view of the famous Corfe Castle, 34052(046) looks completely at home pottering towards Harman's Cross with a demonstration freight train heading for Swanage. 2 April 2017.

Opposite below: Our last few images depict 34092 *City of Wells*, seen in the main line section as one of the locos that pioneered the return steam to former Southern Region back in the late 1980s. Here is a broadside of the loco decked out with 'Golden Arrow' regalia as it passes Creech Bottom crossing, bringing up the rear of a train from Swanage to River Frome Bridge. 2 April 2017.

CITY OF WELLS
34092

Above: The loco is seen approaching Harman's Cross in this view and slows for the stop with a Swanage to Norden train. 2 April 2017.

Opposite above: Recent tree clearance at this location had opened up this shot at Creech Bottom crossing as 34092 approaches with a train from Swanage to the Frome River Bridge. 2 April 2017.

Opposite below: This time we see the loco without the 'Golden Arrow' additions as it is about to cross Corfe Castle viaduct on the rear of a Norden to Swanage train. 7 June 2024.

GOLDEN
ARROW
CITY OF WELLS
34092

34092
CITY OF WELLS
34092

The final image in this volume shows 34092 approaching Corfe Castle, with 34028 *Eddystone* and 35006 *Peninsular & Oriental SN Company* in the sidings awaiting their next workings. This was during the line's superb 'Strictly Bulleid II' gala. 7 June 2024.